MW01088138

INGEBORG BACHMANN was born in 1926 in Klagenfurt, Austria. She studied philosophy at the universities of Innsbruck, Graz, and Vienna, where she wrote her dissertation on Martin Heidegger. In 1953 she received the poetry prize from Gruppe 47 for her first volume, *Borrowed Time (Die gestundete Zeit)*, after which her second collection, *Invocation of the Great Bear (Anrufung des großen Bären)*, appeared in 1956. Her various awards include the Georg Büchner Prize, the Berlin Critics Prize, the Bremen Award, and the Austrian State Prize for literature. Writing and publishing essays, opera libretti, short stories, and novels as well, she divided her time between Munich, Zurich, Berlin, and Rome, where she died in a fire in her apartment in 1973.

Darkness Spoken gathers together Bachmann's two celebrated books of poetry, as well as early and late poems not collected in book form, 129 of them appearing in English for the first time, as well as twenty-five poems which have never before been published in German. Bachmann is considered one of the most important poets to emerge in post-war German letters, and this volume represents the largest collection available of this major voice in 20th-century poetry. Influencing numerous writers from Thomas Bernhard to Christa Wolf to Elfriede Jelinek (winner of the 2004 Nobel Prize in Literature), Bachmann's poetic investigation into the nature and limits of language in the face of historical violence remains unmatched in its ability to combine philosophical insight with haunting lyricism. Just as Bachmann's *Malina* and *The Book of Franza* sought to expand the possibilities of the novel, *Darkness Spoken* contains the bedrock of a vision as far reaching as it is indelible, and as uncompromising as it is bound to hope.

PETER FILKINS has published two volumes of poetry, *What She Knew* (1998) and *After Homer* (2002), and has translated Bachmann's *The Book of Franza* and *Requiem for Fanny Goldmann*, as well as Alois Hotschnig's novel, *Leonardo's Hands*. He is the recipient of an Outstanding Translation Award from the American Literary Translators Association, and the Berlin Prize from the American Academy in Berlin. A graduate of Williams College and Columbia University, he has studied at the University of Vienna with the support of a Fulbright grant. He teaches at Simon's Rock College of Bard in Great Barrington, Massachusetts.

INGEBORG
Darkness Spoken
BACHMANN

The Collected Poems

Translated & Introduced by
PETER FILKINS

Foreword by
CHARLES SIMIC

ZEPHYR PRESS
2006

All photographs courtesy of Foto-Archiv, Piper Verlag GmbH,
München and the Ingeborg Bachmann estate
Proof reading of the German text by Herbert Arnold
Book design by *typeslowly*
Printed in Michigan by Cushing-Malloy, Inc.

Zephyr Press acknowledges with gratitude the financial support of
the Massachusetts Cultural Council and the National Endowment
for the Arts.

NATIONAL
ENDOWMENT
FOR THE ARTS

massculturalcouncil.org

MCC

Zephyr Press books are distributed to the trade in the U.S. and Canada
by Consortium Book Sales and Distribution [www.cbsd.com] and by
Small Press Distribution [www.spdbooks.org].

Library of Congress Control Number: 2006921389

09 08 07 06   98765432 first edition

ZEPHYR PRESS
50 Kenwood Street
Brookline, MA 02446
www.zephyrpress.org

ACKNOWLEDGMENTS

The following translations have appeared in the periodicals listed, some of them in slightly different form.

The American Poetry Review — "After This Flood," "Shadows, Roses, Shadow," "The Native Land," "In the Storm of Roses," "Early Noon," "March Stars"

Paris Review — "Letter in Two Drafts," "In Apulia"

The Seneca Review — "Gloriastrasse"

The Boston Review — "I Know of No Better World"

Two Lines — "The Drugs, The Words"

Harvard Review — "Fall Down, Heart," "The Heavy Cargo," "[On many nights I ask my mother]"

Denver Quarterly — "[I should disappear]"

The Literary Imagination — Departure from England," "To Say to a Third"

Sulfur — "In Twilight," "Psalm"

The Massachusetts Review — "Borrowed Time"

TriQuarterly — "Every Day," "No Delicacies"

Partisan Review — "A Type of Loss"

Ironwood — "Journey Out"

Translation — "Invocation of the Great Bear," "My Bird," "Rome at Night," "Wood and Shavings"

The Bloomsbury Review — "Exile"

Poetry East — "Message"

Visions-International — "Paris"

"Stay" appeared in the 2000 Poetry in Motion Series of the New York Transit Authority.

"To the Sun" appeared in *The 100 Greatest Poems of the Twentieth Century*, edited by Mark Strand. Norton, 2005.

TABLE OF CONTENTS

ANRUFUNG DES GROßEN BÄREN / INVOCATION
OF THE GREAT BEAR

Early and Late Poems

FOREWORD *by* Charles Simic

I am a dead man who wanders
registered nowhere

I first read Ingeborg Bachmann some thirty years ago in Jerome
Rothenberg's small anthology of young German poets. I liked her
poems immediately, even though Hans Magnus Enzensberger, Paul
Celan and Günter Grass with their radical imagery suited my taste
for novelty much more. In fact, there was nothing obviously modern
about Bachmann's poems if one thinks of modernism as a tradition
that includes Expressionism, Dada and Surrealism. Such poems
tend to be programmatically irreverent and anti-poetic. In contrast,
Bachmann wrote in a manner that would not have seemed entirely
unfamiliar to the great Romantic poets, that is, until they started
reading her closely and realized her profound difference.

I myself remember being made uneasy even at my first encounter.
Here was a poetry of sublime lyricism that suggested the knowledge
of the horrors of the Second World War without employing any of
its familiar images. Bachmann had a way of writing about nature such
that it reminded one of concentration camps, as it were. In every new
anthology of German poetry that subsequently came out, I sought
her out, and when I did find the same few poems that kept being
translated over and over again, I experienced once more her spell. Very
simply, I knew that I had just read a poet that I would never forget.

This is one of the true mysteries of literature. What is it that
makes certain poems immediately memorable? Obviously, it could
be the sheer mastery of form and originality of the imagination that
captivate us. Still, this is not always an explanation. Tastes change,
newness wears out. Poems that once seemed unforgettable because
of their shocking imagery or content suddenly cease to seduce us.
Long after the dazzling virtuosity of one kind or another, the ab-
sence of something far more important becomes noticeable. I have
here in mind that elusive property known as the poet's voice. In the
case of Bachmann, it is not so much what she says, or even how she
says it, rather, it is her voice that one always remembers. A voice that

touches the heart. One could go so far as to claim that the sound of a living voice is all that lyric poetry conveys.

The voice is the imprint of individuality. The tone of one's voice, as everybody knows, varies depending on the attitude one takes toward the words one is saying. In poetry, it is the voice that brings the breath of the living human being to us. The tone either persuades us that what is being said matters, or it does not, and that tone cannot be contrived. Here's someone bearing witness to her consciousness and the wonder of its existence. The world is a strange place, and what is ever more strange is that I should be alive in it today! No grammar of that sensation is possible, as Emily Dickinson knew. She also understood that poets aim to recreate in their poems the feel of that *something* which cannot be put into words.

The preoccupation of so much post-1945 poetry in Germany and elsewhere is language. Are there any words still left around that one can trust? It is the weight of the unsayable that gives Bachmann's poetry its tragic dimension.

> Where Germany's earth blackens the sky,
> a cloud seeks words and fills the crater with silence.

She takes into account the profound philosophical and moral difficulty of being a poet in an epoch of history's greatest murderers, an epoch furthermore in which whatever explanations of evil we once turned to for solace have become inadequate. The death of God, you may say, is no big deal if everybody behaves well, but once the slaughter of the innocent starts, how do you catch any sleep at night? An air of permanent crises and terror surrounding all human endeavor is our inheritance.

> War is no longer declared,
> but rather continued. The outrageous
> has become the everyday. The hero
> is absent from battle. The weak
> are moved into the firing zone.
> The uniform of the day is patience,
> the order of merit is the wretched star
> of hope over the heart.

If that was all there was to it, our predicament would be far more clear. But, there is another paradox. Yes, unimaginable crimes and sufferings have occurred, and yes, the world is still beautiful. There are still trees, lovers and children and they go about their business as if nothing had happened. After all the nightmares and gloomy thoughts one has had, it is astonishing to find innocence. Is it possible to be happy in a world that has seen such horrors, Bachmann continuously asks herself? Does that knowledge always doom one to despair and the inability to relish life for what it is?

I am the child of great fear for the world,
who within peace and joy hangs suspended
like the stroke of a bell in the day's passing
and like the scythe in the ripe pasture.

I am the Continual-Thought-Of-Dying.

Bachmann's is a poetry of estrangement and nostalgia. Her poems are elegies for a loss beyond words. She is the one made stranger in the midst of her own people by that knowledge, the one condemned to remain forever standing on the threshold. "Our godhead, history, has ordered for us a grave from which there's no resurrection" she says. Her poems have an awareness of the tragic worthy of the Greeks. She is the poet of the long, dark night of history and the lone human being awake in it. It is her heroic refusal to make things intellectually and morally easy for herself that gives her poems the heroic stature and nobility they have.

In a century of displaced persons, Bachmann's poetry, appropriately, is full of voyages and partings. This prodigal daughter knows that we cannot ever say what our fates truly mean; we can only try to convey endlessly how things appear to us. Every day we say farewell to some small epiphany that made the world so vivid and meaningful yesterday. Whoever in the future wishes to experience that all-pervading sense of exile our age has felt, should read Bachmann, just as we must be immensely grateful that Peter Filkins has now given us the fullest and the best translations we have in English of this magnificent poet.

ON THE BORDER OF SPEECH

When Yeats wrote in *A Vision* of the urge "to hold in a single thought reality and justice," he could just as well have been describing the impetus behind the poetry of Ingeborg Bachmann. Bridging the poetry of experience and the poetry of ideas, Bachmann's vision is one continually fixed upon the terror she perceived within the quotidian, as well as the need to elicit the unspoken, primeval truth that lies just beyond the pale of the "unspeakable." In following this trajectory, Bachmann's poems conduct a journey *in* thought *towards* feeling, for hers is not a poetry of recollected experience, nor a poetry of ideas about experience, but rather a poetry that enacts *the experience of ideas* in order to evoke the nature of true feeling, despite the impediments that exist in cognitive speech.

Born on June 25, 1926, Bachmann grew up in Klagenfurt, Austria, the eldest of three children. Capital of Carinthia, the country's most southern province, Klagenfurt is situated in a deep valley not far from rugged, often snow-capped mountains that provide the natural borders between three countries — Austria, Slovenia, and Italy. Though Bachmann spent her entire adult life living away from the sleepy provincial city, her childhood in Klagenfurt remained a lasting influence. Its fields, lakes, and forest paths continually appear in her work, and it was also there that Bachmann first encountered the brutality of the "real" world when Hitler and his troops marched triumphant into the main square of the city in 1938. Years later, Bachmann would maintain that this moment marked the end of her childhood, a world of innocence shattered by the brutality that the young girl perceived in the marching troops and the hysteria that welcomed them.[1]

The perceived border drawn between Bachmann and her childhood on that day became the central obsession of her imaginative life. Because of the fear that stirred in her, the border between the real and the imagined, as well as the struggle to cross it through language, became "not a problem of logic, but rather a question of existence."[2] Bachmann herself locates this dilemma in the historical terrain of Klagenfurt, for in a short biographical piece found among her papers after her death, she writes:

I spent my childhood in Carinthia, in the South, on the border, in a valley that had two names — one German and the other Slovenian. And the house in which for generations my ancestors had lived — both Austrians and Wends — still bears a name that sounds foreign. Hence, near the border there is still another border: the border of speech — and on either side I was accustomed to stories of good and bad spirits from two or three lands; for an hour away, over the mountains, there also lay Italy.[3]

Thus, whether traveling between the focal points of innocence and guilt, hope and despair, life and death, Bachmann's poetic journey is both localized and universal. In confronting the "border of speech" that she found erected all about her in childhood, as well as the threat of those marching troops, Bachmann encountered early on the duality of "the unspeakable" as a realm of both "good and bad spirits." The need to elicit each through the urge to cross over into "the spoken" would become the central vector of her adult life and work.

That vector was to travel swiftly, for Bachmann's rise to prominence in German letters was meteoric. After studying briefly at the universities of Innsbruck and Graz shortly after the war, she transferred to the University of Vienna, where in 1950 she completed a doctoral thesis on "Die kritische Aufnahme der Existentialphilosophie Martin Heideggers" ("The Critical Reception of the Existential Philosophy of Martin Heidegger"). While employed at Radio Rot-Weiß-Rot in Vienna, in 1952 Bachmann first traveled to Munich to read at the influential gathering of postwar German writers known as Gruppe 47. The poet Paul Celan, whom she had met in Vienna, was instrumental in arranging her appearance, and though the recital of his "Todesfuge" was a stunning event, Bachmann's own reading was lauded with praise and awe. The German literary world was immediately swept away by the young blonde-haired poet reading her poems in a near whisper, and soon her work appeared in leading journals. The following year Bachmann's first collection, *Die gestundete Zeit (Borrowed Time)* was published, and at the age of twenty seven she returned to the congress to receive the coveted Gruppe 47 Prize amid torrents of acclaim.

Bachmann's early success was instantaneous, landing her on the cover of *Der Spiegel* in 1954. She also soon found herself swamped with requests for poems, radio plays, and opera libretti, and these would remain the principal genres that she continued to work in throughout the 1950's. Traveling to the United States in 1955 at the invitation of Harvard University, publishing her second volume of poems, *Anrufung des Großen Bären (Invocation of the Great Bear)* in 1956, and invited to deliver the inaugural lectures for the poetry chair founded at Frankfurt University in 1959, Bachmann was not only the most celebrated writer of the postwar generation, but also was described as the most important German poet since Gottfried Benn.

The reasons for Bachmann's swift rise to fame are both literary and historical. Amid the devastation left behind by the war, Bachmann's poems spoke directly to a historical sense of guilt and despair, while also refusing to see the present as any better. Rather, despite Germany's burgeoning economic "miracle," here was a young poet announcing that "Harder days are coming," and that "The loan of borrowed time/ will be due on the horizon" ("Borrowed Time").[4] Furthermore, the breadth of her range as a poet, which deeply connected to the classical tradition of Goethe and Hölderlin, also enabled her to boldly say that,

Where Germany's sky blackens the earth,
its beheaded angel seeks a grave for hate
and offers you the bowl of the heart
("Early Noon")

and then quickly follow it with echoes of Goethe's "Der König in Thule," as well as Schubert's *Die Winterreise* in the same poem:

Seven years later
it occurs to you again,
at the fountain before the portal,

xxii

don't look too deep within,
as your eyes fill with tears.

Seven years later,
inside a mortuary,
the hangmen of yesterday
drain the golden cup.
Your eyes lower in shame.

The result is a double sense of time, one that was contemporaneous
with Austria's recent history under fascism, as well as a broader, more
pervasive sense of time, the latter being the "historical sense" that
T.S. Eliot described as "a perception, not only of the pastness of the
past, but of its presence."

This quality links Bachmann to the modernist poets, but if
this were the entire scope of her achievement, her work would be
only a footnote to a movement whose heyday had passed. Instead,
Bachmann's vision and career are more complex, harder to pin down,
if only because of the fragmentary nature of each. Hers is a voice
that speaks beyond its time as much as directly to it, for throughout
Bachmann's work the problem of language lifts her writing beyond
the breakthroughs of modernism towards a new conception of lan-
guage that, as Sabine Gölz has observed, "uses the remembrance of
the past not to make it return in the same shape but repeats it in
order to make something new appear"[5]

The influence of Ludwig Wittgenstein's philosophy is central to
this new conception, for Bachmann continually refers to it in her
writing.[6] The last sentence of Wittgenstein's *Tractatus*, "What we
cannot speak about we must pass over in silence,"[7] serves as a kind of
touchstone in her work, though the problem that Wittgenstein sees
in the inability of language to name the "unspeakable" truth is not
one that she is content to treat as unsolvable. Rather, at the end of
her first essay on Wittgenstein, published in 1953, she wonders, "Or
could he mean that we've squandered our language because it con-
tains no word that can touch upon what cannot be spoken?"[8]

The question is an important one, for simply by asking it Bachmann opens up the possibility that, if the right word were to exist or be found, "the unspeakable" might be recovered as a source for "true" speech, thus helping to cleanse language of the imprecision and corruption that cause meaningful speech to be lost or misused. In postwar Germany, this was a particularly important concern for the writers of Gruppe 47 who sought to free language of the fascist overtones that still clung to it, while because of the cataclysm they had experienced, there was also a distaste for the "beautiful" words of the patriotic "Blut und Boden" writings that had appeared under the Nazis. Bachmann was the first poet to come along whose "simplicity of word choice and complexity of meaning"[9] created a poetry that could forward an intelligent philosophy of language on historical terms, but with the recognition that "No country and no group, no idea, can found itself upon the reality of those [the victims] who have died."[10]

This allows Bachmann to face history head on, its "Message" being as hopeless as it is unwavering:

Out of the corpse-warm foyer of heaven steps the sun.
There it is not the immortals,
but rather the fallen, we perceive.

And brilliance doesn't trouble itself with decay. Our godhead,
history, has ordered for us a grave
from which there is no resurrection.

What distinguishes her vision from the merely apocalyptic is the intelligence and control with which she wields it, for in the perception of "the fallen" one also has the sense of a larger fall having occurred, one that implicates the viewer ("history has ordered for us a grave") as much as the viewed. Bachmann's approach, then, is seated within history, as well as outside it. Most often she will attest to a statement such as "Germany's sky blackens the earth" ("Early Noon") by suddenly observing that "A handful of pain vanishes over the hill," the emblematic nature of her imagery bordering on the surreal, but only for the purpose of constructing a mythos in which, at the end of the same poem, "The unspeakable passes, barely spoken, over the land."

Key to this aesthetic is Bachmann's continual employment of linguistic "fragments" (*Scherben*) to construct poems that function as mosaics.[11] In "Great Landscape Near Vienna," for instance, Bachmann describes the oil fields that mercilessly "pump spring from the fields." She then switches to Vienna's Prater and the famed Ferris wheel that "drags the coat that covered our love," only to shift the focus once more outside the city when she reminds us that

> Where the crane completes
> its circle amid the rushes of the marsh's flat water,
> on a reed the hour strikes more resonantly than waves.

Yet, as if this were not enough, we are then given a single line, "Asia's breath lies beyond the river," Bachmann providing neither context nor meaning for it. The effect is both eerie and chilling, for it transports us to a larger dimension, one that sees the boundaries of time and space as transparent demarcations. Similarly, by the end of the poem, after musing about an array of subjects ranging from "the theater of many peopled grief" existing in the Roman settlements upon which Vienna is built, to the fact that "no one is saved, many are stricken" in the present day, Bachmann can speak to the immediate decay created by the threat she sees in the oil fields, but in a manner that is timeless in its implications:

> And so the fish are also dead and float
> towards the black seas that await us.
> But we were washed away long ago, gripped
> by the pull of other streams, where the world
> disappeared and there was little cheer.
> The towers of the plain sing our praises,
> for we came here unwittingly, falling on the rungs
> of depression, then falling deeper,
> with an ear sharply tuned for the fall.

Given this range, the most compelling aspect of Bachmann's

poems is that the reader may often be inclined to wonder about the *where* and the *when* of any poem, but never the *who*, for the continuity of Bachmann's voice is the central source of her poetic authority. "In each of my moments, I'm aware of a strange/ moment," says Prince Myshkin in her monologue for him, echoing the way in which Bachmann speaks on several different planes at the same time. However, throughout her work the localities of place and time are seated within the observing self that names them. In "The Native Land," for instance, the speaker says,

> And when I drank of myself
> and my native land
> rocked with earthquakes,
> I opened my eyes to see.
>
> Then life fell to me.

However, Bachmann displays how the observation of the I *observing* is what defines the "place" of the poem when at the end she notes:

> There the stone is not dead.
> The wick flares
> when lit by a glance.

What's important about this is that, though Bachmann often seems to border on a confessional tone, it is through the voice of an emblematic "I," one that can even be read as a specifically feminine voice speaking to and from within a patriarchy, and which resides in a particular way of seeing, rather than in a particular self that sees. The third of Bachmann's Frankfurt lectures is, in fact, entirely devoted to a discussion of "the writing I" as a literary construct. There she argues that the "I" no longer exists within history, but that "history exists in the I,"[12] an idea perhaps as applicable to a reading of our own "confessionalist" poets as it is crucial to an understanding of how Bachmann seizes control of the self by constructing a vision where "The wick flares/ when lit by a glance" rather than the other way around.

Because the act of "seeing" has no end in itself, it lends itself to the timeless and the utopian. However, when this act is performed in and through words, it encounters the "border of speech," such that another of Wittgenstein's better known propositions in the *Tractatus*, "The limits of my language mean the limits of my world,"[13] can be read for the contrary implications of freedom and impediment that it posits. Language *is* the world in this formulation, though Bachmann was also quick to value the possibility inherent in Wittgenstein's thought that "There are, indeed, things that cannot be put into words. They *make themselves manifest.* They are what is mystical."[14] For her, the effort to evoke the mystical side of "the unspoken" in contrast to the historically "unspeakable" involves the utopian pursuit of a truth that is both transient and real. What complicates her vision, however, is her recognition, as she argued in writing on Robert Musil, that "utopia is not an end, but rather a tendency" for the writer.[15] Thus, Bachmann's poems remain *in pursuit* of the truth, both historical and ideal, but while standing *on* the "border of speech," caught between the actual and the possible.

Language, however, through its insistence on order and cognition, limits the means by which it can address the "unspeakable." Increasingly, Bachmann came to struggle with this limitation at the same time that she sought to reshape and overcome it. The most significant step she made in this process was her switch to prose in mid-career as her primary artistic medium, though it is also clear that she wrote fiction in her early years as well. In publishing only eighteen more poems after 1956, the date of her second and last volume, Bachmann largely ceased to be known as a poet in the sixties. However, as attested to by the large collection of unpublished poems included here, Bachmann did not abandon poetry. Instead, she turned to it as a means to grapple with personal difficulty, as well as to work through a new way to attack the "border of speech." For it is in the poems Bachmann wrote in the early sixties that we find the germ of her later work. Though they lack the singular vision and thematic organization of her earlier volumes, they function as a transparent commentary on the development of her thought and work, much like the early poems that precede her first collection.[16]

Meanwhile, Bachmann's turn to prose was for a long time a real stumbling block in the critical reception of her work. A collection of short stories, *Das dreißigste Jahr (The Thirtieth Year)* appeared in 1961, bringing with it a mixture of lukewarm praise and consternation as to why one of the German language's leading poets had turned to a different genre. Nonetheless, Bachmann continued to write stories and essays while declaring openly that she no longer expected or even wished to write any more poems. Eventually the public came to accept this, her novel *Malina* becoming a popular success when it appeared in 1971 as the first entry into what was planned as a cycle of novels called *Todesarten (Ways of Dying)*. Another collection of stories, *Simultan (Simultaneous,* but available in English as *Three Paths to the Lake)*, was also well received upon publication in 1972. In fact, Bachmann soon became better known, more closely studied for her prose than she was for her poetry. Not only did the growing women's movement find in her work a voice for their trenchant issues, but readers as a whole became interested in her stark portrayal of contemporary men and women locked in the struggle between the diseases of society and the wounds of the private soul, language existing between as both scalpel and sword.

The crucible, however, that produced the major focus of Bachmann's later prose is the poetry she wrote from 1957 to 1964, for it is there that she makes the crucial link between the ills of society and the diseased self, seeing each as symptomatic of the other. This is particularly so in the numerous poems she wrote after her break up with Max Frisch in late 1962. After suffering a breakdown that would eventually leave her addicted to the medications doctors provided her, Bachmann wrote over one hundred poems in two years time, nearly the same amount she had written previously in her entire career. Jotted down in haste, the cries of a woman in desperate circumstances, few of these poems live up to the standard she established in her finest work. Still, they provide a fascinating window onto the shift in Bachmann's thinking, for within them we see a woman at first struggling to comprehend her own pain only to discover that she is the embodiment of the crippled world that surrounds her, thus achieving the solace of a darkness that is "spoken" rather than just suffered.

This process, however, was neither easy nor obvious. Early on, when Bachmann is at her most vulnerable, she seems unable to write about her pain with any degree of irony or insight. Instead, it is as if her poetic voice has failed her, the result being that

> I've misplaced my poems.
> I search for them in each nook and cranny.
> Because of pain I know nothing, not even how
> One writes about pain, for I simply know nothing else.

> [I've misplaced my poems]

At times her desperation borders on self-pity, or at least the formless negation of sorrow and pain at their deepest levels. However, what seems to save Bachmann, or at least restore the connective thread between herself and others, is her identification with the sufferings of others. With this comes an awareness of suffering as an entity often hidden by the society at large. In identifying with the victims silenced by society, Bachmann comes to understand the deeper reasons for her own silence as a victim, such that

> I step outside
> myself, out of my eyes,
> hands, mouth, outside
> of myself I
> step, a bundle
> of goodness and godliness
> that must make good
> this devilry
> that has happened.

> [I step outside myself]

The way to "make good/ this devilry/ that has happened" is of course to describe it and give it imaginative shape through metaphor and story. Bachmann would go on to do just that by coming to see her own pain as a form of "Torture," or even "murder" ("[I Should Disappear]" or "Gently and Softly," etc.) inflicted upon "the entire body, on which a history,/ and not only mine, is inscribed" ("[After Many Years]"). Similarly, in her drafts for her acceptance speech for the Georg Büchner Prize, written in the summer of 1964, Bachmann states, "[N]o one is made crazy through writing, but rather becomes crazy for the same reasons as those who do not write, namely the denial of their rights, power, naked brutality, the loss of their dignity and the threat to their very existence. And this threat can be found not only in war, not just in times of naked power, or the domineering need to survive, but rather before and after, i.e. in times of peace...."[17] This, indeed, would become the central theme to Bachmann's *Todesarten* cycle, but it was the intensity of her own struggle as documented privately in her poems that first brought her to it.

Hans Höller sees this shift in Bachmann's thinking from the inward to the outward as taking place in the poem titled "Sound Barrier" ("Schallmauer"), where "Within the poem's metaphor the inner world and the outer world are condensed, such that the broken physical and psychological identity of the speaker speaks to the destruction of the human realm in general."[18] As such, not only Bachmann finds herself "In Enemy Hands," as she writes elsewhere, but so must the reader when told:

> You are in enemy hands,
> they are already grinding your
> bones, they demand
> that you look,
> they trample on your
> gaze with their feet,
> trilling in your ear
> the whistle
> of alarm.

The shift from the first person to the second here underscores Bachmann's ability to at last stand outside her own experience and make artistic sense of it. However, gone is the longing for an earlier world of pastoral calm, or even the expressed urge for the utopian ideal. Instead, as Höller points out, as Bachmann's writing progresses towards its new plane of regard, "Now the trauma suffered through power and the idea of utopia stand in opposition: on the one hand there are texts in which power possesses the "I," and on the other side are the memories of another, more peaceful existence in which the "I" experiences its urbane realm as a middle European landscape of memory in which it feels at home."[19] Such would become Franza's longing for the "Galicien" of her lost childhood in *The Book of Franza*, as well as the narrator's idea of her Vienna street as a private "Ungargasseland" in *Malina*, though in the end there is no escaping the murderous reality of the society that surrounds it.

Yet given this poetic burst in mid-career, the question still remains: why did Bachmann stop writing poetry, or at least claim to do so in interviews? That she had said all she had to say within it is, of course, the most viable answer, yet there are few easy answers in the work of this writer. Rather, one could argue that the fragmentation of Bachmann's career, namely her success in no less than six different genres — poetry, the short story, the novel, the essay, opera libretti, and radio plays — corresponds to a major strategy of the poetry in its use of "fragments" welded into mosaic patterns by the silence they seek to break. Put another way, Bachmann's turn towards prose does not preclude the fact that the same thread of concern runs throughout her work, or that the stringing of that thread through varying means and materials is as much a part of the nature of her thinking as is any single work or genre.

In fact, it's the protagonist of the title story of her first collection who writes a line in his diary that has since become one of Bachmann's most quoted: "Keine neue Welt ohne neue Sprache" ("No new world without a new language").[20] Not only does this encapsulate what Bachmann was aiming at in all of her writings, it speaks to the many "new worlds" she wished to render in her wide-ranging expression. While it is true that Bachmann simply had more freedom in prose to directly discuss the problems of men and women, history and time, innocence and guilt, etc., it's also true that poetry affords a freer hand with the nuances of speech and metaphor in the search for a "new world" through figurative language. In the end, each dove-tails with the other, Bachmann's poems representing the first and most intense expression of her utopian vision and thought.

First cousin to utopia, however, is disappointment, and there is an increasing sense in Bachmann's later poems that the earlier ideals remain somehow unattainable. Still, in looking at the earliest of her poems that also speak with profound trepidation, one arrives at an appreciation for how Bachmann's late struggle with language and poetry was more with a "type" of expression than with the urge to write itself. For example, the early "Destiny" asks:

> Who knows if we have not already moved
> through many heavens with glazed eyes?
> We, who are banished into time
> and thrust from space,
> we, who are refugees in the night and exiled.

Bachmann's later, uncollected "Exile" would seem a direct extension of "Destiny," yet it approaches its subject from a more grounded perspective, one that acknowledges loss, but also with a greater assurance of what can be retrieved from it. In the last stanzas, the speaker states:

> I with the German language
> this cloud around me
> which I keep as a house
> press through all languages
>
> O how it grows dark
> those muted those rain tones
> only a few fall
>
> Into brighter zones it will lift the dead man up

The "it" being language, here the motions of falling and flight come together and are transformed into a resurrection through words. An exile from her native land (even from the "native" self, given that the speaker is referred to as a "dead *man*" at the beginning of the poem), the writer remains both a prisoner and worshiper of her native tongue. It is all that is left to her, though it as well remains a "cloud." Within it, however, she is able to maintain "a house," just as she can construct a word like "Regentöne" ("rain tones") in order to get at her meaning. Later, in "You Words," Bachmann even goes so far as to address language directly, knowing that

> The word
> will only drag
> other words behind it,
> the sentence a sentence,

but also that her final urge is that "nothing be final/ — not this passion for words/ nor a saying and its contradiction!"

For Bachmann, the objective is clear, namely "To create a single lasting sentence,/ to persevere in the ding-dong of words" ("Truly"). However, in one of her last poems, "No Delicacies," she refuses to forward the battle through the "delicacies" of traditional poetic speech. Declaring that, "Nothing pleases me anymore," she goes on to examine what she has taken from language, as well as what she cannot redress:

> I have learned an insight
> with words
> that exist
> (for the lowest class)
>
> Hunger
>   Shame
>   Tears
> and
>   Darkness.

Knowledge, however, is not enough, nor the determination of her statement that "I despair in the face of despair." Instead, she can only maintain that "I don't neglect writing," refusing "to get by with words" in a watered down fashion. "I am not my assistant," she declares, arguing instead for a defiant act of cancellation at the end of the poem:

> Must I
> with a hail-battered head,
> with the writing cramp in this hand,
> under the pressure of the three hundredth night
> rip up the paper,
> sweep away the scribbled word operas,
> annihilating as well: I you and he she it
>
> we you all?
>
> (Should? The others should.)
>
> My part, it shall be lost.

Though this would seem an ultimate denial of the efficacy of any speech, the conviction behind it is one that still values words. Even in one of the last poems she completed, "Bohemia Lies by the Sea," a poem she claimed she would always stand by,[21] Bachmann recognizes the border set down and accepts it, if only to maintain hope amid profound doubt, as she writes:

> I still border on a word and on another land,
> I border, like little else, on everything more and more,
>
> a Bohemian, a wandering minstrel, who has nothing, who
> is held by nothing, gifted only at seeing, by a doubtful sea,
>   the land of my choice.

All of it, however, the struggle and the hope came to a sudden and tragic end on the night of September 26, 1973, when Bachmann fell asleep in her apartment in Rome while smoking a cigarette in bed. She awoke to find herself and the bed engulfed in flames, but by the time the fire department arrived she was found unconscious and badly burned. Three weeks later, at the age of forty-seven, Bachmann was dead, her life and work having met its own "Early Noon," though writers ranging from Christa Wolf to Uwe Johnson to Thomas Bernhard would continue to press the limits and wonders of

"The unspeakable ... barely spoken" that Bachmann first explored. Where she herself might have headed, or if she would indeed return to poetry, is impossible to say, though clearly she would have soon completed work on the drafts that survive of the novels in her *Todesarten* cycle. What is clear is that Bachmann's implicit urge would and does remain to delineate and step beyond the border of speech first laid down within her poems.

"To become seeing," writes Hans Höller, "to be able to see, is not something sought after but also the curse, the deadly consequence discovered and suffered within the confrontation with historical experience."[22] That Bachmann was met with this curse and challenge as a child only a year before W.H. Auden would write in his elegy to Yeats that "poetry makes nothing happen" illustrates her courage in facing the reality of her times while examining the very language used to perceive it. Though ultimately she might agree with Auden's stoicism, in her flight across the abyss of historical experience just this side of the border of speech, Bachmann is there to remind us that the attempt at meaningful speech must still be made. As she herself writes in "Wozu Gedichte" ("What Good Are Poems"), "The playing field is language, and its borders are the borders of what we gaze on without question, that which is divulged and precisely imagined, experienced in pain, and in happiness celebrated and praised — namely the world."[23] Beyond this, the poet's only responsibility is to endure and embrace what Bachmann expresses best at the end of her "Songs in Flight":

Love has its triumph and death has one,
in time and the time beyond us.
We have none.

Only the sinking of stars. Silence and reflection.
Yet the song beyond the dust
will overcome our own.

Peter Filkins

1. See Bachmann's 1971 interview with Gerda Bödefeld in *Ingeborg Bachmann. Wir müssen wahre Sätze finden: Gespräche und Interviews*, ed. Christine Koschel and Inge von Weidenbaum, (Munich: Piper, 1983) 111-115. Although Bachmann speaks as if she witnessed Hitler's entry into Klagenfurt firsthand, research has shown that she was actually hospitalized with diphtheria on that particular day, though nonetheless she would have been well aware of the public spectacle and hysteria which accompanied the Anschluß. (See Joachim Hoell, *Ingeborg Bachmann* (Munich: Deutsche Taschenbuch, 2001) 21.

2. Holthusen, Hans E. "Kämpfender Sprachgeist. Die Lyrik Ingeborg Bachmanns," in *Kein objektives Urteil — nur ein lebendiges*, ed. Christine Koschel und Inge von Weidenbaum (Munich: Piper, 1989) 25 (my translation). Besides Holthusen's seminal essay, this volume collects together some of the most important criticism on Bachmann in German from the last forty years.

3. Ingeborg Bachmann. *Werke*, ed. Christine Koschel, Inge von Weidenbaum, and Clemens Münster, (Munich: Piper, 1978) 4: 302 (my translation). Hereafter, quotes from Bachmann's collected works, translated by myself, are cited as Werke, followed by the appropriate volume and page number.

4. For a discussion of the historical climate surrounding Bachmann's early career, see George C. Schoolfield, "Ingeborg Bachmann," *Essays on Contemporary German Literature*, ed. Brian Keith-Smith (London: Oswald Wolff, 1969) 4:187–212.

5. Sabine I. Gölz. "Reading in Twilight: Canonization, Gender, the Limits of Language — and a Poem by Ingeborg Bachmann," *New German Critique* 47 (1989): 45.

6. See Sara Lennox, "Bachmann and Wittgenstein," *Modern Austrian Literature* 18.3–4 (1985) 239–259.

7. Wittgenstein, Ludwig. *Tractatus Logico-Philosophicus*, trans. D.F. Pears and B.F. McGuinness (London: Routledge, 1961) 151. Hereafter referred to as *Tractatus*.

8. *Werke* 4:23.

9. Marsch, Edgar. "Ingeborg Bachmann," *Deutsche Dichter der Gegenwart*, ed. Benno von Wiese (Berlin: Erich Schmidt, 1973) 515 (my translation).

10. *Werke* 4:335.

11. See Wolfgang Bender, "Ingeborg Bachmann," *Deutsche Literatur der Gegenwart*, ed. Dietrich Weber (Stuttgart: Kröner, 1976) 585. Die Scherben also means "shards" of glass or pottery. In connection with this meaning, Jo Ann Van Vliet observes that Bachmann's frequent reference to Scherben might also echo the glass shards of "Kristallnacht" on November 9, 1938, "as well as the lines of a Hitler Youth anthem: 'Wir werden weiter marschieren/ wenn alles in Scherben fällt/ denn heute gehört uns Deutschland/ und morgen die ganze Welt.'" See her "'Wie alle Glocken schweigen': Guilt and Absolution in Ingeborg Bachmann's 'Psalm,'" *Modern Austrian Literature* 18:3-4 (1985) 125–126.

12. *Werke* 4:230.

13. *Tractatus*, 115.

14. *Tractatus*, 151.

15. *Werke* 4:27.

16. See Hans Höller, *Ingeborg Bachmann: Das Werk-Von den frühesten Gedichten bis zum "Todesarten"-Zyklus* (Frankfurt: Athenäum, 1987) 170–190. Höller makes a strong argument that Bachmann's early and late poems are best read together.

17. Ingeborg Bachmann: *"Todesarten"* — *Projekt*, 4 vols., eds. Monika Albrecht and Dirk Göttsche, (Munich: Piper, 1995) 1:175-176 (my translation).

18. Höller, Hans. *Ingeborg Bahchmann: Letzte, unveröffentliche Gedichte, Entwürfe und Fassungen* (Frankfurt: Suhrkamp, 1998) 31 (my translation).

19. *Ibid*, 35.

20. *Werke* 2:132.

21. See Kurt Bartsch, *Ingeborg Bachmann* (Stuttgart: Metzler, 1988) 132-133. Bartsch quotes Bachmann's pride in the poem in an unpublished interview from 1973.

22. Hans Höller. *Ingeborg Bachmann: Das Werk-Von den frühesten Gedichten bis zum "Todesarten"-Zyklus* (Frankfurt: Athenäum, 1987) 171.

23. *Werke* 4:304.

TRANSLATOR'S NOTE

The German text for the poems in *Borrowed Time* and *Invocation of the Great Bear*, as well as many of the early and late poems is from the first volume of Ingeborg Bachmann: *Werke*, ed. Christine Koschel, Inge von Weidenbaum, and Clemens Münster (Munich: Piper, 1978). Almost all of the poems in sections III and IV were published in the volume, *Ich weiß keine bessere Welt*, ed. Isolde Moser, Heinz Bachmann, and Christian Moser (Munich: Piper, 2000), though five poems from that volume, "Poliklinik Prag," "Jüdischer Friedhof," "Wenzelplatz," "In Feindeshand," and "Schallmauer," first appeared in Hans Höller's, *Ingeborg Bachmann: Letzte, unveröffentliche Gedichte, Entwürfe und Fassungen* (Frankfurt: Suhrkamp, 1998) . In addition, this volume also draws together twenty-five early and late poems that appear in German for the first time. The manuscripts for them can be found in the Bachmann archive located at the Österreichische Nationalbibliothek in Vienna.

Given the clarity and directness of Bachmann's vocabulary, it is surprising how difficult it can be to render her meaning. However, I have tried to maintain consistency in the imagery and vocabulary that Bachmann uses. I have also tried to remain faithful to meter, stanzaic form, rhyme, and lineation. The rhyme and meter are, of course, the hardest to render, and at times I have had to rely on slant or consonantal rhyme in order not to obscure or violate Bachmann's voice and meaning. However, I have also tried to render those passages in the German where strong rhymes occur in conjunction with alternating soft rhymes.

For the original prodding to read and translate Bachmann's poetry, I am deeply indebted to Joseph Brodsky, as well as to two of my German professors at Columbia University, Howard Stern and Beth Bjorklund, for many insightful conversations years ago about Bachmann and the difficulties of translation. Thanks also go to The Fulbright Commission of Austria for a grant that allowed me to study at the University of Vienna while working on the translations, as well as to both the Österrischische Gesellschaft für Literatur and the Bundekanzleramt für Kunst for grants that allowed me to do valuable research in the Bachmann archive. In addition, I am indebted to Dr. Eva Irblich for her knowledgeable assistance with the archive, and to Isolde Moser, Heinz Bachmann, and Christian Moser for their permission to publish poems from it. I am also grateful to R. Piper Verlag and Suhrkamp Verlag for granting permission for these translations, and for a sabbatical leave granted to me by Simon's Rock College of Bard, part of which was used to complete this book.

Finally, the poet's brother, Heinz Bachmann, has been extremely kind, helpful, and generous with his time in reading every word of the manuscript and offering countless useful corrections and suggestions for the past twenty years. It is to his patient and loyal care of Ingeborg Bachmann's work and memory that this book is dedicated.

Darkness Spoken

DIE GESTUNDETE ZEIT

BORROWED TIME

I

Ausfahrt

Vom Lande steigt Rauch auf.
Die kleine Fischerhütte behalt im Aug,
denn die Sonne wird sinken,
ehe du zehn Meilen zurückgelegt hast.

Das dunkle Wasser, tausendäugig
schlägt die Wimper von weißer Gischt auf,
um dich anzusehen, groß und lang,
dreißig Tage lang.

Auch wenn das Schiff hart stampft
und einen unsicheren Schritt tut,
steh ruhig auf Deck.

An den Tischen essen sie jetzt
den geräucherten Fisch;
dann werden die Männer hinknien
und die Netze flicken,
aber nachts wird geschlafen,
eine Stunde oder zwei Stunden,
und ihre Hände werden weich sein,
frei von Salz und Öl,
weich wie das Brot des Traumes,
von dem sie brechen.

I

Journey Out

Smoke rises from the land.
Remember the tiny fishing huts,
because the sun will sink
before you've set ten miles behind you.

The dark water, thousand-eyed,
opens its white-foamed lashes,
studying you, deep and long,
thirty days long.

Even when the ship pitches hard
and makes each step uncertain,
stand calm on deck.

At the table they eat
the heavily smoked fish;
then the men will kneel
and mend the nets,
though nightly each will sleep
an hour or two,
and their hands will soften,
free from salt and oil,
soft as the bread of the dream
which they break.

Die erste Welle der Nacht schlägt ans Ufer,
die zweite erreicht schon dich.
Aber wenn du scharf hinüberschaust,
kannst du den Baum noch sehen,
der trotzig den Arm hebt
— einen hat ihm der Wind schon abgeschlagen
— und du denkst: wie lange noch,
wie lange noch
wird das krumme Holz den Wettern standhalten?
Vom Land ist nichts mehr zu sehen.
Du hättest dich mit einer Hand in die Sandbank krallen
oder mit einer Locke an die Klippen heften sollen.

In die Muscheln blasend, gleiten die Ungeheuer des Meers
auf die Rücken der Wellen, sie reiten und schlagen
mit blanken Säbeln die Tage in Stücke, eine rote Spur
bleibt im Wasser, dort legt dich der Schlaf hin,
auf den Rest deiner Stunden,
und dir schwinden die Sinne.

Da ist etwas mit den Tauen geschehen,
man ruft dich, und du bist froh,
daß man dich braucht. Das Beste
ist die Arbeit auf den Schiffen,
die weithin fahren,
das Tauknüpfen, das Wasserschöpfen,
das Wändedichten und das Hüten der Fracht.
Das Beste ist, müde zu sein und am Abend
hinzufallen. Das Beste ist, am Morgen,
mit dem ersten Licht, hell zu werden,
gegen den unverrückbaren Himmel zu stehen,
der ungangbaren Wasser nicht zu achten
und das Schiff über die Wellen zu heben,
auf das immerwiederkehrende Sonnenufer zu.

The first wave of night hits the shore,
the second already reaches you.
But if you look hard,
you can still see the tree
which defiantly lifts an arm
— the wind has already knocked one off
— and you think: how much longer,
how much longer
will the twisted timber withstand the weather?
Of land there's nothing more to be seen.
With your hand you should have dug into the sandbank
or tied yourself to the cliff with a strand of hair.

Blowing into conches, sea monsters float
on the crests of waves, they ride and slice
the day to pieces with bright sabers; a red trail
remains in the water, where sleep takes hold of you
for the rest of your hours,
your senses spinning.

But then something happens with the ropes,
you are called and you are happy
that you are needed. Best of all
is the work on ships
that sail far away,
the knotting of ropes, the bailing of water,
the caulking of leaks, the guarding of freight.
Best to be tired and at evening
to collapse. Best in the morning
to awaken clear to the first light,
to rise up beneath the immovable sky,
to ignore the impassable water,
and to lift the ship over the waves
towards the forever recurring shore of the sun.

Abschied von England

Ich habe deinen Boden kaum betreten,
schweigsames Land, kaum einen Stein berührt,
ich war von deinem Himmel so hoch gehoben,
so in Wolken, Dunst und in noch Ferneres gestellt,
daß ich dich schon verließ,
als ich vor Anker ging.

Du hast meine Augen geschlossen
mit Meerhauch und Eichenblatt,
von meinen Tränen begossen,
hieltst du die Gräser satt;
aus meinen Träumen gelöst,
wagten sich Sonnen heran,
doch alles war wieder fort,
wenn dein Tag begann.
Alles blieb ungesagt.

Durch die Straßen flatterten die großen grauen Vögel
und wiesen mich aus.
War ich je hier?

Ich wollte nicht gesehen werden.

Meine Augen sind offen.
Meerhauch und Eichenblatt?
Unter den Schlangen des Meers
Seh ich, an deiner Statt,
das Land meiner Seele erliegen.

Ich habe seinen Boden nie betreten.

Departure from England

I have barely stepped upon your land,
silent country, barely disturbed a stone.
I was lifted so high by your sky,
placed so in clouds, mist, and remoteness,
that I had already left you
the moment I set anchor.

You have closed my eyes
with sea breeze and oak leaf,
upon the tears I cried
you let the grasses feed;
out of my dreams, suns dared
to venture across the land,
yet everything disappeared
as soon as your day began.
Everything remained unspoken.

Through streets flapped the great gray birds
that singled me out for expulsion.
Was I ever here?

I didn't want to be seen.

My eyes are open.
Sea breeze and oak leaf?
Under the serpentine sea
in place of you I see
the country of my soul succumb.

I have never stepped on its land.

Fall ab, Herz

Fall ab, Herz, vom Baum der Zeit,
fallt, ihr Blätter, aus den erkalteten Ästen,
die einst die Sonne umarmt',
fallt, wie Tränen fallen aus dem geweiteten Aug!

Fliegt noch die Locke taglang im Wind
Um des Landgotts gebräunte Stirn,
unter dem Hemd preßt die Faust
schon die klaffende Wunde.

Drum sei hart, wenn der zarte Rücken der Wolken
sich dir einmal noch beugt,
nimm es für nichts, wenn der Hymettos die Waben
noch einmal dir füllt.

Denn wenig gilt dem Landmann ein Halm in der Dürre,
wenig ein Sommer vor unserem großen Geschlecht.

Und was bezeugt schon dein Herz?
Zwischen gestern und morgen schwingt es,
lautlos und fremd,
und was es schlägt,
ist schon sein Fall aus der Zeit.

Fall Down, Heart

Fall down, heart, from the tree of time,
fall, you leaves, from icy branches
that once the sun embraced,
fall, as tears fall from longing eyes.

Though his curls whip for days in the wind
around the land god's umber brow,
under the shirt a fist presses
already to the gaping wound.

Be hard, if the tender backs of clouds
bend yet again to you;
take it as nothing if Hymettus's honeycombs
once more fill you up.

Because one stalk in a drought means little to a farmer,
one summer so little to our great lineage.

And so what can your heart attest to?
Between yesterday and tomorrow it swings,
soundless and strange,
and what it beats
is its own fall out of time.

Dunkles zu sagen

Wie Orpheus spiel ich
auf den Saiten des Lebens den Tod
und in die Schönheit der Erde
und deiner Augen, die den Himmel verwalten,
weiß ich nur Dunkles zu sagen.

Vergiß nicht, daß auch du, plötzlich,
an jenem Morgen, als dein Lager
noch naß war von Tau und die Nelke
an deinem Herzen schlief,
den dunklen Fluß sahst,
der an dir vorbeizog.

Die Saite des Schweigens
gespannt auf die Welle von Blut,
griff ich dein tönendes Herz.
Verwandelt ward deine Locke
ins Schattenhaar der Nacht,
der Finsternis schwarze Flocken
beschneiten dein Antlitz.

Und ich gehör dir nicht zu.
Beide klagen wir nun.

Aber wie Orpheus weiß ich
auf der Seite des Todes das Leben,
und mir blaut
dein für immer geschlossenes Aug.

Darkness Spoken

Like Orpheus I play
death on the strings of life,
and to the beauty of the Earth
and your eyes, which administer heaven,
I can only speak of darkness.

Don't forget that you also, suddenly,
on that morning when your camp
was still damp with dew, and a carnation
slept on your heart,
you saw the dark stream
race past you.

The string of silence
taut on the pulse of blood,
I grasped your beating heart.
Your curls were transformed
into the shadow hair of night,
black flakes of darkness
buried your face.

And I don't belong to you.
Both of us mourn now.

But like Orpheus I know
life on the side of death,
and the deepening blue
of your forever closed eye.

Paris

Aufs Rad der Nacht geflochten
schlafen die Verlorenen
in den donnernden Gängen unten,
doch wo wir sind, ist Licht.

Wir haben die Arme voll Blumen,
Mimosen aus vielen Jahren;
Goldnes fällt von Brücke zu Brücke
atemlos in den Fluß.

Kalt ist das Licht,
noch kälter der Stein vor dem Tor,
und die Schalen der Brunnen
sind schon zur Hälfte geleert.

Was wird sein, wenn wir, vom Heimweh
benommen bis ans fliehende Haar,
hier bleiben und fragen: was wird sein,
wenn wir die Schönheit bestehen?

Auf den Wagen des Lichts gehoben,
wachend auch, sind wir verloren,
auf den Straßen der Genien oben,
doch wo wir nicht sind, ist Nacht.

Paris

Lashed to the wheel of night
the lost ones sleep
in the thunderous passages beneath;
but where we are, it's light.

Our arms are full of blossoms,
mimosa from many years;
goldness showers from bridge after bridge
breathless into the stream.

Cold is the light,
colder yet the stone before the portal,
and the basins of fountains
are already half empty.

What will happen if we, homesick
and dazed with windblown hair,
remain here and ask: what will happen
if we can withstand such beauty?

Lifted onto the wagon of light,
and waking, we are lost
in the alleys of brilliance above;
but where we are not, it's night.

Die große Fracht

Die große Fracht des Sommers ist verladen,
das Sonnenschiff im Hafen liegt bereit,
wenn hinter dir die Möwe stürzt und schreit.
Die große Fracht des Sommers ist verladen.

Das Sonnenschiff im Hafen liegt bereit,
und auf die Lippen der Galionsfiguren
tritt unverhüllt das Lächeln der Lemuren.
Das Sonnenschiff im Hafen liegt bereit.

Wenn hinter dir die Möwe stürtz und schreit,
kommt aus dem Westen der Befehl zu sinken;
doch offnen Augs wirst du im Licht ertrinken,
wenn hinter dir die Möwe stürzt und schreit.

The Heavy Cargo

The summer's heavy cargo has been loaded,
waiting in the harbor a sun ship lies,
as at your back the seagull dips and cries.
The summer's heavy cargo has been loaded.

Waiting in the harbor a sun ship lies,
and there upon the lips of figureheads
the lemur's mocking smile appears and spreads.
Waiting in the harbor a sun ship lies.

As at your back the seagull dips and cries,
from the western horizon comes the order to sink;
you'll drown, open-eyed, in the light you'll drink,
as at your back the seagull dips and cries.

Reigen

Reigen — die Liebe hält manchmal
im Löschen der Augen ein,
und wir sehen in ihre eignen
erloschenen Augen hinein.

Kalter Rauch aus dem Krater
haucht unsre Wimpern an;
es hielt die schreckliche Leere
nur einmal den Atem an.

Wir haben die toten Augen
gesehn und vergessen nie.
Die Liebe währt am längsten
und sie erkennt uns nie.

Round Dance

Round dance: a love can sometimes cease
in the extinguishing of an eye,
and what we come to see
is love's extinguished eye.

Cold smoke from the crater
breathes upon our lashes;
only once did empty terror
not breathe at all upon us.

We've seen the eyes of the dead
and will forget them never.
Love lasts to the end,
but apprehends us never.

Herbstmanöver

Ich sage nicht: das war gestern. Mit wertlosem
Sommergeld in den Taschen liegen wir wieder
auf der Spreu des Hohns, im Herbstmanöver der Zeit.
Und der Fluchtweg nach Süden kommt uns nicht,
wie den Vögeln, zustatten. Vorüber, am Abend,
ziehen Fischkutter und Gondeln, und manchmal
trifft mich ein Splitter traumsatten Marmors,
wo ich verwundbar bin, durch Schönheit, im Aug.

In den Zeitungen lese ich viel von der Kälte
und ihren Folgen, von Törichten und Toten,
von Vertriebenen, Mördern und Myriaden
von Eisschollen, aber wenig, was mir behagt.
Warum auch? Vor dem Bettler, der mittags kommt,
schlag ich die Tür zu, denn es ist Frieden
und man kann sich den Anblick ersparen, aber nicht
im Regen das freudlose Sterben der Blätter.

Laßt uns eine Reise tun! Laßt uns unter Zypressen
oder auch unter Palmen oder in den Orangenhainen
zu verbilligten Preisen Sonnenuntergänge sehen,
die nicht ihresgleichen haben! Laßt uns die
unbeantworteten Briefe an das Gestern vergessen!
Die Zeit tut Wunder. Kommt sie uns aber unrecht,
mit dem Pochen der Schuld: wir sind nicht zu Hause.
Im Keller des Herzens, schlaflos, find ich mich wieder
auf der Spreu des Hohns, im Herbstmanöver der Zeit.

Autumn Maneuver

I don't say: ah, yesterday. With worthless
summer money pocketed, we lie again
on the chaff of scorn, in time's autumn maneuver.
And the escape southward isn't an option for us
as it is for the birds. Across the way, at evening,
trawlers and gondolas pass, and sometimes
a splinter of dream-filled marble pierces me
in the eye, where I am most vulnerable to beauty.

In the papers I read about the cold
and its effects, about fools and dead men,
about refugees, murderers and myriads
of ice floes, but little that comforts me.
Why should it be otherwise? In the face of the beggar
who comes at noon I slam the door, for we live in peacetime
and one can spare oneself such a sight, but not
the joyless dying of leaves in the rain.

Let's take a trip! Let's stroll under cypresses
or even under palms or in the orange groves
to see at reduced rates sunsets
that are beyond compare! Let's forget
the unanswered letters to yesterday!
Time works wonders. But if it arrives inconveniently
with the knocking of guilt: we're not at home.
In the heart's cellar, sleepless, I find myself again
on the chaff of scorn, in time's autumn maneuver.

Die gestundete Zeit

Es kommen härtere Tage.
Die auf Widerruf gestundete Zeit
wird sichtbar am Horizont.
Bald musst du den Schuh schnüren
und die Hunde zurückjagen in die Marschhöfe.
Denn die Eingeweide der Fische
sind kalt geworden im Wind.
Ärmlich brennt das Licht der Lupinen.
Dein Blick spurt im Nebel:
die auf Widerruf gestundete Zeit
wird sichtbar am Horizont.

Drüben versinkt dir die Geliebte im Sand,
er steigt um ihr wehendes Haar,
er fällt ihr ins Wort,
er befiehlt ihr zu schweigen,
er findet sie sterblich
und willig dem Abschied
nach jeder Umarmung.

Sieh dich nicht um.
Schnür deinen Schuh.
Jag die Hunde zurück.
Wirf die Fische ins Meer.
Lösch die Lupinen!

Es kommen härtere Tage.

Borrowed Time

Harder days are coming.
The loan of borrowed time
will be due on the horizon.
Soon you must lace up your boots
and chase the hounds back to the marsh farms.
For the entrails of fish
have grown cold in the wind.
Dimly burns the light of lupines.
Your gaze makes out in fog:
the loan of borrowed time
will be due on the horizon.

There your loved one sinks in sand;
it rises up to her windblown hair,
it cuts her short,
it commands her to be silent,
it discovers she's mortal
and willing to leave you
after every embrace.

Don't look around.
Lace up your boots.
Chase back the hounds.
Throw the fish into the sea.
Put out the lupines!

Harder days are coming.

II

Sterne im März

Noch ist die Aussaat weit. Auf treten
Vorfelder im Regen und Sterne im März.
In die Formel unfruchtbarer Gedanken
fügt sich das Universum nach dem Beispiel
des Lichts, das nicht an den Schnee rührt.

Unter dem Schnee wird auch Staub sein
und, was nicht zerfiel, des Staubes
spätere Nahrung. O Wind, der anhebt!
Wieder reißen Pflüge das Dunkel auf.
Die Tage wollen länger werden.

An langen Tagen sät man uns ungefragt
in jene krummen und geraden Linien,
und Sterne treten ab. Auf den Feldern
gedeihen oder verderben wir wahllos,
gefügig dem Regen und zuletzt auch dem Licht.

II

March Stars

Still it's too early for sowing. Fields
surface in rain, March stars appear.
Like an afterthought, the universe submits
to familiar equations, such as the light
that falls but leaves the snow untouched.

Under the snow there will also be dust
and, what doesn't disintegrate, the dust's
later nourishment. O wind, picking up.
Again the plows rip open the darkness.
Each new day will want to be longer.

It's on long days that we are sown,
unasked, in those neat and crooked rows,
as stars sink away above. In fields
we thrive or rot without a choice,
submitting to rain and also at last the light.

Im Zwielicht

Wieder legen wir beide die Hände ins Feuer,
du für den Wein der lange gelagerten Nacht,
ich für den Morgenquell, der die Kelter nicht kennt.
Es harrt der Blasbalg des Meisters, dem wir vertrauen.

Wie die Sorge ihn wärmt, tritt der Bläser hinzu.
Er geht, eh es tagt, er kommt, eh du rufst, er ist alt
wie das Zwielicht auf unsren schütteren Brauen.

Wieder kocht er das Blei im Kessel der Tränen,
dir für ein Glas — es gilt, das Versäumte zu feiern —
mir für den Scherben voll Rauch — der wird überm Feuer geleert.
So stoß ich zu dir und bringe die Schatten zum Klingen.

Erkannt ist, wer jetzt zögert,
erkannt, wer den Spruch vergaß.
Du kannst und willst ihn nicht wissen,
du trinkst vom Rand, wo es kühl ist
und wie vorzeiten, du trinkst und bleibst nüchtern,
dir wachsen noch Brauen, dir sieht man noch zu!

Ich aber bin schon des Augenblicks
gewärtig in Liebe, mir fällt der Scherben
ins Feuer, mir wird er zum Blei,
das er war. Und hinter der Kugel
steh ich, einäugig, zielsicher, schmal,
und schick sie dem Morgen entgegen.

In Twilight

Again we both swear to what we each hold as true,
you reaching for the wine of the long-seasoned night,
I for morning's wellspring that knows no wine press.
The bellows await the master in whom we trust.

As sorrow warms him, the glassblower steps toward us.
He leaves before dawn, he comes before you call, he is old
as the twilight on our thin brows.

Again he boils the lead in the kettle of tears,
making for you a glass — meaning a toast to what's lost —
for me a shard full of smoke — it's emptied over the fire.
And so I lean into you, making the shadows ring.

Known is he who hesitates now,
known is he who forgot what was meant.
You can't and don't want to know it,
you drink from the rim where it's cool;
and like long ago, you drink and stay sober,
your brows are still growing, you are still seen!

But I am already prepared for the moment
of love; for me the shard falls
into the fire, where it returns to the lead
it once was. And behind the bullet
I stand, one-eyed, almost invisible, with a steady aim,
and shoot it towards the morning.

Holz und Späne

Von den Hornissen will ich schweigen,
denn sie sind leicht zu erkennen.
Auch die laufenden Revolutionen
sind nicht gefährlich.
Der Tod im Gefolge des Lärms
ist beschlossen von jeher.

Doch vor den Eintagsfliegen und den Frauen
nimm dich in acht, vor den Sonntagsjägern,
den Kosmetikern, den Unentschiedenen, Wohlmeinenden,
von keiner Verachtung getroffnen.

Aus den Wäldern trugen wir Reisig und Stämme,
und die Sonne ging uns lange nicht auf.
Berauscht vom Papier am Fließband,
erkenn ich die Zweige nicht wieder,
noch das Moos, in dunkleren Tinten gegoren,
noch das Wort, in die Rinden geschnitten,
wahr und vermessen.

Blätterverschleiß, Spruchbänder,
schwarze Plakate … Bei Tag und bei Nacht
bebt, unter diesen und jenen Sternen,
die Maschine des Glaubens. Aber ins Holz,
solang es noch grün ist, und mit der Galle,
solang sie noch bitter ist, bin ich
zu schreiben gewillt, was im Anfang war!

Seht zu, daß ihr wachbleibt!

Wood and Shavings

Of hornets I will say nothing,
since they are so easy to spot.
Also, the current revolutions
are not that dangerous.
Death has always been chosen
amid a fanfare of noise.

Yet beware the May flies and women,
beware the Sunday hunters,
beauticians, the undecided, the well meaning,
the ones devoid of contempt.

Out of the forests we carried branches and logs,
and for a long time there was no sun.
Intoxicated by paper on the conveyer belt,
I no longer recognize the branches
nor the moss, dyed in darker tints,
nor the word, carved into the bark,
impudent and true.

Wasted paper, banners,
black posters …. By day and by night
the machine of faith rumbles beneath
this or that star. But in wood,
as long as it is still green, and with bile,
as long as it is still bitter, I am
willing to write what happened at the start!

Make sure you stay awake.

Der Spur der Späne, die flogen, folgt
der Hornissenschwarm, und am Brunnen
sträubt sich der Lockung,
die uns einst schwächte,
das Haar.

The swarm of hornets chases the shavings
blown by the wind, while at the fountain,
resisting the curled allure
that once made us weak,
my hair bristles.

Thema und Variation

In diesem Sommer blieb der Honig aus.
Die Königinnen zogen Schwärme fort,
der Erdbeerschlag war über Tag verdorrt,
die Beerensammler kehrten früh nach Haus.

Die ganze Süße trug ein Strahl des Lichts
in einen Schlaf. Wer schlief ihn vor der Zeit?
Honig und Beeren? Der ist ohne Leid,
dem alles zukommt. Und es fehlt ihm nichts.

Und es fehlt ihm nichts, nur ein wenig,
um zu ruhen oder um aufrecht zu stehen.
Höhlen beugten ihn tief und Schatten,
denn kein Land nahm ihn auf.
Selbst in den Bergen war er nicht sicher
— ein Partisan, den die Welt abgab
an ihren toten Trabanten, den Mond.

Der ist ohne Leid, dem alles zukommt,
und was kam ihm nicht zu? Die Kohorte
der Käfer schlug sich in seiner Hand, Brände
häuften Narben in seinem Gesicht und die Quelle
trat als Chimäre vor sein Aug,
wo sie nicht war.

Honig und Beeren?
Hätte er je den Geruch gekannt, er wär ihm längst gefolgt!
Nachtwandlerischer Schlaf im Gehen,
wer schlief ihn vor der Zeit?
Einer, der alt geboren wurde
und früh ins Dunkel muß.
Die ganze Süße trug ein Strahl des Lichts
an ihm vorbei.

Theme and Variation

All summer long the hives produced no honey.
Queen bees gave up and led their swarms away,
the strawberry patch dried up in a day,
and without work, the gatherers went home early.

All sweetness was carried away on a beam of light
in a single night's sleep. Who slept while this happened?
Honey and berries? He knows no misfortune,
he who lacks for nothing. For him, it all comes right.

And he lacks for nothing, except just a little,
whenever he needs to rest or stand erect.
For he's bent double by caves and shadows
because no country gave him asylum.
Even in the mountains he didn't feel safe
— a partisan, whom the world had turned in
to its own dead satellite, the moon.

He knows no misfortune, he who lacks for nothing,
and what did he ever lack? The beetle's
cohort fought in his hand, firebrands
amassed scars upon his face, and the spring
appeared as a chimaera before his eyes
where it was not.

Honey and berries?
Had he known their scent, he would've followed it long ago.
Walking through sleep, sleepwalking,
who slept while this happened?
One who was born already old
and is called to darkness early.
All sweetness was carried away on a beam of light
eluding him.

Er spie ins Unterholz den Fluch,
der Dürre bringt, er schrie
und ward erhört:
die Beerensammler kehrten früh nach Haus!
Als sich die Wurzel hob
und ihnen pfeifend nachglitt,
blieb eine Schlangenhaut des Baumes letzte Hut.
Der Erdbeerschlag war über Tag verdorrt.

Unten im Dorf standen die Eimer leer
und trommelreif im Hof.
So schlug die Sonne zu
und wirbelte den Tod.

Die Fenster fielen zu,
die Königinnen zogen Schwärme fort,
und keiner hinderte sie, fortzufliegen.
Die Wildnis nahm sie auf,
der hohle Baum im Farn
den ersten freien Staat.
Den letzten Menschen traf
ein Stachel ohne Schmerz.

In diesem Sommer blieb der Honig aus.

He spat a curse into the undergrowth
that brought on drought; he screamed
and was heard:
without work, the gatherers went home early!
When the root lifted itself
and, hissing, slithered towards them,
a snakeskin remained, the tree's last defense.
The strawberry patch dried up in a day.

In the village below, the bucket stood empty,
ready to be used as a drum in the square.
And so the sun struck it
and sent death whirling.

The windows slammed shut,
queen bees gave up and led their swarms away,
and no one stopped them from flying off.
The wilderness took them in,
the hollow tree in the ferns
the first free state.
The last living men, pricked
by a thorn, could feel no pain.

All summer long the hives produced no honey.

Früher Mittag

Still grünt die Linde im eröffneten Sommer,
weit aus den Städten gerückt, flirrt
der mattglänzende Tagmond. Schon ist Mittag,
schon regt sich im Brunnen der Strahl,
schon hebt sich unter den Scherben
des Märchenvogels geschundener Flügel,
und die vom Steinwurf entstellte Hand
sinkt ins erwachende Korn.

Wo Deutschlands Himmel die Erde schwärzt,
sucht sein enthaupteter Engel ein Grab für den Haß
und reicht dir die Schüssel des Herzens.

Eine Handvoll Schmerz verliert sich über den Hügel.

Sieben Jahre später
fällt es dir wieder ein,
am Brunnen vor dem Tore,
blick nicht zu tief hinein,
die Augen gehen dir über.

Sieben Jahre später,
in einem Totenhaus,
trinken die Henker von gestern
den goldenen Becher aus.
Die Augen täten dir sinken.

Schon ist Mittag, in der Asche
krümmt sich das Eisen, auf den Dorn
ist die Fahne gehißt, und auf den Felsen
uralten Traums bleibt fortan
der Adler geschmiedet.

Early Noon

Silently the linden greens in incipient summer,
far from the cities there glimmers
the pale brightness of the day moon. Already it's noon,
already a sunbeam flashes in the fountain,
already the fabulous bird's flayed wing
lifts itself beneath the rubble,
and the hand that's cramped from casting stones
sinks into the budding wheat.

Where Germany's sky blackens the earth,
its beheaded angel seeks a grave for hate
and offers you the bowl of the heart.

A handful of pain vanishes over the hill.

Seven years later
it occurs to you again,
at the fountain before the portal,
don't look too deep within,
as your eyes fill with tears.

Seven years later,
inside a mortuary,
the hangmen of yesterday
drain the golden cup.
Your eyes lower in shame.

Already it's noon, in embers
the iron bends, on the thorn
the flag is hoisted, and onto the cliff
of the ancient dream the eagle is welded,
remaining forever.

Nur die Hoffnung kauert erblindet im Licht.

Lös ihr die Fessel, führ sie
die Halde herab, leg ihr
die Hand auf das Aug, daß sie
kein Schatten versengt!

Wo Deutschlands Erde den Himmel schwärzt,
sucht die Wolke nach Worten und füllt den Krater mit
    Schweigen,
eh sie der Sommer im schütteren Regen vernimmt.

Das Unsägliche geht, leise gesagt, übers Land:
schon ist Mittag.

Only hope cowers, blinded in the light.

Throw off its shackles, help it
down the slope, cover
its eyes so that
the shadows don't scorch it!

Where Germany's earth blackens the sky,
a cloud seeks words and fills the crater with silence
before summer hears them in the patter of rain.

The unspeakable passes, barely spoken, over the land:
already it's noon.

Alle Tage

Der Krieg wird nicht mehr erklärt,
sondern fortgesetzt. Das Unerhörte
ist alltäglich geworden. Der Held
bleibt den Kämpfen fern. Der Schwache
ist in die Feuerzonen gerückt.
Die Uniform des Tages ist die Geduld,
die Auszeichnung der armselige Stern
der Hoffnung über dem Herzen.

Er wird verliehen,
wenn nichts mehr geschieht,
wenn das Trommelfeuer verstummt,
wenn der Feind unsichtbar geworden ist
und der Schatten ewiger Rüstung
den Himmel bedeckt.

Er wird verliehen
für die Flucht von den Fahnen,
für die Tapferkeit vor dem Freund,
für den Verrat unwürdiger Geheimnisse
und die Nichtachtung
jeglichen Befehls.

Every Day

War is no longer declared,
but rather continued. The outrageous
has become the everyday. The hero
is absent from the battle. The weak
are moved into the firing zone.
The uniform of the day is patience,
the order of merit is the wretched star
of hope over the heart.

It is awarded
when nothing more happens,
when the bombardment is silenced,
when the enemy has become invisible
and the shadow of eternal armament
covers the sky.

It is awarded
for deserting the flag,
for bravery before a friend,
for the betrayal of shameful secrets
and the disregard
of every command.

Einem Feldherrn

Wenn jenes Geschäft im Namen der Ehre
ergrauter und erblindeter Völker
wieder zustande kommt, wirst du
ein Handlanger sein und dienstbar
unsren Gemarkungen, da du's verstehst,
sie einzufrieden mit Blut.
Voraus in den Büchern schattet
dein Name, und es verleitet
sein Anflug Lorbeer zum Wuchs.

Wie wir's verstehen: opfre keinem vor dir
und rufe auch Gott nicht an. (Verlangte ihn je
teilzuhaben an deiner Beute? War er je
ein Parteigänger deiner Hoffnungen?)

Eins sollst du wissen:
erst wenn du nicht mehr versuchst,
wie viele vor dir, mit dem Degen
den unteilbaren Himmel zu trennen,
treibt der Lorbeer ein Blatt.
Erst wenn du mit einem ungeheuren Zweifel
dein Glück aus dem Sattel hebst und selbst
aufspringst, verheiß ich dir Sieg!

Denn du errangst ihn nicht damals,
als dein Glück für dich siegte;
zwar sanken die Fahnen des Feindes
und Waffen fielen dir zu
und Früchte aus Gärten,
die ein andrer bebaute.

To A General

When that affair in the name of the honor
of blind and grey-haired nations
again comes to pass, you will be
the drudge tending to our boundaries,
because you know
how to fence them in with blood.
Already your name shadows
the books, its presence seducing
a sprig of laurel into growth.

To us, it is so: don't make sacrifices to anyone
and don't invoke God. (Did he ever
demand a cut of your spoils? Was he ever
a party to your hopes?)

There's one thing you should know:
only when you no longer attempt,
as many before you, to part
the unseverable sky with the sword
will the laurel sprout a leaf.
Only when, with monstrous doubt,
you lift your luck out of the saddle
and step down as yourself, will I promise you victory!

For you won no victory then
when your luck won it for you;
indeed, the enemy's flags sank
and weapons fell to you
and fruit from the gardens,
which another tended.

Wo am Horizont der Weg deines Glücks
und der Weg deines Unglücks
in eins verlaufen, richte die Schlacht.
Wo es dunkelt und die Soldaten schlafen,
wo sie dir fluchten und von dir
verflucht wurden, richte den Tod.

Du wirst fallen
vom Berg ins Tal, mit den reißenden Gewässern
in die Schluchten, auf den Grund der Fruchtbarkeit,
in die Samen der Erde, dann in die Minen von Gold,
in den Fluß des Erzes, aus dem die Standbilder
der Großen gehämmert werden, in die tiefen Bezirke
des Vergessens, Millionen Klafter von dort,
und in die Bergwerke des Traums.
Zuletzt aber in das Feuer.

Dort reicht dir der Lorbeer ein Blatt.

Where, on the horizon, the path of your luck
and the path of your bad luck
converge, prepare for battle.
Where darkness falls and the troops sleep,
where they will curse you and by you
are cursed, prepare for death.

You will fall
from the mountain into the valley, with rapids
into the ravine, into fecund soil,
into the seeds of the earth, then into the gold mines,
into the river of ore from which the statues
of the great are hammered, into the deep realm
of forgetfulness, a million fathoms farther
and into the pit of the dream.
Then finally into the fire.

There the laurel will offer you a leaf.

Botschaft

Aus der leichenwarmen Vorhalle des Himmels tritt die Sonne.
Es sind dort nicht die Unsterblichen,
sondern die Gefallenen, vernehmen wir.

Und Glanz kehrt sich nicht an Verwesung. Unsere Gottheit,
die Geschichte, hat uns ein Grab bestellt,
aus dem es keine Auferstehung gibt.

Message

Out of the corpse-warm foyer of heaven steps the sun.
There it is not the immortals,
but rather the fallen, we perceive.

And brilliance doesn't trouble itself with decay. Our godhead,
history, has ordered for us a grave
from which there is no resurrection.

Die Brücken

Straffer zieht der Wind das Band vor den Brücken.

An den Traversen zerrieb
der Himmel sein dunkelstes Blau.
Hüben und drüben wechseln
im Licht unsre Schatten.

Pont Mirabeau … Waterloobridge …
Wie ertragen's die Namen,
die Namenlosen zu tragen?

Von den Verlornen gerührt,
die der Glaube nicht trug,
erwachen die Trommeln im Fluß.

Einsam sind alle Brücken,
und der Ruhm ist ihnen gefährlich
wie uns, vermeinen wir doch,
die Schritte der Sterne
auf unserer Schulter zu spüren.
Doch übers Gefälle des Vergänglichen
wölbt uns kein Traum.

Besser ist's, im Auftrag der Ufer
zu leben, von einem zum andern,
und tagsüber zu wachen,
daß das Band der Berufene trennt.
Denn er erreicht die Schere der Sonne
im Nebel, und wenn sie ihn blendet,
umfängt ihn der Nebel im Fall.

III

The Bridges

Wind tightens the ribbon drawn across bridges.

The sky grinds on the crossbeams
with its darkest blue.
On this side and that our shadows
pass each other in the light.

Pont Mirabeau … Waterloo Bridge …
How can the names stand
to carry the nameless?

Stirred by the lost
that faith could not carry,
the river's drumbeat awakens.

Lonely are all bridges,
and fame is as dangerous for them
as it is for us, yet we presume
to feel the tread of stars
upon our shoulders.
Still, over the slope of transience
no dream arches us.

It's better to follow the riverbanks,
crossing from one to another,
and all day keep an eye out
for the official to cut the ribbon.
For when he does, he'll seize the sun's scissors
within the fog, and if the sun blinds him,
he'll be swallowed by fog when he falls.

Nachtflug

Unser Acker ist der Himmel,
im Schweiß der Motoren bestellt,
angesichts der Nacht,
unter Einsatz des Traums —

geträumt auf Schädelstätten und Scheiterhaufen,
unter dem Dach der Welt, dessen Ziegel
der Wind forttrug — und nun Regen, Regen, Regen
in unserem Haus und in den Mühlen
die blinden Flüge der Fledermäuse.
Wer wohnte dort? Wessen Hände waren rein?
Wer leuchtete in der Nacht,
Gespenst den Gespenstern?

Im Stahlgefieder geborgen, verhören
Instrumente den Raum, Kontrolluhren und Skalen
das Wolkengesträuch, und es streift die Liebe
unsres Herzens vergessene Sprache:
kurz und lang lang ... Für eine Stunde
rührt Hagel die Trommel des Ohrs,
das, uns abgeneigt, lauscht und verwindet.

Nicht untergegangen sind Sonne und Erde,
nur als Gestirne gewandert und nicht zu erkennen.

Wir sind aufgestiegen von einem Hafen,
wo Wiederkehr nicht zählt
und nicht Fracht und nicht Fang.
Indiens Gewürze und Seiden aus Japan
gehören den Händlern
wie die Fische den Netzen.

Night Flight

Our field is the sky
plowed by the engine's sweat,
in the face of night,
at the risk of a dream —

dreamt on Golgotha and on funeral pyres,
under the roof of the world, whose shingles
the wind carried off — and now rain, rain, rain
in our house, and in the mills
the blind flight of the bats.
Who lived there? Whose hands were pure?
Who was lit up in the night,
a ghost to other ghosts?

Protected by steel feathers, instruments
sound out space, control clocks and dials
probe thickets of clouds, and love strokes
the forgotten speech of our heart:
short and long long .... For an hour
hail beats the drum of the ear
that, reluctantly, listens in and endures.

Sun and earth have not sunk,
they only wander as stars, unrecognizable.

We have taken off from a port
where the return doesn't matter,
nor the cargo, nor the haul.
Indian spices and silks from Japan
belong to the dealers
like fish to the nets.

Doch ein Geruch ist zu spüren,
vorlaufend den Kometen,
und das Gewebe der Luft,
von gefallnen Kometen zerrissen.
Nenn's den Status der Einsamen,
in dem sich das Staunen vollzieht.
Nichts weiter.

Wir sind aufgestiegen, und die Klöster sind leer,
seit wir dulden, ein Orden, der nicht heilt und nicht lehrt.
Zu handeln ist nicht Sache der Piloten. Sie haben
Stützpunkte im Aug und auf den Knien ausgebreitet
die Landkarte einer Welt, der nichts hinzuzufügen ist.

Wer lebt dort unten? Wer weint …
Wer veliert den Schlüssel zum Haus?
Wer findet sein Bett nicht, wer schläft
auf den Schwellen? Wer, wenn der Morgen kommt,
wagt's, den Silberstreifen zu deuten: seht, über mir …
Wenn das Wasser von neuem ins Mühlrad greift,
wer wagt's, sich der Nacht zu erinnern?

Yet a smell can be traced
preceding the comets
and the air's fabric
ripped by those fallen.
Call it the status of the lonely
in whom wonder still occurs.
Nothing more.

We have risen, and the cloisters are empty,
since we endure, an order that can't heal or teach.
It's not the pilots' job to act. They have
the air bases in sight, and spread out on their knees
the map of a world, to which nothing can be added.

Who lives below? Who is crying …
Who has lost the key to his house?
Who can't find his bed, who sleeps
on the doorstep? Who, when morning comes,
will dare interpret the silver trail: look, above me …
When water churns the mill wheel again,
who will dare to remember the night?

Psalm

I

Schweigt mit mir, wie alle Glocken schweigen!

In der Nachgeburt der Schrecken
sucht das Geschmeiß nach neuer Nahrung.
Zur Ansicht hängt karfreitags eine Hand
am Firmament, zwei Finger fehlen ihr,
sie kann nicht schwören, daß alles,
alles nicht gewesen sei und nichts
sein wird. Sie taucht ins Wolkenrot,
entrückt die neuen Mörder
und geht frei.

Nachts auf dieser Erde
in Fenster greifen, die Linnen zurückschlagen,
daß der Kranken Heimlichkeit bloßliegt,
ein Geschwür voll Nahrung, unendliche Schmerzen
für jeden Geschmack.

Die Metzger halten, behandschuht,
den Atem der Entblößten an,
der Mond in der Tür fällt zu Boden,
laß die Scherben liegen, den Henkel …

Alles war gerichtet für die letzte Ölung.
(Das Sakrament kann nicht vollzogen werden.)

Psalm

I

Be silent with me, as all bells are silent!

In the afterbirth of terror
the rabble grovels for new nourishment.
On Good Friday a hand hangs on display
in the firmament, two fingers missing,
and it cannot swear that all of it,
all of it didn't happen, and nothing
ever will. It dives into red clouds,
whisks off the new murderers
and goes free.

Each night on this earth
open the windows, fold back the sheets
so that the invalid's secret lies naked,
a sore full of sustenance, endless pain
for every taste.

Gloved butchers cease
the breath of the naked;
the moon in the doorway falls to earth;
let the shards lie, the handle ….

All was prepared for the last rites.
(The sacrament cannot be completed.)

el alles ist.
ine Stadt heran,
_____ lich aus dem Staub dieser Stadt,
übernimm ein Amt
und verstelle dich,
um der Bloßstellung zu entgehen.

Löse die Versprechen ein
vor einem blinden Spiegel in der Luft,
vor einer verschlossenen Tür im Wind.

Unbegangen sind die Wege auf der Steilwand des Himmels.

3

O Augen, an dem Sonnenspeicher Erde verbrannt,
mit der Regenlast aller Augen beladen,
und jetzt versponnen, verwebt
von den tragischen Spinnen
der Gegenwart ...

4

In die Mulde meiner Stummheit
leg ein Wort
und zieh Wälder groß zu beiden Seiten,
daß mein Mund
ganz im Schatten liegt.

2

How vain it all is.
Roll into a city,
rise from the city's dust,
take over a post
and disguise yourself
to avoid exposure.

Fulfill the promises
before a tarnished mirror in the air,
before a shut door in the wind.

Untraveled are the paths on the steep slope of heaven.

3

O eyes, scorched by the Earth's reservoir of sun,
weighted with the rain of all eyes,
and now absorbed, interwoven
by the tragic spiders
of the present …

4

In the hollow of my muteness
lay a word
and grow tall forests on both sides,
such that my mouth
lies wholly in shade.

Im Gewitter der Rosen

Wohin wir uns wenden im Gewitter der Rosen,
ist die Nacht von Dornen erhellt, und der Donner
des Laubs, das so leise war in den Büschen,
folgt uns jetzt auf dem Fuß.

In the Storm of Roses

Wherever we turn in the storm of roses,
the night is lit up by thorns, and the thunder
of leaves, once so quiet within the bushes,
rumbling at our heels.

Salz und Brot

Nun schickt der Wind die Schienen voraus,
wir werden folgen in langsamen Zügen
und diese Inseln bewohnen,
Vertrauen gegen Vertrauen.

In die Hand meines ältesten Freunds leg ich
mein Amt zurück; es verwaltet der Regenmann
jetzt mein finsteres Haus und ergänzt
im Schuldbuch die Linien, die ich zog,
seit ich seltener blieb.

Du, im fieberweißen Ornat,
holst die Verbannten ein und reißt
aus dem Fleisch der Kakteen einen Stachel
— das Zeichen der Ohnmacht,
dem wir uns willenlos beugen.

Wir wissen,
daß wir des Kontinentes Gefangene bleiben
und seinen Kränkungen wieder verfallen,
und die Gezeiten der Wahrheit
werden nicht seltener sein.

Schläft doch im Felsen
der wenig erleuchtete Schädel,
die Kralle hängt in der Kralle
im dunkeln Gestein, und verheilt
sind die Stigmen am Violett des Vulkans.

Von den großen Gewittern des Lichts
hat keines die Leben erreicht.

Salt and Bread

Now the wind sends its rails ahead;
we will follow in slow trains
and inhabit these islands,
trust beside trust.

Into the hand of my oldest friend
I place the key to my post; the rain man will now manage
my darkened house and lengthen
the lines of the ledger which I drew up
since I stayed less often.

You, in fever-white vestments,
gather the exiled and tear
from the flesh of cactus a thorn
— symbol of impotence
to which we meekly bow.

We know
that we'll remain the continent's captives,
and again we'll succumb to its troubled ills,
and the tides of truth
will arrive less often.

For sleeping yet in the cliff
is the barely lit skull,
the claw hangs in the claw
in the dark stone, and the stigmata
are healed in the violet of the volcano.

Of the great storms of light,
none has reached the living.

So nehm ich vom Salz,
wenn uns das Meer übersteigt,
und kehre zurück
und legs auf die Schwelle
und trete ins Haus.

Wir teilen ein Brot mit dem Regen,
ein Brot, eine Schuld und ein Haus.

So I gather the salt
when the sea overcomes us,
and turn back
and lay it on the threshold
and step into the house.

We share bread with the rain;
bread, a debt, and a house.

Große Landschaft bei Wien

Geister der Ebene, Geister des wachsenden Stroms,
zu unsrem Ende gerufen, haltet nicht vor der Stadt!
Nehmt auch mit euch, was vom Wein überhing
auf brüchigen Rändern, und führt an ein Rinnsal,
wen nach Ausweg verlangt, und öffnet die Steppen!

Drüben verkümmert das nackte Gelenk eines Baums,
ein Schwungrad springt ein, aus dem Feld schlagen
die Bohrtürme den Frühling, Statuenwäldern weicht
der verworfene Torso des Grüns, und es wacht
die Iris des Öls über den Brunnen im Land.

Was liegt daran? Wir spielen die Tänze nicht mehr.
Nach langer Pause: Dissonanzen gelichtet, wenig cantabile.
(Und ihren Atem spür ich nicht mehr auf den Wangen!)
Still stehn die Räder. Durch Staub und Wolkenspreu
schleift den Mantel, der unsre Liebe deckte, das Riesenrad.

Nirgends gewährt man, wie hier, vor den ersten Küssen
die letzten. Es gilt, mit dem Nachklang im Mund
weiterzugehn und zu schweigen. Wo der Kranich
im Schilf der flachen Gewässer seinen Bogen vollendet,
tönender als die Welle, schlägt ihm die Stunde im Rohr.

Asiens Atem ist jenseits.

Rhythmischer Aufgang von Saaten, reifer Kulturen
Ernten vorm Untergang, sind sie verbrieft, so weiß ichs
dem Wind noch zu sagen. Hinter der Böschung
trübt weicheres Wasser das Aug, und es will
mich noch anfallen trunkenes Limesgefühl;
unter den Pappeln am Römerstein grab ich
nach dem Schauplatz vielvölkriger Trauer,
nach dem Lächeln Ja und dem Lächeln Nein.

Great Landscape Near Vienna

Spirits of the plain, spirits of the swelling river,
invoked at our final end, don't halt before the city!
Take also with you the vines hanging over
the fragile banks and lead to a channel
whoever demands an exit, and open into the steppes!

Nearby there shrivels the naked crook of a tree,
a flywheel starts spinning, the derricks pump
spring from the fields, erected forests macerate
the degraded torso of greenness, and an iris of oil
watches over the wells of the land.

To what purpose? We dance the dances no longer.
After a long pause: dissonances made clear, barely cantabile.
(And I no longer feel their breath upon my cheeks!)
The wheels stand still. Through dust and cloud husks
the Ferris wheel drags the coat that covered our love.

Nowhere does one grant, as here, the last kisses before
the first. We carry the aftertaste in our mouths
and must go on in silence. Where the crane completes
its circle amid the rushes of the marsh's flat water,
on a reed the hour strikes more resonantly than waves.

Asia's breath lies beyond the river.

The rhythmic sprouting of seeds, the harvest of cultures
before their decline, they've been documented, but I can
still speak of them to the wind. Behind the escarpment,
softer water dulls the eye, and the drunken feeling
of Limes' fortified boundaries can still take hold of me;
under the poplars I dig by a Roman stone,
searching for the theater of many peopled grief,
for the smile of Yes and the smile of No.

Alles Leben ist abgewandert in Baukästen,
neue Not mildert man sanitär, in den Alleen
blüht die Kastanie duftlos, Kerzenrauch
kostet die Luft nicht wieder, über der Brüstung
im Park weht so einsam das Haar, im Wasser
sinken die Bälle, vorbei an der Kinderhand
bis auf den Grund, und es begegnet
das tote Auge dem blauen, das es einst war.

Wunder des Unglaubens sind ohne Zahl.
Besteht ein Herz darauf, ein Herz zu sein?
Träum, daß du rein bist, heb die Hand zum Schwur,
träum dein Geschlecht, das dich besiegt, träum
und wehr dennoch mystischer Abkehr im Protest.
Mit einer andern Hand gelingen Zahlen
und Analysen, die dich entzaubern.
Was dich trennt, bist du. Verström,
komm wissend wieder, in neuer Abschiedsgestalt.

Dem Orkan voraus fliegt die Sonne nach Westen,
zweitausend Jahre sind um, und uns wird nichts bleiben.
Es hebt der Wind Barockgirlanden auf,
es fällt von den Stiegen das Puttengesicht,
es stürzen Basteien in dämmernde Höfe,
von den Kommoden die Masken und Kränze …

Nur auf dem Platz im Mittagslicht, mit der Kette
am Säulenfuß und dem vergänglichsten Augenblick
geneigt und der Schönheit verfallen, sag ich mich los
von der Zeit, ein Geist unter Geistern, die kommen.
Maria am Gestade —
das Schiff ist leer, der Stein ist blind,
gerettet ist keiner, getroffen sind viele,
das Öl will nicht brennen, wir haben
alle davon getrunken — wo bleibt
dein ewiges Licht?

All life has migrated to the tenements,
new misery is eased sanitarily; in the avenues
the chestnuts blossom scentless; the air no longer
smells of candle smoke; over the balustrade
in the park, the hair sways so lonesome; in the water
the balls sink, dropping from the child's hand
to the bottom, until the dead eye encounters
the blue one that it once was.

The wonders of disbelief are innumerable.
Does a heart insist on being a heart?
Dream that you are pure, lift your hand to swear,
dream your lineage, which masters you, dream
and yet still, in protest, resist the mystic's retreat.
In a different manner numbers and analyses
win, and they disenchant you.
What separates you, is you. Wash away,
return wise, in a new manner of farewell.

The sun sails ahead of the hurricane toward the west;
two thousand years gone, and nothing of us will remain.
The wind lifts baroque garlands,
the cherub's face falls from the steps,
the bastions plunge into darkening courtyards,
from dressers fall the masks and wreathes …

Only in the square, in midday light, chained to
the column's base and toward the most fleeting moment
inclined and seized by beauty, do I break loose
from time, a spirit among spirits arriving.
Maria am Gestade —
the nave is empty, the stone is blind,
no one is saved, many are stricken,
the oil will not burn, we have all
drunk from it — where remains
your eternal light?

So sind auch die Fische tot und treiben
den schwarzen Meeren zu, die uns erwarten.
Wir aber mündeten längst, vom Sog
anderer Ströme ergriffen, wo die Welt
ausblieb und wenig Heiterkeit war.
Die Türme der Ebene rühmen uns nach,
daß wir willenlos kamen und auf den Stufen
der Schwermut fielen und tiefer fielen,
mit dem scharfen Gehör für den Fall.

And so the fish are also dead and float
towards the black seas that await us.
But we were washed away long ago, gripped
by the pull of other streams, where the world
disappeared and there was little cheer.
The towers of the plain sing our praises,
for we came here unwittingly, falling on the rungs
of depression, then falling deeper,
with an ear sharply tuned for the fall.

Ein Monolog des Fürsten Myschkin
zu der Ballettpantomime >Der Idiot<

Mit puppenhaften Schritten treten die Personen des Spiels — Parfion Rogoschin, Nastassia Filipowna, Totzki, Ganja Iwolgin, General Epantschin und Aglaja — auf. Die Pantomime endet mit dem Schlußtakt der Intrada, und Fürst Myschkin tritt in die Mitte der Szene. Er spricht den ganzen Monolog ohne Musik.

Ich habe das Wort, ich nahm's
aus der Hand der Trauer,
unwürdig, denn wie sollte ich
würdiger sein als einer der andern —
selbst ein Gefäß für jene Wolke,
die vom Himmel fiel und in uns tauchte,
schrecklich und fremd
und teilhaft der Schönheit
und jeder Verächtlichkeit dieser Welt.

(O Qual der Helle, Qual
des Fiebers, nah an anderen Fiebern,
unsrer gerechten Krankheit
gemeinsamer Schmerz!)

Laß den stummen Zug durch mein Herz gehen,
bis es dunkel wird
und, was mich erleuchtet,
wieder zurückgegeben ist
an das Dunkel.

Wahrhaftig, weil dieser Schmerz
in euch ist, tut ihr,
was ihr für euer Leben tut,
nicht für euer Leben,

A Monologue of Prince Myshkin
to the Ballet Pantomime "The Idiot"

*Walking like puppets, the characters of the play enter — Parfyon
Rogozhin, Nastasya Filippovna, Totski, Ganya Ivolgin, General
Epanchin and Aglaia. The pantomime ends with the last mea-
sure of the prelude as Prince Myshkin steps into the middle of the
scene. He speaks the entire monologue without music.*

I have the word, I took it
from the hand of sorrow,
unworthy, for how could I
be more worthy than the next —
myself a vessel for that cloud
that fell from the sky, plunging into us,
terrible and strange
and sharing the beauty
and all that's contemptible in this world.

(O torment of light, torment
of the fever, similar to other fevers,
the justified illness
of our common pain!)

Let the silent thrust pass through my heart
until it becomes dark
and what sets me alight
again is given back
to the darkness.

Truly, because this pain exists
in all of you, you do
what you do for the sake of it,
and not for the sake of your lives,

und was ihr zu eurer Ehre tut,
geschieht nicht zu eurer Ehre.

In der Dämonen Gelächter gebrannt,
bodenlos, sind die Schalen
dieses glücklosen Lebens,
das bis zum Rand uns bedenkt.
Trifft eine die andre, so klingen
sie nicht, denn kein Einhalt
ist den Tränen geboten, sprachlos
stürzen sie ab, von Grund
zu Grund, und es verweigert
der letzte, in den sie vergehn,
sich immer unsrem Gehör.
O Stummheit der Liebe!

Jetzt nimmt er jede Person, die er nennt, an der Hand.

Parfion Rogoschin, der Kaufmannssohn,
weiß nichts von einer Million.
In den Winternächten hält sein Gespann
vor den käuflichen Straßen der Welt
und kann sie nicht fahren.
Er schüttet sein Geld in den Schnee,
denn der Schnee ist das Maß

deiner Wangen, Nastassia Filipowna,
dein Name ist eine gefährliche Kurve
in jedem Mund, sie sagen, am Schnee
nähmst du das Maß für deine Wangen,
in deinem Haar wohnten die Winde,
(ich sage nicht: sie sind launisch),
dein Aug sei ein Hohlweg,
in dem ihre Wagen stürzen,
es zählt sie der Schnee, und vom Schnee

and what you do in the name of honor
does nothing for your honor.

Fired by the laughter of demons,
the bottomless drinking cups
of this unfortunate life
study us from their depths.
If one cup strikes another, they make
no sound, for no end to the tears
is ordered, as speechless
they fall from realm
to realm, the last one,
in which they cease, denied
to us and our hearing.
O the muteness of love!

He takes by the hand each person that he names.

Parfyon Rogozhin, the merchant's son,
cares nothing about a million rubles.
During winter nights, he halts his team
before the affordable streets of the world,
but he cannot drive through them.
He tosses his money into the snow,
for snow is the essence

of your cheeks, Nastasya Filippovna,
your name a dangerous curve
in every mouth, for they say from snow
you took the measure for your cheeks,
in your hair lived the winds,
(I wouldn't say so: they're just being funny)
your eye could be the gorge
into which their carriages will plunge
like falling snow, and from the snow

erhältst du das Maß
für deine Wangen.

Totzki — dies ist wohl zuviel,
eh man zu Ruhe geht: eines Kindes Augenblick
in den Armen war die Vergangenheit, und jetzt
ist die Zeit von Blicken, die Zeit
von Lippen über euch beide gekommen.

Ganja Iwolgin, wenn ein Band zwischen allen
gesponnen ist,
werden deine Hände die Knoten sein,
die es spannen,
denn du lächelst nicht gut.
Du forderst zu viel für dich
und verlangst zu wenig von dir.
Dich gängelt nur ein Verlangen:
die Wagen stürzen zu sehn,
in denen die anderen fahren,
eh du selbst unter Rädern verendest.

General Epantschin — es sind nicht Zufälle,
die uns in die Nähe derer führen, die wir meiden.
Wie wir uns in den Kindern entgleiten,
gleiten wir uneingestandenen Wünschen nach
und halten vor fremden Türen als Hüter,
die wir uns selbst so wenig zu hüten vermögen.

Was aber entglitt? Der weiße,
erkaltete Traum einer Jugend,
die nicht Nachsicht verlangt?
Vollkommenes also? Und Schönheit
in solcher Gestalt, daß wir uns
mit ihrem Rätsel begnügen? Aglaja,
so werde ich in dir nichts sehen

you received the measure
of your cheeks.

Totski — this is much too much
before one's final rest: the past was a moment
held like a babe in arms, and now
the time of glancing eyes, the time
of lips has taken hold of both of you.

Ganya Ivolgin, when a cord is stretched
between everyone,
your hands will be the knots
that tighten it,
for you don't laugh easily.
You want too much for yourself
and ask too little from yourself.
Only one desire leads you on:
to see the carriages plunge
in which the others ride
before you are crushed under the wheels.

General Epanchin — it's no accident
that led us into your realm, which now we shun.
Just as we give way to our children,
we give in to inadmissable desires
and stand as guards before strange doors
which we ourselves are so incapable of guarding.

But what did we give up? The white,
chilly dream of youth
that asks for no leniency?
Or perfection? And beauty
rendered such that we've
had enough of its puzzle? Aglaia,
I will see nothing in you

als die Botschaft einer Welt,
in die ich nicht eintreten,
ein Versprechen, das ich nicht halten,
und einen Besitz, den ich nicht wahren kann.

Er wendet sich um und steht mit dem Gesicht zum Publikum.

Erwacht zum Leben im Schein,
von Planeten verführt,
die von uns Ausdruck verlangen,
seh ich zur grenzenlosen Musik
die Bewegung der Stummen.

Hier münden seine Worte in einen marionettenhaft starren Tanz.

Unsere Schritte sind nur die wenig
genauen Anschläge weniger Töne,
die uns erreichen.

*In den Tanz, der die Einsamkeit jedes einzelnen zum
Ausdruck bringen soll, wird auch Myschkin hineingezogen.*

but the message of a world
into which I cannot enter,
a promise, which I cannot keep,
a possession, which I cannot protect.

He turns and faces the audience.

Awakened to life amid radiance,
seduced by the planets
that demand from us expression,
I witness borderless music
in the movement of the mute.

Here his words accompany a stiff marionette dance.

Our steps are only the few
precise strokes of the even fewer tones
that reach us.

*Myshkin is drawn into a dance in which the loneliness of each
character is expressed.*

Ein Interieur, das die Atmosphäre einer Zirkusarena schafft.
Nastassia gängelt Totzki, Ganja und den General an weißen
Bändern und spielt in einem tragischen, gewagten, gefährlichen
Tanz ihre Macht über die drei Männer aus. Dann erscheint
Rogoschin, und Nastassia dreht sich an den Männern vorbei. Ihr
Kostüm fällt stückweise von ihr ab, so daß sie zuletzt, nur mit
einem weißen Trikot bekleidet, unter einer goldenen Kugel steht.
Sie hebt eine Hand zum Ball und reicht die andere Rogoschin,
der abwartend abseits gestanden ist. In diesem Augenblick tritt
Myschkin auf sie zu.

Halt ein! Dich beschwör ich,
Gesicht der einzigen Liebe,
bleib hell und schlag mit den Wimpern
das Auge zur Welt zu, bleib schön,
Gesicht der einzigen Liebe,
und heb deine Stirn
aus dem Wetterleuchten der Zweifel.
Deine Küsse werden sie teilen,
dich entstellen im Schlaf,
wenn du nach Spiegeln blickst,
in denen du jedem gehörst!

Myschkin führt Nastassia zur Vorderbühne und steigt mit ihr
in ein Trapez, das aus dem Schnürboden herabgelassen wurde.
Während die beiden langsam in die Höhe schweben, erklingen
nur wenige Takte einer sehr zarten Musik.

Sei wahr und gib dem Schnee die Jahre zurück,
nimm Maß an dir selbst und laß die Flocken
dich nur von ungefähr streifen.

Auch dies ist die Welt:
ein früher Stern, den wir als Kinder
bewohnen; verteilt an die Brunnen

An interior that gives off the atmosphere of a circus arena. Nasta-
sya leads around Totski, Ganya, and the General on white cords
and expresses her power over the three men in a tragic, bold, dan-
gerous dance. Then Rogozhin appears and Nastasya turns away
from the three men. Her costume falls off her piece by piece, so that
she stands finally under a golden ball dressed only in white tights.
She lifts one hand to the ball and gives the other to Rogozhin,
who stands waiting at her side. At this moment, Myshkin steps
up to her.

Stop! I beg of you,
face of my only love,
stay lovely, and with your lashes,
shut out the world, stay beautiful,
face of my only love,
and turn your brow
from the heat lightning of doubt.
They will share your kisses,
disfigure you when you are asleep,
when you glance in the mirror
in which you belong to everyone!

Myshkin leads Nastasya downstage and climbs with her into a
trapeze that is lowered from above. As they both swing slowly
through the air, only a few bars of very tender music are heard.

Be true and give the years back to the snow,
from it take measure of yourself and let the flakes
graze you only now and then.

The world is also this:
a former star, which as children
we inhabited, showering into the fountain
as the content and rain of hours,
as the remains of a brighter time.

als Inhalt und Regen der Stunden,
als Vorrat von heiterer Zeit.
Auch dies ist schon Geist, eines armen
fröhlichen Spiels Einerlei, die Schaukel
im Wind und ein Lachen oben und unten;
dies ist das Ziel, von uns selbst
nicht besessen zu sein
und jedes Ziel zu verfehlen;
und auch dies ist Musik,
mit einem törichten Ton,
immer demselben,
einem Lied nachzugehen,
das uns ein spätres verspricht.

Fall nicht in den Tumult des Orchesters,
in dem die Welt sich verspielt.
Du stürzt, wenn du jetzt deinen Bogen
vergibst, und redest mit deinem Fleisch
eine vergängliche Sprache.

Doch Nastassia gleitet vom Trapez in Rogoschins Arme.

This is also the spirit, a poor
merry game of monotony, the swing swaying
in the wind, laughter above and below;
this is the goal, not to be
obsessed with ourselves
and thus miss our true purpose;
and this is also music
with its foolish tone,
always the same,
pursuing a song
that promises us a later one.

Don't fall into the orchestra's tumult
in which the world plays itself out.
You'll plummet if you toss away your bow
and speak with your flesh
a fleeting speech.

However, Nastasya slips from the trapeze into Rogozhin's arms.

Vor einer riesigen roten Ikone steht eine Leiter, auf der Myschkin sitzt. Rogoschin liegt rücklings auf einer Pritsche, hört mit zunehmender Spannung der Erzählung Myschkins zu und beobachtet erregt, wie Myschkin langsam von der Leiter heruntersteigt.

Jedem meiner Augenblicke zähle ich einen fremden
Augenblick zu, den Augenblick eines Menschen,
den ich in mir verborgen trage zu jeder Zeit,
und sein Gesicht in diesem Augenblick,
das ich nie vergessen werde, mein Leben lang nicht.

(Kein Gesicht, das abends von innen reift!)
Bedeckt vom Reif einer Kerkernacht
und frostgrün, weht es dem Morgen entgegen,
mit dem Gitter über den Augen, die doch dem Himmel
einmal aufgetan waren.

Durch die kalten Gänge der Glieder verläßt den Gefangenen
    der Schlaf.
Die Schritte des Wärters hallen in seiner Brust.
Ein Schlüssel sperrt seinen Seufzern auf.

Weil er keine Worte hat,
weil keiner ihn versteht,
bringt man ihm Fleisch und Wein
und übt Nächstenliebe an ihm.

Er aber, versunken
in die Zeremonien des Ankleidens,
kann Wohltaten nicht begreifen,
auch nichts von der Vermessenheit
dessen, was befohlen ist.

Before a huge red icon there stands a ladder on which Myshkin sits. Rogozhin lies behind it on a plank bed, listening intently to Myshkin's story and watching in agitation as Myshkin climbs down slowly from the top of the ladder.

In each of my moments, I'm aware of a strange
moment, the moment of a person
whom I carry concealed for every occasion,
as well as his face within this moment,
which I will never forget my entire life.

(Not the face that blossoms for them nightly!)
Covered with the frost of a prison night
and itself frost green, it floats before morning
with bars before the eyes that nonetheless once
were opened to the sky.

Through the cold vessels of each limb, sleep abandons
    the prisoner.
The warden's footsteps echo in his chest.
A key unlocks his sighs.

Because he has no word,
because no one understands him,
he is brought meat and wine
so charity can be practiced on him.

But he, sunk within
the ceremony of simply dressing,
cannot appreciate good deeds,
nor the audacity
of what has been ordered.

Es beginnt ja ein langes Leben,
wenn die Tür aufgeht und offen bleibt,
wenn die Straßen in Straßen
münden und das Gefälle der Stimmen
des ganzen Volkes ihn hinunterträgt
an die Gestade des Blutmeers,
das von den verbrecherischen
Gerichten der ganzen Welt
mit Todesurteilen
gespeist wird.

Nun ist aber eine Gemeinsamkeit zwischen uns
und dem Urteil, das auch sagt, daß dieser Mann
mit einem vollkommen wahren Gesicht zu der einen
Wahrheit kommt, eh er den Kopf
genau auf das Brett legt
(obwohl sein Gesicht
weiß ist und ohne Bewegung,
und die Gedanken, die er denken mag,
sind vielleicht ohne Bedeutung, er sieht
nur den rostigen Knopf an der Jacke
des Scharfrichters).

Eine Gemeinsamkeit ist auch zwischen uns
und dem Verurteilten, da er uns zu überzeugen vermag,
daß dem Mord, den wir bereiten,
und dem Mord, der für uns bereitet wird,
die Wahrheit vorangeht.
Und es liegt einer vor mir,
und ich stehe vor einem
mit allen Möglichkeiten zu dieser Wahrheit
und mit dem Mut zu ihrem Leben
und zu unserem Tode.

No doubt a long life begins
when the door opens and stays open,
when the streets flow into
streets and the cascade of voices
from all the people carries him down
to the bank of the sea of blood
which is fed sentences
of death
by the corrupt courts
of the entire world.

But now there is a commonness between us
and the sentence that also says this man,
with a completely honest face, attains
the one truth, before he lays his head
directly upon the block
(although his face
is white and motionless,
and the thoughts he likes to think
are perhaps without meaning, he sees
the corroded button on the jacket
of the executioner).

There's also a commonness between us
and the sentenced, for he can convince us
that the murder, for which we prepare,
and the murder, which for us is prepared,
is preceded by the truth.
And one lies before me,
and I stand before another
with all the possibilities of this truth
and with the courage needed to live
and for us to die.

Doch in meiner Sterblichkeit
kann ich nichts lehren
und könnt' ich's, so selbst
nur in dem Augenblick, von dem ich spreche,
und ich hätte in diesem Augenblick
nichts mehr zu sagen.

Jetzt springt Rogoschin auf und wirft Myschkin, der gegen Ende der Erzählung die unterste Sprosse erreicht hat, zu Boden. Es erklingt wieder die sehr zarte Musik. Verwandelt geht Rogoschin auf Myschkin zu, hebt ihn auf und hält ihn in den Armen. Sie tauschen ihre Kreuze.

Yet in my mortality
I can teach nothing, and even
if I could, it would only be
at the moment in which I speak,
and at this moment I would
have nothing more to say.

Rogozhin jumps up and throws Myshkin to the ground just as he reaches the bottom rung. Again, very tender music starts up. Transformed, Rogozhin goes to Myshkin, lifts him up, and holds him in his arms. They exchange crosses.

*Auf der leeren schwarzen Bühne ist in ganz dünnen, weißen
Umrissen ein schloßartiges Haus aufgebaut. Durch das Haus
ist eine gleichfalls weiße Ballettstange gezogen, an der Aglaja,
in ein blendend weißes Tutu gekleidet, steht. Myschkin, der die
Variation auf Puschkins Ballade vom armen Ritter auf der
Vorderbühne mit dem Gesicht zum Publikum spricht, dreht sich
zu Aglaja kein einziges Mal um, die jedes Mal, wenn der Text
von der Musik — einem Ritornell — unterbrochen wird, an der
Ballettstange ein kristallklares Ballettexercise vollbringt. Die
Szene beginnt mit Musik.*

Bürgschaft übernehm ich für einen,
der auf dieser Welt lebte vor langer Zeit
und als sonderbar galt, einen Ritter,
aber wie nenn ich ihn heute,
da's kein Verdienst ist, in Armut
und nicht auf Schlössern zu leben?

Sorglos kleidete er sich in die Tage,
bis einer um seine Schultern
franste und ihm ein Licht
auflud, in dessen Umkreis
die Scham nicht geduldet war
und der endliche Friede der Langmut.

Die den Krieg verdammen, sind auserwählt,
zu kämpfen in diesem Licht.
Sie streuen das Korn
auf die toten Äcker der Welt,
sie liegen in den Feuerlinien
einen Sommer lang,
sie binden die Garben für uns
und fallen im Wind.

*On the empty black stage there stands the skeletal white frame of
a palatial house. Made of the same material as the house frame, a
white ballet bar runs through the house, at which stands Aglaia
dressed in a bright white tutu. Myshkin, who speaks the varia-
tion on Pushkin's "Ballad of the Poor Knight" while facing the
audience downstage, never once turns to Aglaia. When the text
is interrupted by a score — a ritornelle — she completes a very
precise ballet exercise at the bar. The scene begins with music.*

I put up bail for one
who lived in this world long ago
and was strange as a knight,
but what should I call him today,
given there's little merit in living
in poverty and not in castles?

Without worry he draped the day
around his shoulders, until
one day he stood fringed by an aura
of radiant light, in whose circle
shame was not tolerated,
nor the ultimate peace of patience.

Those who damn the war are chosen
to battle in this light.
They scatter the grain
on the dead fields of the world,
they lie in the firing lines
all summer long,
they bind the sheaves for us
and float away upon the wind.

Aglaja wiederholt zum ersten Teil des Ritornells ihre Variation.

In der Zeit der Vorbereitung mied ich die Städte
und lebte gefährlich, wie man es aus Liebe tut.

Später geriet ich in eine Abendgesellschaft
und erzählte von einer Hinrichtung. So fehlte ich abermals.

Meinen ersten Tod empfing ich aus der Hand eines Gewitters
und ich dachte: so hell ist die Welt und so außer sich,

wo ich die Wiesen verdunkle, schaufelt der Wind Erde
über eine Kreuz, laßt mich liegen mit dem Gesicht nach unten!

Blaue Steine flogen nach mir und erweckten mich vom Tode.
Sie rührten von einem Sternengesicht, das zerbrach.

Aglaja wiederholt zum ersten Teil des Ritornells ihre Variation.

Und ausgestoßen aus dem Orden der Ritter,
verwiesen aus den Balladen,
nehme ich einen Weg durch die Gegenwart,
zu auf den Horizont, wo die zerrissenen
Sonnen im Staub liegen,
wo die Schattenspiele
auf der unerhörten Wand des Himmels
zu Verwandlungen greifen und ihr
einen Stoff einbilden
aus dem alten
Glauben meines Kindergebets.

Wenn auch die Kränze entzwei sind,
abgesprungen die Perlen, wenn der Kuß
in die blauen Falten der Madonnen,
abgeschmackt nach den Ekstasen

During training, I avoided the cities
and lived on the run, like someone in love.

Later I turned up at an evening party
and told of an execution. I felt out of place again.

I received my first death at the hands of a thunderbolt
and I thought: the world is so bright and exceptional;

where I darken the fields, the wind shovels earth
over a cross, allowing me to lie with my face down!

Blue stones flew at me and awakened me from death.
They came from the face of a star that had shattered.

Aglaia repeats her variation to the first part of the ritornelle.

And banished from the order of knights,
exiled from the ballads,
I follow a path through the present
to the horizon, where ragged suns
lie in the dust,
where the play of shadows
grips the unbelievable wall of heaven
in order to transform it and create
something new from it
out of the old beliefs
of my childhood prayers.

Even if it means the garlands are broken in two
and the pearls fall off, if the kiss
placed in the blue folds of the Madonna
becomes tasteless after the ecstasies

so vieler Nächte, beim ersten Hauch
das Licht in den Nischen löscht,
trete ich aus dem schwarzen
Blut der Ungläubigen in mein eignes
und höre auf den Abgesang
einer Geschichte,
die unsre Opfer verachtet.

Aglaja wiederholt zum ersten Teil des Ritornells ihre Variation.

Mir will eine Schwäche, der Wahnsinn
willkommen ist, meinen Weg
vertreten und mich der Freiheit entziehen.

Hörig dem Sog, wich mein Fleisch
früh den Messern aus, die ich hob,
um es aufzureißen. Mit dem Hauch,
den es umklammert, will es hinab,
mit meinem Atem, den ich zurückgeben werde
zum Beweis, daß mein Mund
nicht gefragt hat nach meinem Leben
und den Bedingungen, unter denen
wir für die Schöpfung
zu zeugen haben.

*Mit dem zweiten Teil des Ritornells endet die Szene, und Aglaja
erstarrt auf der Spitze, in der letzten ihrer Attituden.*

of so many nights, like the first breath
of the candles blown out in niches,
I would step out of the black
blood of the infidel within me
and listen to the final stanza
of a history
that scorns our victims.

Aglaia repeats her variation to the first part of the ritornelle.

A weakness that welcomes madness
wants to obstruct my path
and take away my freedom.

Vulnerable to its pull, my flesh
soon learned to avoid the knife I raised
to cut it open. The breath
that clings to my flesh, keeping it earthbound
is the breath that I will give back,
as evidence that my mouth
didn't ask about my life
and the terms by which
we were witnesses
to the Creation.

The scene ends with the second part of the ritornelle, and Aglaia freezes on the tip of a toe and in her final position.

Wir sehen eine Kurpromenade mit einem Orchestertempelchen im Hintergrund. Eine Gesellschaft von Vögeln hat sich hier versammelt — gemeint ist die Petersburger Hautevolee. Wenn der Vorhang sich öffnet, hält der Dirigent der kleinen Kapelle den Taktstock hoch. Die Vogelgesellschaft steht regungslos. Jeder ist in seiner Pose erstarrt, so daß die Szene den Eindruck eines kolorierten Druckes macht. Im Vordergrund steht Myschkin, der sich sehr fremd in dieser Umgebung fühlt.

Die leicht fliegen, werde ich nicht
beneiden, die Gesellschaft der Vögel,
die viele Orte berührt
und noch im raschesten Flug
voll Überdruß ist.

Myschkin geht ab. Der Dirigent des kleinen Orchesters bewegt seinen Taktstock zur Musik, und die erstarrte Vogelgesellschaft löst sich in eine »Kurpromenade« auf. Wenn die Musik endet, wenden sich alle dem Kapellmeister zu und applaudieren. Etwas vor Schluß des Tanzes treten Myschkin und Aglaja auf. Sie nehmen an dem Treiben teil und gehen dann zur Vorderbühne. Und Myschkin erklärt sich Aglaja.

Wo ich hinkam, fand ich mich unter Steinen,
wie sie ergraut und von Vertrauen befangen.

Mir ist gewiß, daß auch dein Gesicht
so alt herabfiel und sich neben mich legte
unter den eisweißen Wasserfall,
unter dem ich zuerst mein Bett aufschlug
und unter dem ich in meinem Tode
liegen werde, den Absturz
der Reinheit vor Augen.

We see a resort promenade with a bandstand in the background. A Society of Birds has assembled here, meaning the cream of Petersburg's society. As the curtain opens, the conductor of the tiny band holds the baton high. The Society of Birds stands by motionless. Each is frozen in his or her pose, so the scene gives the impression of a colored print. Myshkin stands downstage, feeling very strange in these surroundings.

Those who flit about, I will not
envy, namely the Society of Birds
that touches down in many places,
though in its hasty flight
it's full of ennui.

Myshkin departs. The conductor of the tiny band moves his baton to the music, and stiffly the society begins to move about in a promenade. As the music ends, they all turn to the band leader and applaud. Just before the end of the dance, Myshkin and Aglaia enter. They take part in the proceedings and then walk downstage. Myshkin speaks to Aglaia.

When I came to, I found myself mingling with stones.
I turned as gray as they and felt full of trust.

I'm certain that also your face
has become old and has lain next to me
under the ice cold waterfall
under which I first laid out my bed,
and under which I will lie
in my death, purity falling
before my eyes.

Myschkin und Aglaja gehen ab. Es wird Abend. Einige Lampions leuchten auf, die Kapelle hört zu spielen auf, die Gesellschaft findet sich paarweise zusammen und verläßt die Bühne. Blaue Versatzstücke kommen von oben, und die Bühne wird von einem klaren Blau überströmt. Dann fliegt Aglaja herein, von weißen Tänzern gefolgt, und Myschkin erscheint ihr als Wunschbild in einem weißen Kostüm. Doch Nastassias Erscheinung tritt zwischen die Liebenden und trennt sie. Die blauen Versatzstücke werden weggehoben. Allein im nächtlichen Garten sieht Aglaja sich ernüchtert um und wirft sich weinend auf eine Bank. Myschkin, in realer Gestalt, kommt und kniet vor ihr nieder.

Ich habe Zutrauen gefaßt zum Verzicht.
Du weinst, weil ich dich meinen Wünschen vorziehe?
Du wählst ein kurzes Los: meine Zeit, und ich will
die Verheerungen aller Träume, mit denen
du schläfst und herausreichst aus der Welt.

Für dich habe ich keinen Trost.
Wir werden beisammen liegen,
wenn die Bewegung der Berge geschieht,
mit einem Steingefühl, alterslos,
auf dem Boden der Nachtfurcht
und im Anfang einer großen Verstörung.

Einmal nur hatte der Mond das Nachsehn.
Ins Geäst unsres Herzens
fiel das einsamere
Licht der Liebe.
Wie kalt die Welt ist
und wie rasch die Schatten
sich auf unsre Wurzeln niederlegen!

Myshkin and Aglaia depart. Evening falls. Some street lamps are lit, the band stops playing, the Society comes together in twos and moves offstage. A blue background is lowered from above and the stage is lit with a clear blue light. Then Aglaia rushes in followed by dancers in white, and she is smitten by the sight of Myshkin in a white costume. Yet Nastasya's entrance falls between the two and separates them. The blue background is lifted up and away. Alone in the night garden and disillusioned, Aglaia looks around and in tears throws herself onto the bench. Myshkin, revealing his true character, comes and kneels before her.

I have become resigned to our separation.
You cry because I prefer my own wishes to you?
You drew a short straw: my time, and I want
the destruction of all the dreams with which
you sleep and escape to the world.

For you I have no comforting words.
We will lie side by side
when the mountains begin to move,
ourselves feeling like stones, ageless,
on the firm ground of night's fear
and at the start of vast disorder.

Once the moon was abandoned.
Onto the branches of our heart
fell the lonelier
light of love.
How cold the world is
and how swiftly the shadows
lay themselves upon our roots.

Aglaja hört Myschkin verständnislos zu; ihre Erwartungen sind enttäuscht worden, sie springt auf und läßt Myschkin betroffen stehen. Die Vögel kehren in den nächtlichen Garten zurück, diesmal um Nastassia Filipowna versammelt, die durch ihre faszinierende Schönheit in einem herausfordernden Tanz alles in Atem hält. Dann stehen die beiden Frauen voreinander. Nastassia beleidigt Aglaja und wird von einem der Begleiter Aglajas wieder beleidigt. Myschkin geht ab, und die aufgescheuchte Vogelgesellschaft flieht. Das Licht ist auf den Vordergrund gerichtet, während die Kulissen fortgetragen werden; nur ein schwarzumkleidetes Podium mit zwei Seitenleitern bleibt auf der Bühne, und Aglaja und Nastassia tanzen mit schwarzgekleideten Partnern ihre Variationen, als kämpften sie mit unsichtbaren Floretten auf Leben und Tod. Wenn Myschkin zurückkommt, steigen die beiden Frauen auf je eine der Leitern und bedeuten ihm, daß sie seine Erklärung erwarten. Aglaja sieht Myschkins Zögern, wirft sich vom Podium herunter und wird von ihrem Partner weggetragen. Ehe Myschkin ihr folgen kann, bricht Nastassia wie leblos vor ihm zusammen. Er hebt sie auf und hält sie in den Armen.*

*Aglaia listens disbelieving to Myshkin. Her expectations hav-
ing been disappointed, she jumps up and lets Myshkin stand
there dismayed. The Birds return to the night garden, this time
gathering around Nastasya Filippovna, who holds them breath-
less through her compelling beauty during a provocative dance.
Then both women face each other. Nastasya gestures insultingly
to Aglaia and is insulted in turn by one of Aglaia's companions.
Myshkin departs and the embarrassed Society flees. The light is
directed downstage while the scenery is carried off. Only a po-
dium clad in black with a ladder on each side remains on stage,
and Aglaia and Nastasya dance their variations with partners
dressed in black as if fighting a life or death battle with invisible
foils. As Myshkin returns, both women climb up a ladder on each
side of the podium and signal to him that they expect an explana-
tion. Aglaia notes Myshkin's hesitation, jumps from the podium,
and is carried away by her partner. Before Myshkin can follow
her, Nastasya collapses, as if lifeless, before him. He lifts her up
and holds her in his arms.*

Auf der leeren Bühne stehen, in schwarzen Kostümen, mit
dem Rücken zum Publikum, Menschen mit Kandelabern,
während Myschkin, zum Publikum gewendet, spricht.

Mit einem geliehenen Wort bin ich,
und nicht mit dem Feuer, gekommen
und schuld an allem, o Gott!
Es sind die Kreuze getauscht,
und das eine wird nicht getragen.
Schwach lob ich die Strenge
Deines Gerichts und ich denke
schon an Vergebung, ehe Du sie gewährst.

Wo die Angst in mir aufspringt
und Helle vor mir herwirft, entdeck ich
Schreckliches und meine Schuld
an allem, an dem Verbrechen,
mit dem ich noch diese Nacht
in Deine Nacht kommen muß,
und mein heilloses Wissen will ich
nicht preisgeben an mein Gewissen.

Sei Du die Liebe, ich bin nur in leisem
Fieber aus Dir hervorgegangen
und unter Fiebernden hinfällig
geworden. Deine Blindheit erkennend,
vor der wir eins sind im Dunkel,
bekenn ich, daß ich schuld bin
an allem, denn Du, seit Du uns nicht
mehr siehst, zählst auf ein Wort.

On the empty stage a number of people stand in black costumes, holding candelabras and with their backs to the audience as Myshkin faces the audience and speaks.

With a borrowed word I have come,
and not with the fire, for I am
to blame for everything, O God!
The crosses have been exchanged,
but one will not be carried.
Weakly I praise the severity
of Your justice, and already I hope
for pardon before You even grant it.

Where fear leaps up inside me
and blinding light opens before me, I discover
the horror and my guilt
for everything, for the crime
with which, on this night,
into Your night I must come,
though I don't want to relinquish
my wretched knowledge to my belief.

Let it be that You are Love, for I am only
a light fever that came from You,
one who, between the delirium, became
weak. Knowing Your blindness,
before which we are as one in darkness,
I acknowledge that I'm guilty
of everything, for You, since You no longer
see us, depend upon a word.

Ein roter Teppich wird herausgerollt. Myschkin dreht sich um und steht jetzt auch mit dem Rücken zum Publikum. Nastassia erscheint und versucht, auf die Vorderbühne zu Myschkin zu gelangen, doch Rogoschin springt einige Male, mit einem Messer in der Hand, dazwischen. Die schwarzen Gestalten führen an Ort und Stelle entsprechende Schritte zu einem Bolero aus. Schließlich ergreift Rogoschin Nastassia und trägt sie, mit dem Rücken zum Publikum, von der Bühne. Auch die schwarzen Gestalten gehen ab. Die Ikone senkt sich aus dem Schnürboden herunter. Myschkin steht ohnmächtig davor.

Öffne mir!
Alle Tore sind zugefallen, es ist Nacht,
und was zu sagen ist, ist noch nicht gesagt.
Öffne mir!
Die Luft ist voll von Verwesung, und mein Mund
hat den blauen Mantel noch nicht geküßt.
Öffne mir!
Ich lese schon in den Linien deiner Hand, mein Geist,
der meine Stirne berührt und mich heimholen will.
Öffne mir!

Endlich tritt Rogoschin heraus, und Myschkin geht ihm entgegen.

Geheim ist der Mund, mit dem ich morgen rede. Ich will diese Nacht mit dir wachen und werde dich nicht verraten.

Behutsam führt Rogoschin Myschkin hinter die Ikone. Die Bühne wird ganz dunkel, und im Dunkeln spricht Myschkin die beiden Terzinen.

A red carpet is rolled out. Myshkin turns around and stands with his back to the audience as well. Nastasya appears and tries to go to Myshkin downstage, but Rogozhin jumps between them a few times with a knife in his hand. The figures in black perform steps that correspond to a bolero right where they stand. Finally, Rogozhin carries off Nastasya with his back to the audience. The figures in black also depart. The icon is lowered from above. Myshkin stands powerless before it.

Open the door!
All gates are closed, it is night,
and what must be said has not been said.
Open the door!
The air is full of decay, and my mouth
has not yet kissed the blue mantle.
Open the door!
Spirit, who touches my forehead and wants
to take me home, I can read it in the lines of your hand.
Open the door!

Finally Rogozhin steps forward and Myshkin towards him.

Sealed is the mouth with which I'll speak tomorrow.
I want to wake with you tonight and not betray you.

Rogozhin leads Myshkin behind the icon with care. The stage becomes completely dark, and in darkness Myshkin speaks both tercets.

In den Strängen der Stille hängen die Glocken
und läuten den Schlaf ein,
so schlafe, sie läuten den Schlaf ein.

In den Strängen der Stille kommen die Glocken
zur Ruhe, es könnte der Tod sein,
so komm, es muß Ruhe sein.

*Es wird etwas hell. Aus dem Schnürboden kommen weiße Stricke
zu den Klängen der Apotheose herab. Myschkin bleibt unbeweglich
stehen, und während immer mehr Stricke herabsinken, erscheinen
Tänzer, die in verhaltenen, feierlichen Bewegungen den Ausbruch
des Wahnsinns darstellen.*

Choreographie: Tatjana Gsovsky
Musik: Hans Werner Henze

From the cords of silence hang the bells,
and they toll as a prelude to sleep,
so sleep, they toll as a prelude to sleep.

On the cords of silence finally the bells
come to rest; this could be death,
so come, there must be rest.

*It becomes somewhat brighter. White cords are lowered from
above to the strains of an apotheosis. Myshkin remains motion-
less, and as more and more cords are lowered, dancers appear who,
with restrained, solemn movements depict the onset of madness.*

Choreography: Tatyana Gsovsky
Music: Hans Werner Henze

ANRUFUNG DES GROSSEN BÄREN

INVOCATION OF THE GREAT BEAR

Das Spiel ist aus

Mein lieber Bruder, wann bauen wir uns ein Floß
und fahren den Himmel hinunter?
Mein lieber Bruder, bald ist die Fracht zu groß
und wir gehen unter.

Mein lieber Bruder, wir zeichnen aufs Papier
viele Länder und Schienen.
Gib acht, vor den schwarzen Linien hier
fliegst du hoch mit den Minen.

Mein lieber Bruder, dann will ich an den Pfahl
gebunden sein und schreien.
Doch du reitest schon aus dem Totental
und wir fliehen zu zweien.

Wach im Zigeunerlager und wach im Wüstenzelt,
es rinnt uns der Sand aus den Haaren,
dein und mein Alter und das Alter der Welt
mißt man nicht mit den Jahren.

Laß dich von listigen Raben, von klebriger Spinnenhand
und der Feder im Strauch nicht betrügen,
iß und trink auch nicht im Schlaraffenland,
es schäumt Schein in den Pfannen und Krügen.

Nur wer an der goldenen Brücke für die Karfunkelfee
das Wort noch weiß, hat gewonnen.
Ich muß dir sagen, es ist mit dem letzten Schnee
im Garten zerronnen.

I

The Game is Over

My dearest brother, when will we build a raft
and sail down through the sky?
My dearest brother, the weight's too much for our craft
and we will sink and die.

My dearest brother, we sketch out on paper
countries and railway lines.
Watch out, close to the set of tracks right here
you'll be blown high by mines.

My dearest brother, to a stake I want to be tied,
raising then a cry.
But out of the valley of death you choose to ride,
and off together we fly.

Awake in the gypsy camp and the desert tent,
the sand runs out of our hair;
your age, my age, and the age of the planet
in years can have no measure.

Don't be fooled by the spider, the clever raven,
or in a bush, by the feather;
however, don't eat and drink inside a fool's haven,
lies foam in skillets and pitchers.

On the golden bridge, only he who might know
the troll's secret word can win.
I'm sorry to say, along with our last snow,
it melted in the garden.

Von vielen, vielen Steinen sind unsre Füße so wund.
Einer heilt. Mit dem wollen wir springen,
bis der Kinderkönig, mit dem Schlüssel zu seinem Reich
    im Mund,
uns holt, und wir werden singen:

Es ist eine schöne Zeit, wenn der Dattelkern keimt!
Jeder, der fällt, hat Flügel.
Roter Fingerhut ist's, der den Armen das Leichentuch
    säumt,
und dein Herzblatt sinkt auf mein Siegel.

Wir müssen schlafen gehn, Liebster, das Spiel ist aus.
Auf Zehenspitzen. Die weißen Hemden bauschen.
Vater und Mutter sagen, es geistert im Haus,
wenn wir den Atem tauschen.

From many stones our feet are sore. One can heal.
Let's hop to the fairytale king,
for it's in his mouth that the castle key's sealed,
and he'll lead us away to sing:

It is a happy time when the date pit sprouts!
Everyone who falls has wings.
Red foxglove is what hems the poor's shrouds,
and your bud is sealed in my ring.

We must go to sleep, my dearest, the game is over.
Off on tiptoe. Our nightshirts billowing white.
The house is always haunted, say Father and Mother,
when we exchange breaths at night.

Von einem Land, einem Fluß und den Seen

I

Von einem, der das Fürchten lernen wollte
und fortging aus dem Land, von Fluß und Seen,
zähl ich die Spuren und des Atems Wolken,
denn, so Gott will, wird sie der Wind verwehn!

Zähl und halt ein — sie werden vielen gleichen.
Die Lose ähneln sich, die Odysseen.
Doch er erfuhr, daß wo die Lämmer weiden,
schon Wölfe mit den Fixsternblicken stehn.

Er fühlte seine Welle ausgeschrieben,
eh sie ihn wegtrug und ihm Leid geschah;
sie sprang im See auf und sie schwang die Wiege,
in die sein Sternbild durch die Schleier sah.

Er schüttelte und trat die tauben Nüsse,
den Hummeln schlug er schärfre Töne vor,
und Sonntag war ihm mehr als Glockensüße —
Sonntag war jeder Tag, den er verlor.

Er zog den Karren aus verweichten Gleisen,
von keinem leichten Rädergang verführt,
beim Aufschrei, den die Wasser weiterreichten
an Seen, vom ersten Steinschlag aufgerührt.

Doch sieben Steine wurden sieben Brote,
als er im Zweifel in die Nacht entwich;
er tauchte durch den Duft und streute Krumen
im Gehn für den Verlornen hinter sich.

Of a Land, a River and Lakes

I

Left behind by one who wished to learn of dread
in leaving the land of his birth, a river and lakes,
it's footprints that I count, a breath's own cloud,
which later, as God wills, the wind will take.

Count up, and stop — finding they're much the same.
Each journey has its twin, as well as each destiny.
For, in fact, he learned that beside the grazing lambs
the wolves already stand, eyes fixed and starry.

In waves he felt his destiny was written
before it pulled him out into sorrow's lake;
as the wave sprang up, his cradle was aswim,
his star looked on through veils at the baby awake.

He shook and kicked about the empty nutshells,
he returned sharp tones to the bumblebee's buzz,
and Sunday meant more than sweet ringing bells —
Sunday meant every day that no longer was.

Out of softened, muddy tracks he pulled his wagon,
never having an easy path he could call his own;
a scream was what, as ripples, the water passed on
across the lake when he threw his first stone.

Yet when, full of doubt, one night he disappeared,
the seven stones turned into seven loaves;
he plunged into the meadow's fragrant air,
scattering crumbs for the lost in forest groves.

Erinnre dich! Du weißt jetzt allerlanden:
wer treu ist, wird im Frühlicht heimgeführt.
O Zeit gestundet, Zeit uns überlassen!
Was ich vergaß, hat glänzend mich berührt.

II

Im Frühlicht rücken Brunnen in die Mitte,
der Pfarrer, das Brevier, der Sonntagsstaat,
die kalten Pfeifen und die schwarzen Hüte,
Leib, Ehr und Gut vor allerhöchsten Rat.

Untätig steht der Fluß, die Weiden baden,
die Königskerzen leuchten bis ins Haus,
das schwere Essen ist schon aufgetragen,
und alle Sprüche gehn auf Amen aus.

Die Nachmittage, hell und ungeheuer —
die Nadel springt im Strumpf, Gewöll zerreißt,
und das Geschirr der Pferde wird gescheuert,
bis eins erklirrt, mit dem Fallada reist.

Die Alten liegen in den dumpfen Stuben,
das Testament im Arm, im zweiten Schlaf,
und ihre Söhne zeugen wortlos Söhne
mit Mägden, die der Gott als Regen traf

Gestillte Lippen und gestillte Augen —
die Raupen hängen eingepuppt im Schrein,
und Dunggeruch steigt mit den Fliegentrauben
bei früher Dämmrung durch die Fenster ein.

Remember it now! For you know it's obvious:
who's faithful is led home in the early light.
O borrowed time, the time still left to us!
What I forgot now stirs inside me bright.

II

In early light, the fountains quell their splash,
the parson, the breviary, the Sunday finery,
the pipes extinguished, rows of formal black hats,
body, honor, and goods sit before the Deity.

Still stands the river, beside it willows bask,
the house is bathed by the yellow light of mullein,
as the trays of heavy food are served at last
and all prayers finish with a muttered Amen.

The afternoons so bright and so immense —
the needle darns the sock, dwindling the skein,
outside the horse's harness is being cleansed,
until the buggy sets off, the fairytale begun.

The elderly lie inside their musty dens,
holding the Bible, old couples 'rest their eyes',
as wordlessly their sons beget more sons
with girls who only by rain have been baptized.

Sated eyes and sated lips as well —
caterpillars that hang cocooned in their wrappings;
at dusk, above dung heaps, the flies now circle
wafting the odor through the window's casing.

Am Abend Stimmenauflauf an den Zäunen,
Andacht und Rosen werden laut zerpflückt,
die Katzen scheuchen auf aus ihren Träumen,
und rote Mieder hat der Wind verrückt.

Die Zöpfe lösen sich, die Schattenpaare
im Nebel auf, vom nahen Hügel rollt
der unfruchtbare Mond, besetzt die Äcker
und nimmt das Land für eine Nacht in Sold.

III

Dem Hügelzug ist eine Burg geblieben,
vom Berg geschützt, der Felsen um sie stellt,
den Geier ausschickt mit dem Krallensiegel,
dem Königswappen, eh sie ganz verfällt.

Es sind drei Tote hinterm Wall verborgen;
von einem weht vom Wachtturm noch das Haar,
von einem heißt es, daß er Steine schleudert,
von einem, daß er doppelköpfig war.

Der stiftet Brand, dem sie zu dritt befehlen,
der mordet, den ein schwarzes Haar umschlingt,
und wer den Stein aufhebt, wird selber sterben,
noch diesen Abend, eh die Amsel singt.

Die unbeschuhten Geister auf den Zinnen,
der unbewehrte Leichnam im Verlies,
im Gästebuch die Namen der Beschauer —
die Nacht vertuscht sie, die uns kommen hieß.

At evening, voices are gathered by the fence,
prayers and roses are plucked apart with a din,
as cats asleep are frightened from their trance,
and a corset's red flaps madly in the wind.

The pigtails now undone, the pairs of shadows
dissolve in fog, while over the nearest hill
the barren moon now rolls, occupies meadows,
and for a night commands the land at will.

III

There still remains a fortress in the hills
secured by the mountain and the cliffs surrounding
that dispatch vultures, their claws' sharp seals
and coat of arms, as the fortress falls to ruin.

Where atop the tower a corpse's hair still blows,
ensconced behind the wall remain three dead;
of these, the second is known to still sling stones,
while it's said that the third has a pair of heads.

The three together order one to set a fire;
the murderer's the one to whom the black hair clings;
and whoever lifts the stone will himself expire
this very evening before the blackbird sings.

The barefoot spirits that haunt the parapets,
the unarmed corpse that lies within the dungeon,
the guest book filled with names of those who visit —
night sweeps them under, though it still spurs us on.

Sie schlägt den Erdplan auf, verschweigt die Ziele;
sie trägt die Zeit als eine Eiszeit ein,
die Schottterstege über die Moränen,
den Weg zu Grauwack und zu Kreidestein.

Die Drachenzeichnung lobt sie und die Festung,
vom Faltenwurf der frühen Welt umwallt,
wo oben unten war und unten oben.
Die Scholle tanzt noch überm blauen Spalt.

Ins Schwemmland führt die Nacht. Es schwemmt uns wieder
ins Kellerland der kalten neuen Zeit.
So such im Höhlenbild den Traum vom Menschen!
Die Schneehuhnfeder steck dir an das Kleid.

IV

In andren Hüllen gingen wir vorzeiten,
du gingst im Fuchspelz, ich im Iltiskleid;
noch früher waren wir die Marmelblumen,
in einer tiefen Tibetschlucht verschneit.

Wir standen zeitlos, lichtlos in Kristallen
und schmolzen in der ersten Stunde hin,
uns überrann der Schauer alles Lebens,
wir blühten auf, bestäubt vom ersten Sinn.

Wir wanderten im Wunder und wir streiften
die alten Kleider ab und neue an.
Wir sogen Kraft aus jedem neuen Boden
und hielten nie mehr unsren Atem an.

For night unfolds the map, keeps secret its aim;
it grinds time slowly along, as in an ice age,
the gravel path left by the glacial moraine,
the process that creates both chalk and clay.

Both fortress and fossil by night are celebrated,
as earlier worlds appear when the curtain lifts,
where down was up, and up was stood on its head.
The firmament still dances above a deep blue rift.

Night settles into alluvium. We're sinking again
into an icy new age's cavernous soil.
Within cave murals look for the dream of man!
Fasten a ptarmigan feather to your lapel.

IV

In earlier times we wandered in other garments,
you in fox fur and I in a polecat's skin;
still earlier yet we were flowers of adamant
buried in the snow of a Tibetan ravine.

We stood there timeless, lightless in the crystals,
melting only when the first hour had begun,
feeling the shower of life wash over us,
we blossomed, carrying seeds of initial perception.

We wandered within a marvel, shedding old clothes,
and donning new clothes as we moved along.
From each new soil we drew more strength for ourselves,
and never again did we hold our breath so long.

Wir waren leicht als Vögel, schwer als Bäume,
kühn als Delphin und still als Vogelei.
Wir waren tot, lebendig, bald ein Wesen
und bald ein Ding. (Wir werden niemals frei!)

Wir konnten uns nicht halten und wir zogen
in jeden Körper voller Freude ein.
(Und niemand sag ich, was du mir bedeutest —
die sanfte Taube einem rauhen Stein!)

Du liebtest mich. Ich liebte deine Schleier,
die lichten Stoffe, die den Stoff umwehn,
und ohne Neugier hielt ich dich in Nächten.
(Wenn du nur liebst! Ich will dich ja nicht sehn!)

Wir kamen in das Land mit seinen Quellen.
Urkunden fanden wir. Das ganze Land,
so grenzenlos und so geliebt, war unser.
Es hatte Platz in deiner Muschelhand.

V

Wer weiß, wann sie dem Land die Grenzen zogen
und um die Kiefern Stacheldrahtverhau?
Der Wildbach hat die Zündschnur ausgetreten,
der Fuchs vertrieb den Sprengstoff aus dem Bau.

Wer weiß, was sie auf Grat und Gipfel suchten?
Ein Wort? Wir haben's gut im Mund verwahrt;
es spricht sich schöner aus in beiden Sprachen
und wird, wenn wir verstummen, noch gepaart.

We were light as birds, and as still as their eggs;
we were as bold as dolphins, heavy as trees.
We were dead, yet fully alive — now a being
and now a thing. (We will never be free!)

We couldn't help changing, and into each body
each of us moved, experiencing our full splendor.
(And I'll tell no one what you mean to me —
as to the rugged stone, the dove so tender!)

It's then you loved me. And I loved your veil,
the luminous light wound through its luminous tulle,
and nightly, uncurious, it was you I held.
(If you only loved me! I don't want to see you!)

We came into this country with its spring waters.
We found deeds they left behind. The entire land
was so open and so loved, all of it ours.
It fit perfectly inside the shell of your hand.

V

Who knows when they divided up the land
with borders, wrapping barbed wire around each fir?
The mountain's roaring stream douses the fuse's brand,
the fox hauls out explosives from his lair.

Who knows just what they sought on summit and ridge?
A word? Inside our mouths it's hidden well away;
it's made more beautiful by each separate language
and will, when we fall silent, still conjugate.

Wo anders sinkt der Schlagbaum auf den Pässen;
hier wird ein Gruß getauscht, ein Brot geteilt.
Die Handvoll Himmel und ein Tuch voll Erde
bringt jeder mit, damit die Grenze heilt.

Wenn sich in Babel auch die Welt verwirrte,
man deine Zunge dehnte, meine bog —
die Hauch- und Lippenlaute, die uns narren,
sprach auch der Geist, der durch Judäa zog.

Seit uns die Namen in die Dinge wiegen,
wir Zeichen geben, uns ein Zeichen kommt,
ist Schnee nicht nur die weiße Fracht von oben,
ist Schnee auch Stille, die uns überkommt.

Daß uns nichts trennt, muß jeder Trennung fühlen;
in gleicher Luft spürt er den gleichen Schnitt.
Nur grüne Grenzen und der Lüfte Grenzen
vernarben unter jedem Nachtwindschritt.

Wir aber wollen über Grenzen sprechen,
und gehn auch Grenzen noch durch jedes Wort:
wir werden sie vor Heimweh überschreiten
und dann im Einklang stehn mit jedem Ort.

VI

Der Schlachttag naht mit hellem Messerwirbel,
die matten Klingen schleift der Morgenwind,
und aus der Brise gehn gestärkt die Schürzen
der Männer, die ums Vieh versammelt sind.

Elsewhere, on mountain passes barriers fall;
here a greeting's exchanged, some bread is shared.
A handful of sky and a pocketful of soil
are brought along so that the border's repaired.

When the world became confused in Babel,
your tongue was stretched and also mine was bent —
breath and lip sounds, that still can make us fools,
were spoken by the spirit, who through Judea went.

Since names have cradled us to the nature of things,
since we've posited signs, and to us signs have come;
snow not only means the white weight falling,
snow means the silence by which we're overcome.

To stay together, each must feel separation;
within the same air, he feels the same chill within.
Only the borders of air and the borders of green
can be healed at night by each step of the wind.

And yet we are determined to speak across borders,
even if borders pass through every word:
in longing still for home, we will cross over,
and again with every place stand in accord.

VI

Bright knives whirling, the day of slaughter nears,
in morning wind the dull knife blades are sharpened,
as around the cattle the men begin to gather,
wearing their aprons that by the breeze are stiffened.

Die Stricke werden fester angezogen,
die Mäuler schäumen, und die Zunge schwimmt;
der Nachbar sorgt für Salz und Pfefferkörner,
und das Gewicht der Opfer wird bestimmt.

Es wollen hier die Toten leichter wiegen,
denn das Lebendige, dem Blut nicht fehlt,
— und mehr als Leben wehrt sich auf der Waage! —
gibt hier den Ausschlag, den kein Zeiger zählt.

Drum meid die Hunde mit den heißen Lefzen
und den Gemeinen, der mit rohem Blut
sich volltrinkt, bis es Schatten übersetzen
in schwarzer Lachen herrenloses Gut.

Und einen Blutsturz später: Wangenflecken —
die erste Scham, weil Schmerz und Schuld bestehn
und Eingeweide ausgenommner Tiere
in Zeichen erster Zukunft übergehn;

weil süßem Fleisch und markgefüllten Knochen
ein Atem ausbleibt, wo der deine geht.
Den Ahnenrock am abgestellten Rocken
hat unversehens Spinnweb überweht.

Die Augen gehen über. Jahre sinken.
Die junge Braue fühlt den weißen Stift.
Und die Gerippe steigen aus dem Anger,
die Kreuze mit der dürren Blumenschrift.

The binding ropes are drawn a little tighter,
muzzles begin to foam, the thick tongues swim;
a neighbor checks his salt and pepper shakers,
while one determines the weight of another victim.

The dead here, in general, tend to weigh much less,
because the living, whose blood is lacking never,
— and what is weighed is more than life itself! —
tip here the balance, which no scale can measure.

Beware the dog nearby with its hot lips,
and the criminal who is sated on raw blood,
until the shadows eventually transform it
into standing black pools of ownerless goods.

And a spurt of blood later: the cheeks aflush —
the first felt shame, since pain and guilt exist;
what follows are entrails, the animals' guts,
that as symbols spill into the future first;

meanwhile it's marrow bones and their sweet flesh
that breathe a breath, as you do yours, no longer.
On a spinning wheel that's stopped, a cobweb mesh
has stealthily covered the dress of an ancestor.

The eyes fill up with tears. Years sink away.
Young eyebrows feel the prick of white thorns.
The skeletons are climbing out of silent graves
past crosses that only withered flowers adorn.

VII

Zum Fest sind alle Seelen rein gewaschen,
der Bretterboden wird gelaugt vorm Tanz,
die Kinder hauchen gläubig in das Wasser,
am Halm erscheint der schöne Seifenglanz.

Der Maskenzug biegt um die Häuserzeile,
Strohpuppen torkeln an die Weizenwand,
die Reiter sprengen über Blumenbarren,
und die Musik zieht in das Sommerland.

Maultrommeln klagen zu den Flötenstimmen.
Die Axt der Nacht fällt in das morsche Licht.
Der Krüppel reicht den Buckel zum Befingern.
Der Idiot entdeckt sein Traumgesicht.

Der Holzstoß flammt: die Werke und die Tage
holt er vorm Anlauf, vor dem neuen Mond;
die Samen und die Funken gehn zu Sternen,
und sie erfahren, was im Himmel lohnt.

Die Schüsse überfliegen Tannenzüge.
Ein Schuß fällt immer, der im Fleisch verhallt.
Und Einer bleibt am Ort, verscharrt in Nadeln
und stumm gemacht vom Moos im schwarzen Wald.

Zum Kehraus drängen traurige Gendarmen.
Die Füße stampfen einen wilden Reim,
und umgestimmt vom strömenden Wacholder
schwanken verloren die Betrunkenen heim.

Im Dunkel flattern lange die Girlanden,
und das Papier treibt schaurig übers Dach.
Der Wind räumt auf in den verlassnen Buden
und trägt den Träumern Zuckerherzen nach.

VII

Made ready for celebration, all souls are cleansed,
as children blow faithfully into the water;
the floorboards are scrubbed down before the dance,
on blades of grass appears the dew's white lather.

The masquerade now winds around the houses,
scarecrows begin to wheel in fields of wheat,
as riders leap on horses over flowered trusses,
and music drifts over fields with summer's heat.

To the voices of the flutes, the Jew's harp laments.
The night's axe sinks into the decaying light.
So others can finger his hump, the cripple bends.
The idiot discovers the face he dreamt of last night.

The pile of wood burns: the gathered works and days
go up in smoke before the new moon ascends;
to the stars, the seeds and rising sparks float away,
and learn what reward exists in heaven.

Gunshots now fly above the firs.
One shot always sinks within the thud of flesh.
And one stays buried where pine needles gather,
and by the black wood's moss is silently enmeshed.

By sad gendarmes the final dance is ordered.
The dancers' feet stomp out their own wild rhythms,
while, senses still aswim with flowing liquor,
lost drunkards stagger slowly towards home.

Long into the night remain the fluttering garlands,
and above rooftops drift ghostly paper streamers.
The wind cleans out the abandoned market stands
and tumbles hearts of sugar back to the dreamers.

VIII

(Habe ich sie nicht erfunden, diese Seen
und diesen Fluß! Und kennt noch wer den Berg?
Geht einer durch ein Land mit Riesenschritten,
verläßt sich einer auf den guten Zwerg?

Die Himmelsrichtung? Und die Wendekreise?
Du fragst noch?! Nimm dein feurigstes Gespann,
fahr diesen Erdball ab, roll mit den Tränen
die Welt entlang! Dort kommst du niemals an.

Was ruft uns, daß sich so die Haare sträuben?
Tollkirschen schwingen um das heiße Ohr.
Die Adern lärmen, überfüllt von Stille.
Die Totenglocke schaukelt überm Tor.

Was kümmern uns die ländlich blinden Fenster,
das Lämmerzeug, der Schorf, das Altenteil?
Nach Unverwandtem trachten Mund und Augen.
Uns wird die bleibende Figur zuteil.

Was sind uns Pferde und die braunen Wolken,
Windwolf und Irrlicht, braver Hörnerschall!
Wir sind zu andren Zielen aufgestiegen,
und andre Hürden bringen uns zu Fall.

Was kümmern uns der Mond und was die Sterne,
uns, deren Stirnen dunkeln und erglühn!
Beim Untergang des schönsten aller Länder
sind wir's, die es als Traum nach innen ziehn.

Wo ist Gesetz, wo Ordnung? Wo erscheinen
uns ganz begreiflich Blatt und Baum und Stein?
Zugegen sind sie in der schönen Sprache,
im reinen Sein …)

VIII

(Have I not invented them, these very lakes,
also this river! Who knows that peak at a glance!
Through a land is it the giant's steps one takes?
Does anyone rely on the good dwarf's guidance?

Which quadrant of the sky? Which latitude?
You're asking me still? Harness your fieriest mare,
drive all around this globe, with tears roll through
the world! You'll never get there.

What cries to us, causing our hair to bristle?
Belladonna swings next to the feverish ear.
The veins beat loudly on, aflood with quiet.
The death bell tolls above the doorway here.

The blind and rustic window, what's it to us,
lamb's wool, the scaly skin, land sold to retire?
Towards a fixed point the eyes and mouth face.
We're left behind, the abandoned figure.

What do horses mean to us, or even brown clouds,
hunting horns, greyhounds, or the will-o'-the-wisp!
It is towards other goals that we have climbed,
it's attempting quite other hurdles that we trip.

What is the moon to us, and what do stars mean,
to us, or to brows so dark and glowing bright!
At the downfall of the most beautiful of lands
we are the ones who absorb it like a dream at night.

Where is there law, where order? Where do we see
the wholly comprehensible leaf or tree or stone?
They are only present in language's beauty,
in Being's pure tone ….)

127

IX

Es kommt der Bruder mit den Weißdornaugen,
den Hecken auf der Brust, dem Vogelleim;
die Amsel fliegt im Sturz auf seine Rute
und treibt mit ihm die Rinderherde heim.

In seinen blonden Haaren wird sie nisten,
im Stall, wenn er in Halmen untergeht,
den Tierdunst atmet, nach dem Schattenhalfter
und einem Rappen für den Sattel späht.

Ins Rosenöl wird sie den Schnabel tunken,
in seine Augen tropft sie Rosenlicht.
Die Nacht steigt in ihr schwellendes Gefieder
und hebt sie auf im seligen Verzicht.

»O Schwester sing, so sing von fernen Tagen!«
»Bald sing ich, bald, an einem schönren Ort.«
»O sing und web den Teppich aus den Liedern
und flieg auf ihm mit mir noch heute fort!

Halt mit mir Rast, wo Bienen uns bewirten,
mich Engelschön im Engelhut besucht …«
»Bald sing ich — doch im Turm beginnt's zu schwirren,
schlaf ein! es ist die Zeit der Eulenflucht.«

Die Kürbisleuchter machen ihre Runde,
der Knecht springt auf, die Peitsche in der Hand,
er starrt ins Licht und überrascht die Amsel
am Ausgang in das letzte Hirtenland.

Die Sense ficht mit ihren wilden Flügeln,
die Gabel sticht die Flatternde ans Tor.
Doch eh den Schläfer ihre Schreie wecken,
erschrickt sein Herz im ersten Rosenflor.

IX

My brother is approaching with hawthorn eyes,
past hedgerows laced with birdlime at chest level;
landing upon his stick, the blackbird dives
helping him drive home the herd of cattle.

In his blond hair it will later build its nest
when he collapses on straw inside the stable,
breathing in the fumes of the animal scents,
searching for a halter and a black horse's saddle.

It will dip its beak into the oil of roses,
and then into his eyes it will drip rose light.
Into its swollen plumage the night now rises,
the blackbird absorbing it, blessedly resigned.

"O sister sing, O sing of days long gone!"
"Soon I will sing; soon in a lovelier place."
"O sing and weave together the carpet of song,
and together upon it today, come, let us race!

Then rest with me, where bees will entertain us,
myself an angelic beauty whom angels attend …."
"Soon I will sing — yet in the tower there rustles
a bird — so sleep, for the owl will soon ascend."

The jack-o-lanterns begin to make their rounds,
the farm boy jumps up from straw, a whip in hand,
he stares into the light as the blackbird bounds
from the gate into the distant pasture land.

The scythe now slices at the blackbird's wings,
a pitchfork nails the fluttering to the stake.
Yet before the sleeper is woken by the bird's screams,
his heart, at dawn's first light, startles him awake.

X

Im Land der tiefen Seen und der Libellen,
den Mund erschöpft ans Urgestein gepreßt,
ruft einer nach dem Geist der ersten Helle,
eh er für immer dieses Land verläßt.

Im Schaumkraut badet er die wehen Augen;
kalt und entzaubert sieht er, was er sah.
Was unbesiegbar macht, wird ihm gegeben:
das weite Herz und die Harmonika.

Es ist die Zeit des Apfelmosts, der Schwalben;
den Fässern wird das Spundloch eingedrückt.
Wer jetzt trinkt, trinkt auf schwarze Vogelzüge,
und jede Ferne macht sein Herz verrückt.

Er schließt die Schmieden, Mühlen und Kapellen,
er geht durchs Maisfeld, schlägt die Kolben ab,
die Körner springen auf mit goldnen Funken,
und es erlischt schon, was ihm Nahrung gab.

Zum Abschied schwören die Geschwister
auf ihren Bund aus Schweigen und Vertraun.
Der Klettenkranz wird aus dem Haar gerissen,
und keines wagt, vom Boden aufzuschaun.

Die Vogelnester stürzen aus den Ästen,
der Zunder brennt, das Feuer wühlt im Laub,
und an den blauen Bienenstöcken rächen
die Engel den verjährten Honigraub.

O Engelstille, wenn im Gehn die Fäden
in alle Lüfte ausgeworfen sind!
Zu allem frei, wird sich die Hand nicht lösen,
die einen fängt vorm Gang ins Labyrinth.

X

In the land of deep lakes and the dragonflies,
having placed a tired kiss on the ancient stone,
he calls to the spirit of the morning's first light
before he leaves this land he called his own.

He bathes his weary eyes in the cardamine;
cold and disenchanted, he sees again what he saw.
What will keep him from harm, he will be given:
the ample yearning heart and the harmonica.

It is the time of apple cider and swallows,
as all around the spigot pierces the cask.
Whoever drinks now toasts the birds flying south,
though distance maddens his heart because it's so vast.

He closes up the foundries, the mills and chapels;
he pulls off ears of corn as he walks through fields;
the corn heaps up in piles of golden sparkles,
extinguished when he consumes his yield.

In leaving, the siblings swear to one another
to remain by silence and trust still bound.
A garland of burdocks is torn out from the hair,
and no one dares lift his eyes from the ground.

Bird nests outside fall down from the branches;
the tinder burns, the fire engulfs each leaf;
meanwhile, atop blue beehives the angels plan
to avenge, from ages past, the honey's thief.

O the peace of angels, when in passing, threads
haphazardly are scattered upon the winds!
Though free to move, the hand remains enmeshed,
which keeps one from entering the labyrinth.

Anrufung des Großen Bären

Großer Bär, komm herab, zottige Nacht,
Wolkenpelztier mit den alten Augen,
Sternenaugen,
durch das Dickicht brechen schimmernd
deine Pfoten mit den Krallen,
Sternenkrallen,
wachsam halten wir die Herden,
doch gebannt von dir, und mißtrauen
deinen müden Flanken und den scharfen
halbentblößten Zähnen,
alter Bär.

Ein Zapfen: eure Welt.
Ihr: die Schuppen dran.
Ich treib sie, roll sie
von den Tannen im Anfang
zu den Tannen am Ende,
schnaub sie an, prüf sie im Maul
und pack zu mit den Tatzen.

Fürchtet euch oder fürchtet euch nicht!
Zahlt in den Klingelbeutel und gebt
dem blinden Mann ein gutes Wort,
daß er den Bären an der Leine hält.
Und würzt die Lämmer gut.

's könnt sein, daß dieser Bär
sich losreißt, nicht mehr droht
und alle Zapfen jagt, die von den Tannen
gefallen sind, den großen, geflügelten,
die aus dem Paradiese stürzten.

Invocation of the Great Bear

Great Bear, shaggy night, come down.
Cloud-furred one with old eyes,
starry eyes,
glimmering you break through the brush
on your pads with claws,
starry claws,
while watchful we tend the flocks,
spellbound, mistrusting
your weary flanks and sharp
half-exposed teeth,
old Bear.

Your world: a fir cone.
You: the fir cone's scales.
I nudge them, roll them
from the fir in the beginning
to the fir in the end,
sniff them, give them a lick or two,
and bat them about with my paws.

Afraid or not afraid,
pay into the basket and give
the blind man a good word
so that he keeps the Bear on a leash.
And season the lambs well.

For it just might be that this Bear
will break loose, threaten no more,
and hunt all cones, those fallen
from firs, the great, the wingéd,
those that from Paradise plunged.

Mein Vogel

Was auch geschieht: die verheerte Welt
sinkt in die Dämmrung zurück,
einen Schlaftrunk halten ihr die Wälder bereit,
und vom Turm, den der Wächter verließ,
blicken ruhig und stet die Augen der Eule herab.

Was auch geschieht: du weißt deine Zeit,
mein Vogel, nimmst deinen Schleier.
und fliegst durch den Nebel zu mir.

Wir äugen im Dunstkreis, den das Gelichter bewohnt.
Du folgst meinem Wink, stößt hinaus
und wirbelst Gefieder und Fell —

Mein eisgrauer Schultergenoß, meine Waffe,
mit jener Feder besteckt, meiner einzigen Waffe!
Mein einziger Schmuck: Schleier und Feder von dir.

Wenn auch im Nadeltanz unterm Baum
die Haut mir brennt
und der hüfthohe Strauch
mich mit würzigen Blättern versucht,
wenn meine Locke züngelt,
sich wiegt und nach Feuchte verzehrt,
stürzt mir der Sterne Schutt
doch genau auf das Haar.

Wenn ich vom Rauch behelmt
wieder weiß, was geschieht,
mein Vogel, mein Beistand des Nachts,
wenn ich befeuert bin in der Nacht,
knistert's im dunklen Bestand,
und ich schlage den Funken aus mir.

My Bird

Whatever happens: the devastated world
sinks back into twilight,
the forest holds its night potion ready,
and from the tower, which the sentry deserted,
the owl's eyes gaze downward, steady and calm.

Whatever happens: you know your time,
my bird, you take your veil
and fly through the fog to me.

We peer through smoke which the riffraff inhabit.
You obey my sign, fly off
and whirl your plumage and down.

My hoary gray shoulder-mate, my weapon,
bedecked with a feather, my only weapon!
My only adornment: veil and feather from you.

Although the fir's dance of needles
singes my skin
and the hip-high bush
tempts me with fragrant leaves,
when my curls leap up,
sway and long for dampness,
stardust still tumbles
directly onto my hair.

When I, crowned with smoke,
know again, whatever happens,
my bird, my nightly accomplice,
when I am ablaze at night,
a dark grove begins to crackle
and I strike the sparks from my body.

Wenn ich befeuert bleib wie ich bin
und vom Feuer geliebt,
bis das Harz aus den Stämmen tritt,
auf die Wunden träufelt und warm
die Erde verspinnt,
(und wenn du mein Herz auch ausraubst des Nachts,
mein Vogel auf Glauben und mein Vogel auf Treu!)
rückt jene Warte ins Licht,
die du, besänftigt,
in herrlicher Ruhe erfliegst —
was auch geschieht.

When I remain as I am, ablaze,
loved by the fire,
until the resin seeps from the stems,
drips onto the wounds and, warm,
spins down to the earth,
(and also when you rob my heart at night,
my bird of belief and my bird of trust!)
that watchtower moves into the light
to which you, calmly,
in splendid quiet fly —
whatever happens.

II

Landnahme

Ins Weideland kam ich,
als es schon Nacht war,
in den Wiesen die Narben witternd
und den Wind, eh er sich regte.
Die Liebe graste nicht mehr,
die Glocken waren verhallt
und die Büschel verhärmt.

Ein Horn stak im Land,
vom Leittier verrannt,
ins Dunkel gerammt.

Aus der Erde zog ich's,
zum Himmel hob ich's
mit ganzer Kraft.

Um dieses Land mit Klängen
ganz zu erfüllen,
stieß ich ins Horn,
willens im kommenden Wind
und unter den wehenden Halmen
jeder Herkunft zu leben!

II

Settlement

Into pasture land I came
just after night had fallen,
smelling the scars in the meadows
and the wind before it rose.
Love no longer grazed,
the bells had faded away
and the sheaves stood bent and ragged.

A horn had been stuck in the earth
stubbornly by the herd's leader,
rammed into the darkness.

I drew it from the earth,
I lifted it to the sky
with all my might.

Wanting to fill this land
completely with music,
I blew the horn,
resolved in the rising wind
to live among the swaying grasses
of every true origin!

Curriculum Vitae

Lang ist die Nacht,
lang für den Mann,
der nicht sterben kann, lang
unter Straßenlaternen schwankt
sein nacktes Aug und sein Aug
schnapsatemblind, und Geruch
von nassem Fleisch unter seinen Nägeln
betäubt ihn nicht immer, o Gott,
lang ist die Nacht.

Mein Haar wird nicht weiß,
denn ich kroch aus dem Schoß von Maschinen,
Rosenrot strich mir Teer auf die Stirn
und die Strähnen, man hatt' ihr
die schneeweiße Schwester erwürgt. Aber ich,
der Häuptling, schritt durch die Stadt
von zehnmalhunderttausend Seelen, und mein Fuß
trat auf die Seelenasseln unterm Lederhimmel, aus dem
zehnmalhunderttausend Friedenspfeifen
hingen, kalt. Engelsruhe
wünscht' ich mir oft
und Jagdgründe, voll
vom ohnmächtigen Geschrei
meiner Freunde.

Mit gespreizten Beinen und Flügeln,
binsenweis stieg die Jugend
über mich, über Jauche, über Jasmin ging's
in die riesigen Nächte mit dem Quadrat-
wurzelgeheimnis, es haucht die Sage
des Tods stündlich mein Fenster an,

Curriculum Vitae

Long is the night,
long for the man
who cannot die, long
the feel of his shifting naked eye
under streetlamps, and his eye
blind drunk on schnapps, and the smell
of moist flesh under his nails
is the briefest of drugs, oh God,
long is the night.

My hair will not turn white
for I crawled out of the womb of machines,
Rose Red smeared tar on my forehead
and hair, someone had strangled
her snow-white sister. But I,
the Indian chief, marched through the city
of ten hundred thousand souls, and my foot
lowered onto the scurrying soul-centipedes
a leather sky, from which ten hundred thousand
pipes of peace hung cold. Often I've wished
for the quiet of angels
and hunting grounds filled
with the powerless cries
of my friends.

With outspread legs and wings,
the young like tall rushes
tower over me, over dung, over jasmine
with the square root of a secret
into the towering nights, the saga of death
breathing against my window each hour.

Wolfsmilch gebt mir und schüttet
in meinen Rachen das Lachen
der Alten vor mir, wenn ich in Schlaf
fall über den Folianten,
in den beschämenden Traum,
daß ich nicht taug für Gedanken,
mit Troddeln spiel,
aus denen Schlangen fransen.

Auch unsere Mütter haben
von der Zukunft ihrer Männer geträumt,
sie haben sie mächtig gesehen,
revolutionär und einsam,
doch nach der Andacht im Garten
über das flammende Unkraut gebeugt,
Hand in Hand mit dem geschwätzigen
Kind ihrer Liebe. Mein trauriger Vater,
warum habt ihr damals geschwiegen
und nicht weitergedacht?

Verloren in den Feuerfontänen,
in einer Nacht neben einem Geschütz,
das nicht feuert, verdammt lang
ist die Nacht, unter dem Auswurf
des gelbsüchtigen Monds, seinem galligen
Licht, fegt in der Machttraumspur
über mich (das halt ich nicht ab)
der Schlitten mit der verbrämten
Geschichte hinweg.
Nicht daß ich schlief: wach war ich,
zwischen Eisskeletten sucht' ich den Weg,
kam heim, wand mir Efeu
um Arm und Bein und weißte
mit Sonnenresten die Ruinen.
Ich hielt die hohen Feiertage,

Give me spurge milk and pour
the laughter of the ancients
into my throat, as in sleep
I stumble over tomes
in the shameful dream
where I'm not worthy of knowledge,
twirling tassels
whose fringes are snakes.

Our mothers have also dreamed
of the future of their men,
seeing them as powerful,
revolutionary, and lonesome,
yet after prayers in the garden,
bent over the flaming weeds,
hand in hand with the babbling
child of their love. My sad father,
why then did you all stay silent
and think no farther?

Lost among flaming fountains,
in a night next to a cannon
that will not fire, damned long
is the night, as under the detritus
of the jaundiced moon, its bilious light,
a sled brocaded with history
sweeps over me (I cannot stop it),
rushing along the trail
left by the dream of power.
Not that I was sleeping: I was awake,
and seeking the path between ice skeletons,
I came home, wound the ivy
around my arm and leg, and painted
the ruins white with the sun's remains.
I observed the holy days,

und erst wenn es gelobt war,
brach ich das Brot.

In einer großspurigen Zeit
muß man rasch von einem Licht
ins andre gehen, von einem Land
ins andre, unterm Regenbogen,
die Zirkelspitze im Herzen,
zum Radius genommen die Nacht.
Weit offen. Von den Bergen
sieht man Seen, in den Seen
Berge, und im Wolkengestühl
schaukeln die Glocken
der einen Welt. Wessen Welt
zu wissen, ist mir verboten.

An einem Freitag geschah's
— ich fastete um mein Leben,
die Luft troff vom Saft der Zitronen
und die Gräte stak mir im Gaumen —
da löst' ich aus dem entfalteten Fisch
einen Ring, der, ausgeworfen
bei meiner Geburt, in den Strom
der Nacht fiel und versank.
Ich warf ihn zurück in die Nacht.

O hätt ich nicht Todesfurcht!
Hätt ich das Wort,
(verfehlt ich's nicht),
hätt ich nicht Disteln im Herz,
(schlüg ich die Sonne aus),
hätt ich nicht Gier im Mund,
(trünk ich das wilde Wasser nicht),
schlüg ich die Wimper nicht auf,
(hätt ich die Schnur nicht gesehn).

and only when it was blessed
did I break the bread.

In an arrogant age
one must rush from one light
into another, from one land
into another, beneath the rainbow,
the compass points stuck in the heart
and night the radius.
Then the open view. From the mountains
one sees lakes, in the lakes,
mountains, and in the belfries of clouds
swing the bells of the one
and only world. To know
just whose world is forbidden to me.

It happened on a Friday
— I fasted for my life,
the air dripped with the juice of lemons,
and a fish bone stuck in my gums —
then out of the gutted fish I lifted
a ring that, tossed away
at my birth, had fallen into
the stream of night and sunk.
I threw it back into the night.

O if only I had no fear of death!
If I had the word
(I wouldn't misplace it),
if I had no thistles in my heart
(I would put out the sun),
if I had no greed in my mouth
(I wouldn't drink the wild water),
if I didn't open my eyelids
(I wouldn't have seen the rope).

Ziehn sie den Himmel fort?
Trüg mich die Erde nicht,
läg ich schon lange still,
läg ich schon lang,
wo die Nacht mich will,
eh sie die Nüstern bläht
und ihren Huf hebt
zu neuen Schlägen,
immer zum Schlag.
Immer die Nacht.
Und kein Tag.

Are they dragging away the sky?
If the Earth had not turned
I'd long be lying still.
I'd long be lying
where the night wants me,
before it flares its nostrils
and lifts its hoof
to strike yet another blow,
always a blow.
Always the night.
And never day.

Heimweg

Nacht aus Schlüsselblumen
und verwunschnem Klee,
feuchte mir die Füße,
daß ich leichter geh.

Der Vampir im Rücken
übt den Kinderschritt,
und ich hör ihn atmen,
wenn er kreuzweis tritt.

Folgt er mir schon lange?
Hab ich wen gekränkt?
Was mich retten könnte,
ist noch nicht verschenkt.

Wo die Halme zelten
um den Felsenspund,
bricht es aus der Quelle
altem, klarem Mund:

»Um nicht zu verderben,
bleib nicht länger aus,
hör das Schlüsselklirren,
komm ins Wiesenhaus!

Reinen Fleischs wird sterben,
wer es nicht mehr liebt,
über Rausch und Trauer
nur mehr Nachricht gibt.«

The Way Home

In the night of cowslip
and bewitching clover,
I moisten my feet
so my step is lighter.

The vampire behind me
mimics my own stride,
and I hear him breathe
whenever he steps aside.

How long has he followed?
Have I offended someone?
A means for being rescued
has not yet been given.

Where the grasses ring
the edge of the rocky pool,
there rises from the spring
a voice ancient and cool:

"So as not to come to ruin
don't stay out much longer;
listen, the key is rattling,
run for shelter!

As a body no longer cared for
will surely meet its end,
it's delirium and sorrow
we hear about more often."

Mit der Kraft des Übels,
das mich niederschlug,
weitet seine Schwinge
der Vampir im Flug,

hebt die tausend Köpfe,
Freund- und Feindgesicht,
vom Saturn beschattet,
der den Ring zerbricht.

Ist das Mal gerissen
in die Nackenhaut,
öffnen sich die Türen
grün und ohne Laut.

Und die Wiesenschwelle
glänzt von meinem Blut.
Deck mir, Nacht, die Augen
mit dem Narrenhut.

With the power so menacing
that knocked me to the ground,
the vampire spreads his wings,
and away he bounds,

lifting over a thousand
faces of friends and enemies
in the shadow of Saturn's bands
that smash to smithereens.

Should the mark of his bite
sink into your skin,
doors will open wide
that are soundless and green.

It's then the meadow's edge
glistens with my blood.
My eyes, O night, protect
beneath a fool's hood.

Nebelland

Im Winter ist meine Geliebte
unter den Tieren des Waldes.
Daß ich vor Morgen zurückmuß,
weiß die Füchsin und lacht.
Wie die Wolken erzittern! Und mir
auf den Schneekragen fällt
eine Lage von brüchigem Eis.

Im Winter ist meine Geliebte
ein Baum unter Bäumen und lädt
die glückverlassenen Krähen
ein in ihr schönes Geäst. Sie weiß,
daß der Wind, wenn es dämmert,
ihr starres, mit Reif besetztes
Abendkleid hebt und mich heimjagt.

Im Winter ist meine Geliebte
unter den Fischen und stumm.
Hörig den Wassern, die der Strich
ihrer Flossen von innen bewegt,
steh ich am Ufer und seh,
bis mich Schollen vertreiben,
wie sie taucht und sich wendet.

Und wieder vom Jagdruf des Vogels
getroffen, der seine Schwingen
über mir steift, stürz ich
auf offenem Feld: sie entfiedert
die Hühner und wirft mir ein weißes
Schlüsselbein zu. Ich nehm's um den Hals
und geh fort durch den bitteren Flaum.

Fog Land

In winter my lover
lives among the beasts of the forest.
The vixen knows I must return
by morning, and she laughs.
How the clouds tremble! On my
snow collar a shower
of brittle ice falls.

In winter my lover
is a tree among trees, inviting
the hapless crows to nest
in her beautiful limbs. She knows
that the wind, when dusk falls,
will lift her stiff, frost-covered
evening dress and chase me home.

In winter my lover
is a fish among fish and mute.
A slave to waters that her fins
stroke from within,
I stand on the bank and watch,
till ice floes drive me away,
how she dives and turns.

And hearing again the bird's hunting call
as above me it arches
its wings, I fall
onto an open field: she plucks
the hens and tosses me a white
collar bone. I hang it around my neck
and walk off through the bitter down.

Treulos ist meine Geliebte,
ich weiß, sie schwebt manchmal
auf hohen Schuh'n nach der Stadt,
sie küßt in den Bars mit dem Strohhalm
die Gläser tief auf den Mund,
und es kommen ihr Worte für alle.
Doch diese Sprache verstehe ich nicht.

Nebelland hab ich gesehen,
Nebelherz hab ich gegessen.

Faithless is my lover,
for I know she sometimes slips off
on high heels to town,
kissing the glasses in bars
deep in the mouth with a straw,
finding a spare word for everyone.
But I don't understand this talk.

For it's fog land I have seen.
Fog heart I have eaten.

Die blaue Stunde

Der alte Mann sagt: mein Engel, wie du willst,
wenn du nur den offenen Abend stillst
und an meinem Arm eine Weile gehst,
den Wahrspruch verschworener Linden verstehst,
die Lampen, gedunsen, betreten im Blau,
letzte Gesichter! nur deins glänzt genau.
Tot die Bücher, entspannt die Pole der Welt,
was die dunkle Flut noch zusammenhält,
die Spange in deinem Haar, scheidet aus.
Ohne Aufenthalt Windzug in meinem Haus,
Mondpfiff — dann auf freier Strecke der Sprung,
die Liebe, geschleift von Erinnerung.

Der junge Mann fragt: und wirst du auch immer?
Schwör's bei den Schatten in meinem Zimmer,
und ist der Lindenspruch dunkel und wahr,
sag ihn her mit Blüten und öffne dein Haar
und den Puls der Nacht, die verströmen will!
Dann ein Mondsignal, und der Wind steht still.
Gesellig die Lampen im blauen Licht,
bis der Raum mit der vagen Stunde bricht,
unter sanften Bissen dein Mund einkehrt
bei meinem Mund, bis dich Schmerz belehrt:
lebendig das Wort, das die Welt gewinnt,
ausspielt und verliert, und Liebe beginnt.

Das Mädchen schweigt, bis die Spindel sich dreht.
Sterntaler fällt. Die Zeit in den Rosen vergeht: —
Ihr Herren, gebt mir das Schwert in die Hand,
und Jeanne d'Arc rettet das Vaterland.
Leute, wir bringen das Schiff durchs Eis,
ich halte den Kurs, den keiner mehr weiß.

The Blue Hour

The old man says: my angel, as you will,
if only you nursed the empty evening so still,
when, with you upon my arm, together we go,
sharing the linden's secret, which only you know,
and streetlamps bloating, embarrassed in the blue,
the day's last faces! while only yours shines through.
The books shut, dead, the world free of its axis,
what holds the flood of dark in place still is
your hair's bright comb, till it as well falls out.
Without delay then, a draft puffs through my house,
a moon's low whistle — then on open tracks the churn
into love that, dragged from memory, at last returns.

The young man asks: you'll always love me most of all?
Swear it by the shadows upon my bedroom wall,
and should the linden's whisper be dark and true,
recite it with blossoms, and let your hair loose —
its pulse of night that so badly wants to spill!
Then a signal from the moon and the wind falls still.
In evening's blue light, the lamps seem intimate,
till space breaks through, its hours indeterminate,
as with soft nibbling lips your own mouth turns
to seek my own, until with pain you learn:
what wins the world is still a living word,
one played and already lost, before love is stirred.

The girl is silent until the spindle spins.
Coins fall from the sky. The time of roses ends.
You men, just pass the sword into my hand
and Joan of Arc will save the fatherland.
People, we'll sail the ship through icy floes,
for I know the course to take that no one knows.

Kauft Anemonen! drei Wünsche das Bund,
die schließen vorm Hauch eines Wunsches den Mund.
Vom hohen Trapez im Zirkuszelt
spring ich durch den Feuerreifen der Welt,
ich gebe mich in die Hand meines Herrn,
und er schickt mir gnädig den Abendstern.

Buy anemones! Three wishes to a bundle;
with every wish you breathe, they close each petal.
As from the circus tent's trapeze I swoop,
I spring clear through the world's own flaming hoop,
surrendering myself to the hands of my partner,
who gives me, like a gentleman, the evening star.

Erklär mir, Liebe

Dein Hut lüftet sich leis, grüßt, schwebt im Wind,
dein unbedeckter Kopf hat's Wolken angetan,
dein Herz hat anderswo zu tun,
dein Mund verleibt sich neue Sprachen ein,
das Zittergras im Land nimmt überhand,
Sternblumen bläst der Sommer an und aus,
von Flocken blind erhebst du dein Gesicht,
du lachst und weinst und gehst an dir zugrund,
was soll dir noch geschehen —

Erklär mir, Liebe!

Der Pfau, in feierlichem Staunen, schlägt sein Rad,
die Taube stellt den Federkragen hoch,
vom Gurren überfüllt, dehnt sich die Luft,
der Entrich schreit, vom wilden Honig nimmt
das ganze Land, auch im gesetzten Park
hat jedes Beet ein goldner Staub umsäumt.

Der Fisch errötet, überholt den Schwarm
und stürzt durch Grotten ins Korallenbett.
Zur Silbersandmusik tanzt scheu der Skorpion.
Der Käfer riecht die Herrlichste von weit;
hätt ich nur seinen Sinn, ich fühlte auch,
daß Flügel unter ihrem Panzer schimmern,
und nähm den Weg zum fernen Erdbeerstrauch!

Erklär mir, Liebe!

Tell Me, Love

Your hat tips slightly, greets, sways in the wind
your uncovered head has touched the clouds,
your heart is busy elsewhere,
your mouth takes on new tongues,
the quack-grass is taking over,
summer blows asters to and fro,
blinded by tufts you lift your face,
you laugh and cry and fall to pieces,
what will become of you —

Tell me, love!

The peacock spreads its tail in festive wonder,
the dove lifts high its feathered collar,
bursting with coos, the air expands,
the drake cries, the whole land eats
wild honey, while in the tranquil park
each flower bed is edged with golden dust.

The fish blushes, overtakes the school
and plunges through grottoes into the coral bed.
To silver sand music the scorpion shyly dances.
The beetle scents his mate from afar;
if only I had his sense, I'd also feel
wings shimmering beneath their armored shells,
and I'd take the path to distant strawberry patches!

Tell me, love!

Wasser weiß zu reden,
die Welle nimmt die Welle an der Hand,
im Weinberg schwillt die Traube, springt und fällt.
So arglos tritt die Schnecke aus dem Haus!

Ein Stein weiß einen andern zu erweichen!

Erklär mir, Liebe, was ich nicht erklären kann:
sollt sich die kurze schauerliche Zeit
nur mit Gedanken Umgang haben und allein
nichts Liebes kennen und nichts Liebes tun?
Muß einer denken? Wird er nicht vermißt?

Du sagst: es zählt ein andrer Geist auf ihn …
Erklär mir nichts. Ich seh den Salamander
durch jedes Feuer gehen.
Kein Schauer jagt ihn, und es schmerzt ihn nichts.

Water knows how to speak,
a wave takes a wave by the hand,
the grape swells in the vineyard, bursts and falls.
The guileless snail creeps out of his house.

One stone knows how to soften another!

Tell me, love, what I cannot explain:
should I spend this brief, dreadful time
only with thoughts circulating and alone,
knowing no love and giving no love?
Must one think? Will he be missed?

You say: another spirit is relying on him …
Tell me nothing. I watch the salamander
slip through every fire.
No dread haunts him, and he feels no pain.

Scherbenhügel

Vom Frost begattet die Gärten —
das Brot in den Öfen verbrannt —
der Kranz aus den Erntelegenden
ist Zunder in deiner Hand.

Verstumm! Verwahr deinen Bettel,
die Worte, von Tränen bestürzt,
unter dem Hügel aus Scherben,
der immer die Furchen schürzt.

Wenn alle Krüge zerspringen,
was bleibt von den Tränen im Krug?
Unten sind Spalten voll Feuer,
sind Flammenzungen am Zug.

Erschaffen werden noch Dämpfe
beim Wasser- und Feuerlaut.
O Aufgang der Wolken, der Worte,
dem Scherbenberg anvertraut!

Shard Mound

Frost beds down the gardens —
in the oven the bread is burning —
the garland of harvest legends
in your hand is a piece of kindling.

Hush! Hide your pleading words,
aghast with tears of sorrow,
beneath the mound of shards
that's always skirted the furrows.

When all the pitchers are smashed,
what's left of the tears in the pitcher?
Below us are burning cracks,
and flaming tongues prevail there.

Steam will still be unfurled
in the hiss of water and fire.
O the ascent of clouds, of words,
entrusted to the shard mound's pyre!

Tage in Weiß

In diesen Tagen steh ich auf mit den Birken
und kämm mir das Weizenhaar aus der Stirn
vor einem Spiegel aus Eis.

Mit meinem Atem vermengt,
flockt die Milch.
So früh schäumt sie leicht.
Und wo ich die Scheibe behauch, erscheint,
von einem kindlichen Finger gemalt,
wieder dein Name: Unschuld!
Nach so langer Zeit.

In diesen Tagen schmerzt mich nicht,
daß ich vergessen kann
und mich erinnern muß.

Ich liebe. Bis zur Weißglut
lieb ich und danke mit englischen Grüßen.
Ich hab sie im Fluge erlernt.

In diesen Tagen denk ich des Albatros',
mit dem ich mich auf-
und herüberschwang
in ein unbeschriebenes Land.

Am Horizont ahne ich,
glanzvoll im Untergang,
meinen fabelhaften Kontinent
dort drüben, der mich entließ
im Totenhemd.

Ich lebe und höre von fern seinen Schwanengesang!

Days in White

These days I rise with the birches
and brush the corn hair from my brow
before a mirror of ice.

Blended with my breath,
milk is beaten.
This early it foams easily.
And where I fog the pane there appears,
traced by a child-like finger,
again your name: Innocence!
After all these years.

These days it doesn't pain me
that I can forget
or that I must remember.

I love. Incandescently
I love and give thanks with angelic prayers.
I learned them with ease.

These days I think of the albatross
with whom I swung
up and over
into an uncharted land.

On the horizon I can sense,
splendid in the sunset,
my marvelous continent
just over there, which will release me
wrapped in a shroud.

I live, and from afar, I hear its swan song!

Harlem

Von allen Wolken lösen sich die Dauben,
der Regen wird durch jeden Schacht gesiebt,
der Regen springt von allen Feuerleitern
und klimpert auf dem Kasten voll Musik.

Die schwarze Stadt rollt ihre weißen Augen
und geht um jede Ecke aus der Welt.
Die Regenrhythmen unterwandert Schweigen.
Der Regeblues wird abgestellt.

Harlem

With barrel staves made loose by all the clouds,
the rain seeps out from every opened slit,
as rain from fire ladders leaps to the ground
and on a crate full of music drums its beat.

The ghetto rolls along with wide white eyes
and slips around each corner out of the world.
The rhythms of rain into the silence slide.
The blues of rain are no longer heard.

Reklame

Wohin aber gehen wir
ohne sorge sei ohne sorge
wenn es dunkel und wenn es kalt wird
sei ohne sorge
aber
mit musik
was sollen wir tun
heiter und mit musik
und denken
heiter
angesichts eines Endes
mit musik
und wohin tragen wir
am besten
unsre Fragen und den Schauer aller Jahre
in die Traumwäscherei ohne sorge sei ohne sorge
was aber geschieht
am besten
wenn Totenstille

eintritt

Advertisement

But where are we going
carefree be carefree
when it grows dark and when it grows cold
be carefree
but
with music
what should we do
cheerful and with music
and think
cheerful
in facing the end
with music
and to where do we carry
best of all
our questions and dread of all the years
to the dream laundry carefree be carefree
but what happens
best of all
when dead silence

sets in

Toter Hafen

Feuchte Flaggen hängen an den Masten
in den Farben, die kein Land je trug,
und sie wehen für verschlammte Sterne
und den Mond, der grün im Mastkorb ruht.

Wasserwelt aus den Entdeckerzeiten!
Wellen überwuchern jeden Weg,
und von oben tropft das Licht aus Netzen
neuer Straßen, in die Luft verlegt.

Drunten blättern Wasser in den Bibeln,
und die Kompaßnadel steht auf Nacht.
Aus den Träumen wird das Gold gewaschen,
und dem Meer bleibt die Verlassenschaft.

Nicht ein Land, nicht eins blieb unbetreten!
Und zerrissen treibt das Seemannsgarn,
denn die tollen, lachenden Entdecker
fielen in den toten Wasserarm.

Dead Harbor

Damp flags hang upon the many masts,
colors that no country has ever flown;
under murky stars and a moon that rests
green within the lookout, they flutter on.

Watery world that explorers once traversed!
Waves obliterate each route they sailed,
as up above light trickles from the gridwork
of new flight paths, which on the air are laid.

Under the surface, water leafs through bibles,
and the compass needle is pointing straight at night.
Out of our dreams, gold can still be filtered,
while under the sea our legacy still lies.

Not one land, not one remains untrodden!
The seaman's tattered nets float in place
of those explorers, laughing and wanton,
who fell into a watery dead embrace.

Rede und Nachrede

Komm nicht aus unsrem Mund,
Wort, das den Drachen sät.
's ist wahr, die Luft ist schwül,
vergoren und gesäuert schäumt das Licht,
und überm Sumpf hängt schwarz der Mückenflor.

Der Schierling bechert gern.
Ein Katzenfell liegt aus,
die Schlange faucht darauf,
der Skorpion tanzt an.

Dring nicht an unser Ohr,
Gerücht von andrer Schuld,
Wort, stirb im Sumpf,
aus dem der Tümpel quillt.

Wort, sei bei uns
von zärtlicher Geduld
und Ungeduld. Es muß dies Säen
ein Ende nehmen!

Dem Tier beikommen wird nicht, wer den Tierlaut nachahmt.
Wer seines Betts Geheimnis preisgibt, verwirkt sich alle Liebe.
Des Wortes Bastard dient dem Witz, um einen Törichten
    zu opfern.

Wer wünscht von dir ein Urteil über diesen Fremden?
Und fällst du's unverlangt, geh du von Nacht zu Nacht
mit seinen Schwären an den Füßen weiter, geh! komm
    nicht wieder.

Spoken and Rumored

Do not pass from our mouth,
word, the one that sows the dragon.
It's true, the air is muggy,
steeped and sour, the light foams,
and over the swamp floats a black cloud of mosquitoes.

The hemlock is fond of drinking.
A cat skin lies on display,
the snake hissing at it,
as the scorpion joins the party.

Do not press at our ears,
rumor of another's guilt;
word, die in the swamp
where the murky pool begins.

Word, remain for us
composed of tender patience
and impatience. This sowing
must come to an end!

The beast will not be caught by the one who mimics its call.
He who betrays the secret of his bed forfeits all love.
The word's bastard serves the joke, sacrificing a fool.

Who expects a judgment from you about this stranger?
And if you give it freely, walk then night after night
with his sores on your feet, walk on, and don't come back.

Wort, sei von uns,
freisinnig, deutlich, schön.
Gewiß muß es ein Ende nehmen,
sich vorzusehen.

(Der Krebs zieht sich zurück,
der Maulwurf schläft zu lang,
das weiche Wasser löst
den Kalk, der Steine spann.)

Komm, Gunst aus Laut und Hauch,
befestig diesen Mund,
wenn seine Schwachheit uns
entsetzt und hemmt.

Komm und versag dich nicht,
da wir im Streit mit soviel Übel stehen.
Eh Drachenblut den Widersacher schützt,
fällt diese Hand ins Feuer.
Mein Wort, errette mich!

Word, be that part of us
enlightened, clear, and beautiful.
Certainly an end must come,
so take it as warning.

(The crab skitters back,
the mole sleeps too long,
soft water loosens the stones
once embedded in the lime.)

Come, grace of sound and breath,
fortify this mouth,
even when its weakness
frightens and stifles us.

Come, and do not falter,
for we battle so much evil.
Before dragon's blood protects an enemy,
this hand will fall into the fire.
Deliver me, my word!

Was wahr ist

Was wahr ist, streut nicht Sand in deine Augen,
was wahr ist, bitten Schlaf und Tod dir ab
als eingefleischt, von jedem Schmerz beraten,
was wahr ist, rückt den Stein von deinem Grab.

Was wahr ist, so entsunken, so verwaschen
in Keim und Blatt, im faulen Zungenbett
ein Jahr und noch ein Jahr und alle Jahre —
was wahr ist, schafft nicht Zeit, es macht sie wett.

Was wahr ist, zieht der Erde einen Scheitel,
kämmt Traum und Kranz und die Bestellung aus,
es schwillt sein Kamm und voll gerauften Früchten
schlägt es in dich und trinkt dich gänzlich aus.

Was wahr ist, unterbleibt nicht bis zum Raubzug,
bei dem es dir vielleicht ums Ganze geht.
Du bist sein Raub beim Aufbruch deiner Wunden;
nichts überfällt dich, was dich nicht verrät.

Es kommt der Mond mit den vergällten Krügen.
So trink dein Maß. Es sinkt die bittre Nacht.
Der Abschaum flockt den Tauben ins Gefieder,
wird nicht ein Zweig in Sicherheit gebracht.

Du haftest in der Welt, beschwert von Ketten,
doch treibt, was wahr ist, Sprünge in die Wand.
Du wächst und siehst im Dunkeln nach dem Rechten,
dem unbekannten Ausgang zugewandt.

What's True

What's true does not throw sand into your eyes;
what's true is that sleep and death seek confirmation
from you through every pain's advice;
what's true, from your tomb, will remove the stone.

What's true is so sunken in, so undefined
in a seed or leaf, and in lazy tongues embedded
for a year, another year, then for all time —
what's true does not buy time, it cancels it.

What's true can part the earth just like a comb
that rakes away dreams, commands, and laurel crowns,
till, full of plucked fruit, its proud and swollen comb
can set its teeth in you and strike you down.

What's true does not occur until the raid
that forces you to give your all.
Your open wounds make clear that you're the prey;
though nothing conquers you that isn't a betrayal.

The moon is rising, and mugs full of regret.
So drink your fill. The night slides down so bitter.
The dove's own feathers will be covered by the dregs
if not a single branch is made secure.

You still cling to the world, burdened by chains,
and yet what's true still causes the wall to split.
You wake in darkness, note everything is the same,
aware there still exists an unknown exit.

III

Das erstgeborene Land

In mein erstgeborenes Land, in den Süden
zog ich und fand, nackt und verarmt
und bis zum Gürtel im Meer,
Stadt und Kastell.

Vom Staub in den Schlaf getreten
lag ich im Licht,
und vom ionischen Salz belaubt
hing ein Baumskelett über mir.

Da fiel kein Traum herab.

Da blüht kein Rosmarin,
kein Vogel frischt
sein Lied in Quellen auf.

In meinem erstgeborenen Land, im Süden
sprang die Viper mich an
und das Grausen im Licht.

O schließ
die Augen schließ!
Preß den Mund auf den Biß!

Und als ich mich selber trank
und mein erstgeborenes Land
die Erdbeben wiegten,
war ich zum Schauen erwacht.

III

The Native Land

Into my native land, into the South,
I moved and found, naked and poor
and up to their waists in the sea,
a town and fortress.

Driven by dust into sleep,
I lay in the light,
and above hung a skeleton tree
covered with Ionian salt.

There no dream fell down.

There no rosemary blooms,
no bird renews
its song in spring waters.

In my native land, in the South,
the viper sprang at me
in that brutal light.

O shut
your eyes, shut them!
Press your mouth to the bite!

And when I drank of myself
and my native land
rocked with earthquakes,
I opened my eyes to see.

Da fiel mir Leben zu.

Da ist der Stein nicht tot.
Der Docht schnellt auf,
wenn ihn ein Blick entzündet.

Then life fell to me.

There the stone is not dead.
The wick flares
when lit by a glance.

Lieder von einer Insel

Schattenfrüchte fallen von den Wänden,
Mondlicht tüncht das Haus, und Asche
erkalteter Krater trägt der Meerwind herein.

In den Umarmungen schöner Knaben
schlafen die Küsten,
dein Fleisch besinnt sich auf meins,
es war mir schon zugetan,
als sich die Schiffe
vom Land lösten und Kreuze
mit unsrer sterblichen Last
Mastendienst taten.

Nun sind die Richtstätten leer,
sie suchen und finden uns nicht.

––––––

Wenn du auferstehst,
wenn ich aufersteh,
ist kein Stein vor dem Tor,
liegt kein Boot auf dem Meer.

Morgen rollen die Fässer
sonntäglichen Wellen entgegen,
wir kommen auf gesalbten
Sohlen zum Strand, waschen
die Trauben und stampfen
die Ernte zu Wein,
morgen am Strand.

Songs from an Island

Ripe shadows cascade from the walls,
moonlight whitewashes the house, and ashes
from the cold crater drift in the sea breeze.

The coast sleeps in the embrace
of beautiful boys;
your flesh considers mine,
still as fond of me
as when the ships
broke loose from land,
and the crosses
hung with our mortal weight
kept watch from the masts.

Now the gallows are empty,
they search but find us gone.

———

When you rise again,
when I rise again,
no stone is before the gate,
no boat lies on the sea.

Tomorrow the barrels will roll
towards the Sunday waves.
We will walk the sand
on anointed soles, washing
the grapes and stomping
the harvest to wine,
tomorrow on the beach.

Wenn du auferstehst,
wenn ich aufersteh,
hängt der Henker am Tor,
sinkt der Hammer ins Meer.

———

Einmal muß das Fest ja kommen!
Heiliger Antonius, der du gelitten hast,
heiliger Leonhard, der du gelitten hast,
heiliger Vitus, der du gelitten hast.

Platz unsren Bitten, Platz den Betern,
Platz der Musik und der Freude!
Wir haben Einfalt gelernt,
wir singen im Chor der Zikaden,
wir essen und trinken,
die mageren Katzen
streichen um unseren Tisch,
bis die Abendmesse beginnt,
halt ich dich an der Hand
mit den Augen,
und ein ruhiges mutiges Herz
opfert dir seine Wünsche.

Honig und Nüsse den Kindern,
volle Netze den Fischern,
Fruchtbarkeit den Gärten,
Mond dem Vulkan, Mond dem Vulkan!

Unsre Funken setzten über die Grenzen,
über die Nacht schlugen Raketen
ein Rad, auf dunklen Flößen
entfernt sich die Prozession und räumt
der Vorwelt die Zeit ein,

When you rise again,
when I rise again,
the hangman hangs on the gate,
the hammer sinks in the sea.

———

And yet the feast must come!
Saint Antonius, you who have suffered,
Saint Leonhard, you who have suffered,
Saint Vitus, you who have suffered.

Make way for our pleas, make way for the worshipers,
make way for music and joy!
We have learned a simpleness,
we sing in a chorus of cicadas,
we eat and drink,
while lean cats
rub against our table
until the evening mass begins,
and I hold your hand
with my eyes
and a quiet, courageous heart
offers you up its wishes.

Give honey and nuts to the children,
full nets to the fishermen,
fruitfulness to the gardens,
and a moon to the volcano! a moon to the volcano!

Our sparks crossed the borders,
above the night the rockets wheeled,
on dark rafts
the procession withdraws and yields
time to the prehistoric world,

den schleichenden Echsen,
der schlemmenden Pflanze,
dem fiebernden Fisch,
den Orgien des Winds und der Lust
des Bergs, wo ein frommer
Stern sich verirrt, ihm auf die Brust
schlägt und zerstäubt.

Jetzt seid standhaft, törichte Heilige,
sagt dem Festland, daß die Krater nicht ruhn!
Heiliger Rochus, der du gelitten hast,
o der du gelitten hast, heiliger Franz.

———

Wenn einer fortgeht, muß er den Hut
mit den Muscheln, die er sommerüber
gesammelt hat, ins Meer werfen
und fahren mit wehendem Haar,
er muß den Tisch, den er seiner Liebe
deckte, ins Meer stürzen,
er muß den Rest des Weins,
der im Glas blieb, ins Meer schütten,
er muß den Fischen sein Brot geben
und einen Tropfen Blut ins Meer mischen,
er muß sein Messer gut in die Wellen treiben
und seinen Schuh versenken,
Herz, Anker und Kreuz,
und fahren mit wehendem Haar!
Dann wird er wiederkommen.
Wann?
    Frag nicht.

———

to the creeping lizards,
gluttonous plants,
feverish fish,
the wind's orgies
and the mountain's pleasure,
where a pious star strays and falls,
exploding upon the crest.

Now be steadfast, foolish saints,
tell the coast the craters are not resting!
Saint Rochus, you who have suffered,
O you who have suffered, Saint Franz.

————

When one goes away, he must fling
his hat of mussels gathered
over the summer into the sea
and sail with windblown hair.
He must plunge the table
set for his love into the sea.
He must pour the last of the wine
left in the glass into the sea.
He must feed the fish his bread
and mix a drop of blood into the sea.
He must throw his knife to the waves
and toss away his shoes,
heart, anchor, and cross,
and sail with windblown hair.
Only then will he return.
When?
        Don't ask.

————

Es ist Feuer unter der Erde,
und das Feuer ist rein.

Es ist Feuer unter der Erde
und flüssiger Stein.

Es ist ein Strom unter der Erde,
der strömt in uns ein.

Es ist ein Strom unter der Erde,
der sengt das Gebein.

Es kommt ein großes Feuer,
es kommt ein Strom über die Erde.

Wir werden Zeugen sein.

There's a fire under the earth
and the fire burns clean.

There's a fire under the earth
and a molten stream.

There's a stream under the earth
and we feel it in our souls.

There's a stream under the earth
and it singes our bones.

There will be a great fire.
There will be a great flood.

We shall witness each.

Nord und Süd

Zu spät erreichten wir der Gärten Garten
in jenem Schlaf, von dem kein dritter weiß.
Im Ölzweig wollte ich den Schnee erwarten,
im Mandelbaum den Regen und das Eis.

Wie aber soll die Palme es verwinden,
daß du den Wall aus warmen Lauben schleifst,
wie soll ihr Blatt sich in den Nebel finden,
wenn du die Wetterkleider überstreifst?

Bedenk, der Regen machte dich begangen,
als ich den offnen Fächer zu dir trug.
Du schlugst ihn zu. Dir ist die Zeit entgangen,
seit ich mich aufhob mit dem Vogelzug.

North and South

Too late we reached within our private sleep
the garden of gardens that no third can know.
I'd hoped to find within the almond tree
both rain and ice, and on olive branches, snow.

But how will the palm survive it when you raze
the embankment's warm arbors, making them scatter,
or find its own leaf in the fog's thick haze
when you impose on it your coat of weather.

Remember how much the rain disturbed you
when I offered you the palm, its open fan.
You closed it up. Its season left you
as soon as, with the birds, I fled your land.

Brief in zwei Fassungen

Rom im November abends besten Dank
das glatte Marmorriff die kalten Fliesen
die Gischt der Lichter eh die Tore schließen
der Klang mit dem erfrorne Gläser springen
der Singsang den sie aus Gitarren wringen
eh sie die Schädel in die Münzen stanzen
auf die Arena mit Zypressenlanzen!
der Holzwurm ist bei mir zu Tisch gesessen —
wie wohl ein Blatt aussieht das Raupen fressen?
und Herbst in Nebelland die bunten Lumpen
der Wälder unter großen Regenpumpen
ob es die Käuzchen gibt das Todeswerben
die Drachen die in warmen Sümpfen sterben
das Segel schwarz den Unglücksschrei der Raben
den Nordwind um die Wasser umzugraben
das Geisterschiff die Halden und die Heiden
schuttüberhäuft das Haus die Trauerweiden
verschuldet und vertränt am Strom aus Särgen
den Wahnsinn den sie aus der Tiefe bergen
Immer und Nimmermehr gemischt zum Trank
dein wehes Herz vergötternd alle Leiden
vernichtet und verloren liebeskrank …

Nachts im November Rom Einklang und Ruh
der Abschied ohne Kränkung ist vollzogen
die Augen hat ein reiner Glanz beflogen
die Säulen wachsen aus den Tamarinden
o Himmel den die blauen Töne binden!
es landen Disken in den Brunnenmitten
sie drehen sich zu leichten Rosenschritten
wollüstig dehnen Katzen ihre Krallen
der Schlaf hat einen letzten Stern befallen

Letter in Two Drafts

Rome in November evening many thanks
the smooth marble reef the cold tile-faces
the spray of lights before the gate closes
the sound that frozen glasses make when shattering
the singsong tune that from guitars keeps wringing
before more heads and tails into coins are pressed
down at the coliseum with lances of cypress!
the woodworm sits beside me at the table —
how juicy does a leaf look that caterpillars nibble?
and autumn in a land of fog the gaudy tatters
of forests that are soaked by great rain showers
whether it be a screech owl's longing for death
the dragons that in the marsh's warmth perish
the blackened sail the ominous call of ravens
the north wind over the water deviating
the ghostly ship the hillsides and the meadows
buried under rubble the house the willows
penniless and weeping at the stream of coffins
its madness from the depths they keep recovering
Forever and No More mixed as a single drink
your pained heart glorifying every sorrow
destroyed completely lost lovesick you sink …

Rome a night in November harmonious and quiet
the goodbye without insult has been accomplished
the eyes by a pure luminescence have been brushed
the columns shoot up out of tamarinds
O the sky through which the blue tones wind!
petals are landing in the middle of fountains
like light rose-steps they continue turning
sensuously the cats stretch out their claws
sleep has seized hold of a last falling star

der Mund entkommt den Küssen ohne Kerben
der Seidenschuh ist unverletzt von Scherben
rasch sinkt der Wein durch dämmernde Gedanken
springt wieder Licht mit seinen hellen Pranken
umgreift die Zeiten schleudert sie ins Heute
die Hügel stürmt die erste Automeute
vor Tempeln paradieren die Antennen
empfangen Morgenchöre und entbrennen
für jeden Marktschrei Preise Vogelrufe
ins Pflaster taucht die Spiegelschrift der Hufe
die Chrysanthemen schütten Gräber zu
Meerhauch und Bergwind mischen Duft und Tränen
ich bin inmitten — was erwartest du?

the mouth escapes a kiss without a scratch
the silken slipper is not harmed by glass
the wine sinks fast through fading twilight thoughts
the light leaps up once more with its bright claws
embraces ages past flings them into today
up hillsides roar the hordes of cars at bay
around the temples antennas are parading
receiving morning's chorus amid the blazing
for every market cry of prices birds calling
into pavement horse hooves dip their mirror writing
chrysanthemums amass on graves like morning dew
sea breeze and mountain wind mix aromas and tears
I'm in the midst of it — what about you?

Römisches Nachtbild

Wenn das Schaukelbrett die sieben Hügel
nach oben entführt, gleitet es auch,
von uns beschwert und umschlungen,
ins finstere Wasser,

taucht in den Flußschlamm, bis in unsrem Schoß
die Fische sich sammeln.
Ist die Reihe an uns,
stoßen wir ab.

Es sinken die Hügel,
wir steigen und teilen
jeden Fisch mit der Nacht.

Keiner springt ab.
So gewiß ist's, daß nur die Liebe
und einer den andern erhöht.

Rome at Night

When the swing seat carries off
the seven hills, it also glides,
burdened and embraced by us,
into dark water,

diving into river mud, till in our lap
the fish gather.
Then when it's our turn
we push off.

The hills sink away,
we climb and share
each fish with the night.

No one jumps off.
Proving that only by the love
of one is another lifted.

Unter dem Weinstock

Unter dem Weinstock im Traubenlicht
reift dein letztes Gesicht.
Die Nacht muß das Blatt wenden.

Die Nacht muß das Blatt wenden,
wenn die Schale zerspringt,
und aus dem Fruchfleisch die Sonne dringt.

Die Nacht muß das Blatt wenden,
denn dein erstes Gesicht
steigt in dein Trugbild, gedämmt vom Licht.

Unter dem Weinstock im Traubenstrahl
prägt der Rausch dir ein Mal —
Die Nacht muß das Blatt wenden!

Under the Grapevine

Under the grapevine in the light of grapes
there ripens your last face.
The night must turn a new leaf.

The night must turn a new leaf
when the peel bursts open
and out of the pulp there presses the sun.

The night must turn a new leaf
because your first face
is now a phantom held by light that fades.

Under the grapevine within the grapes' luster
delirium stamps you with its cipher —
The night must turn a new leaf!

In Apulien

Unter den Olivenbäumen schüttet Licht die Samen aus,
Mohn erscheint und flackert wieder,
fängt das Öl und brennt es nieder,
und das Licht geht nie mehr aus.

Trommeln in den Höhlenstädten trommeln ohne Unterlaß,
weißes Brot und schwarze Lippen,
Kinder in den Futterkrippen
will der Fliegenschwarm zum Fraß.

Käm die Helle von den Feldern in den Troglodytentag,
könnt der Mohn aus Lampen rauchen,
Schmerz im Schlaf ihn ganz verbrauchen,
bis er nicht mehr brennen mag.

Esel stünden auf und trügen Wasserschläuche übers Land,
Schnüre stickten alle Hände,
Glas und Perlen für die Wände —
Tür im klingenden Gewand.

Die Madonnen stillten Kinder und der Büffel ging' vorbei,
Rauch im Horn, zur grünen Tränke,
endlich reichten die Geschenke:
Lammblut, Fisch und Schlangenei.

Endlich malmen Steine Früchte, und die Krüge sind gebrannt.
Öl rinnt offnen Augs herunter,
und der Mohn geht trunken unter,
von Taranteln überrannt.

In Apulia

Under the olive trees the light pours out its seeds,
poppies appear and begin to flicker,
burning the oil that feeds their fire,
a light that never recedes.

Drums inside cavernous cities drum their endless beat.
White bread and lips, blackened,
manger cribs filled with children,
these attract flies that want to feed.

If the light of fields revealed the prehistoric,
poppies would smoke inside the lanterns,
pain would consume their sleeping forms,
till their burning was exhausted.

Donkeys would rise to carry water over the land,
hands would embroider lacy curls,
adorning the walls with glass and pearls —
passages for the tinkling of raiment.

Children are nursed by Madonnas, and the buffalo roam
munching green grass, smoke in their horns;
finally worthy gifts are borne:
snake eggs, fish, blood of the lamb.

Finally the stones crush fruit, the waiting jugs are fired.
Oil drops float like eyes on water,
poppies sink, drunken, as they falter,
overrun by deadly spiders.

Schwarzer Walzer

Das Ruder setzt auf den Gong mit dem schwarzen Walzer ein,
Schatten mit stumpfen Stichen nähn die Gitarren ein.

Unter der Schwelle erglänzt im Spiegel mein finsteres Haus,
Leuchter treten sich sanft die flammenden Spitzen aus.

Über die Klänge verhängt: Eintracht von Welle und Spiel;
immer entzieht sich der Grund mit einem anderen Ziel.

Schuld ich dem Tag den Marktschrei und den blauen Ballon —
Steinrumpf und Vogelschwinge suchen die Position

zum Pas de deux ihrer Nächte, lautlos mir zugewandt,
Venedig, gepfählt und geflügelt, Abend- und Morgenland!

Nur Mosaiken wurzeln und halten im Boden fest,
Säulen umtanzen die Bojen, Fratzen- und Freskenrest.

Kein August war geschaffen, die Löwensonne zu sehn,
schon am Eingang des Sommers ließ sie die Mähne wehn.

Denk die abgöttische Helle, den Prankenschlag auf den Bug
und im Gefolge des Kiels den törichten Maskenzug,

überm ersäuften Parkett zu Spitze geschifft ein Tuch,
brackiges Wasser, die Liebe und ihren Geruch,

Introduktion, dann den Auftakt zur Stille und nichts nachher,
Pausen schlagende Ruder und die Coda vom Meer!

Black Waltz

The oar dips at the sound of a gong, the black waltz starts,
with thick dull stitches, shadows string guitars.

Beneath the threshold, in a mirror, my dark house floats,
the flaring points of light now softly radiate out.

Hanging above the sounds: the harmony of waves in motion,
always the surface shifts towards another destination.

I owe the day its market cries and blue balloon —
stone torsos, the whirling flight of birds, the *pas de deux*

that they perform each night, silently turned towards me,
Venice, on pylons and floating, East and West in harmony!

Only mosaics strike roots and hold fast to the ground,
about a buoy — pillars, frescoes, and grimaces spin around.

There never was an August that saw the lion's sun,
for its mane was set adrift when the summer had begun.

Consider idolatrous light, the claw marks on the bow,
and in the wake of the keel, the carnival masks in tow,

as over the flooded plaza, to the tower, sails a garment,
also the brackish water, as well as love and its scent,

the introduction, a prelude to stillness, not another beat,
the oar striking intervals and the coda of the sea!

Nach vielen Jahren

Leicht ruht der Pfeil der Zeit im Sonnenbogen.
Wenn die Agave aus dem Felsen tritt,
wird über ihr dein Herz im Wind gewogen
und hält mit jedem Ziel der Stunde Schritt.

Schon überfliegt ein Schatten die Azoren
und deine Brust der zitternde Granat.
Ist auch der Tod dem Augenblick verschworen,
bist du die Scheibe, die ihm blendend naht.

Ist auch das Meer verwöhnt und glanzerfahren,
erhöht's den Spiegel für die Handvoll Blut,
und die Agave blüht nach vielen Jahren
im Schutz der Felsen vor der trunknen Flut.

After Many Years

Time's arrow rests easily in the sun's drawn bow.
As soon as the agave blossoms from the cliffs,
your heart will sway above in the wind that blows
each hour's length through its every tick.

Already a shadow drifts above the Azores
and over your breast's own quaking garnet.
Death is also the moment's conspirator,
and you, towards whom it streaks, the target.

The sea is also spoiled and vain, a mere
shift of its mirror swallowing a handful of blood,
just as the agave blooms after many years
in the shelter of cliffs, before the drunken flood.

Schatten Rosen Schatten

Unter einem fremden Himmel
Schatten Rosen
Schatten
auf einer fremden Erde
zwischen Rosen und Schatten
in einem fremden Wasser
mein Schatten

Shadows Roses Shadow

Under an alien sky
shadows roses
shadow
on an alien earth
between roses and shadows
in alien waters
my shadow

Bleib

Die Fahrten gehn zu Ende,
der Fahrtenwind bleibt aus.
Es fällt dir in die Hände
ein leichtes Kartenhaus.

Die Karten sind bebildert
und zeigen jeden Ort.
Du hast die Welt geschildert
und mischst sie mit dem Wort.

Profundum der Partien,
die dann im Gange sind!
Bleib, um das Blatt zu ziehen,
mit dem man sie gewinnt.

Stay

Now the journey is ending,
the wind is losing heart.
Into your hands it's falling,
a rickety house of cards.

The cards are backed with pictures
displaying all the world.
You've stacked up all the images
and shuffled them with words.

And how profound the playing
that once again begins!
Stay, the card you're drawing
is the only world you'll win.

Am Akragas

Das geklärte Wasser in den Händen,
an dem Mittag mit den weißen Brauen,
wird der Fluß die eigne Tiefe schauen
und zum letzten Mal die Dünen wenden,
mit geklärtem Wasser in den Händen.

Trägt der Wind aus Eukalyptushainen
Blätter hochgestrichen, hauchbeschrieben,
wird der Fluß die tiefren Töne lieben.
Festen Anschlag von den Feuersteinen
trägt der Wind zu Eukalyptushainen.

Und geweiht vom Licht und stummen Bränden
hält das Meer den alten Tempel offen,
wenn der Fluß, bis an den Quell getroffen,
mit geklärtem Wasser in den Händen
seine Weihen nimmt von stummen Bränden.

At Agrigento

The purified water held within its hands,
at midday, under the eyebrows of its white caps,
the river gazes deep into its depths,
winding its final stage through dunes of sand
with purified water held within its hands.

As from the eucalyptus groves, the wind
lifts leaves that carry the finest trace of dust,
the river begins to love the sea's deep thrust.
The readiness of sparks to be struck from flints
is carried to the eucalyptus groves by the wind.

Consecrated by light from silent fiery brands,
the sea still holds the ancient temple open,
as the river, returning to its origin,
with purified water held within its hands,
takes consecration from the silent fiery brands.

An die Sonne

Schöner als der beachtliche Mond und sein geadeltes Licht,
Schöner als die Sterne, die berühmten Orden der Nacht,
Viel schöner als der feurige Auftritt eines Kometen
Und zu weit Schönrem berufen als jedes andre Gestirn,
Weil dein und mein Leben jeden Tag an ihr hängt, ist die Sonne.

Schöne Sonne, die aufgeht, ihr Werk nicht vergessen hat
Und beendet, am schönsten im Sommer, wenn ein Tag
An den Küsten verdampft und ohne Kraft gespiegelt die Segel
Über dein Aug ziehn, bis du müde wirst und das letzte verkürzt.

Ohne die Sonne nimmt auch die Kunst wieder den Schleier,
Du erscheinst mir nicht mehr, und die See und der Sand,
Von Schatten gepeitscht, fliehen unter mein Lid.

Schönes Licht, das uns warm hält, bewahrt und wunderbar sorgt,
Daß ich wieder sehe und daß ich dich wiederseh!

Nichts Schönres unter der Sonne als unter der Sonne zu sein …

Nichts Schönres als den Stab im Wasser zu sehn und den
    Vogel oben,
Der seinen Flug überlegt, und unten die Fische im Schwarm,
Gefärbt, geformt, in die Welt gekommen mit einer
    Sendung von Licht,
Und den Umkreis zu sehn, Geviert eines Felds, das
    Tausendeck meines Lands
Und das Kleid, das du angetan hast. Und dein Kleid,
    glockig und blau!

To the Sun

More beautiful than the remarkable moon and its noble light,
More beautiful than the stars, the celebrated orders of night,
Much more beautiful than the fiery display of a comet,
And so much more beautiful than any other star,
Because your life and my life depend on it daily, is the sun.

Beautiful sun, which rises, remembering its tasks
And completing them, most beautiful in summer, when a day
Shimmers on the coast and the calm mirror of sails
Passes over your eye, until you tire and eventually doze.

Without the sun, even art puts on a veil again.
You cease to appear to me, and the sea and the sand,
Lashed by shadows, hide beneath my lids.

Beautiful light, which keeps us warm, sustains and marvelously
    ensures
That I see again, and that I see you again!

Nothing more beautiful under the sun than to be under the
    sun ….

Nothing more beautiful than to see the reed in the water
    and the bird above
Pondering its flight and, below, the fish in their school,
Colorful, shapely, come into the world on a beam of light,
And to see the circumference, the square of a field, the
    thousand corners of my land,
And the dress you have put on. Your dress, bell-shaped
    and blue!

Schönes Blau, in dem die Pfauen spazieren und sich verneigen,
Blau der Fernen, der Zonen des Glücks mit den Wettern
    für mein Gefühl,
Blauer Zufall am Horizont! Und meine begeisterten Augen
Weiten sich wieder und blinken und brennen sich wund.

Schöne Sonne, der vom Staub noch die größte Bewundrung
    gebührt,
Drum werde ich nicht wegen dem Mond und den Sternen
    und nicht,
Weil die Nacht mit Kometen prahlt und in mir einen
    Narren sucht,
Sondern deinetwegen und bald endlos und wie um
    nichts sonst
Klage führen über den unabwendbaren Verlust
    meiner Augen.

A beautiful blue in which peacocks strut and bow,
The blue of distances, zones of joy with climates for my
        every mood,
The horizon's blue chance! And my enchanted eyes
Widen again and blink and burn themselves sore.

Beautiful sun, which even from dust deserves the highest praise,
Causing me to raise a cry, not to the moon,
The stars, the night's garish comets that name me a fool,
But rather to you, and ultimately to you alone,
As I lament the inevitable loss of my sight.

IV

Lieder auf der Flucht

> *Dura legge d'Amor! ma, ben che obliqua,*
> *Servar convensi; però ch'ella aggiunge*
> *Di cielo in terra, universale, antique.*
>
> Petrarca, ›I Trionfi‹

I

Der Palmzweig bricht im Schnee,
die Stiegen stürzen ein,
die Stadt liegt steif und glänzt
im fremden Winterschein.

Die Kinder schreien und ziehn
den Hungerberg hinan,
sie essen vom weißen Mehl
und beten den Himmel an.

Der reiche Winterflitter,
das Mandarinengold,
treibt in den wilden Böen.
Die Blutorange rollt.

IV

Songs in Flight

Dura legge d'Amor! ma, ben che obliqua,
Servar convensi; però ch'ella aggiunge
Di cielo in terra, universale, antique.

Petrarch, *I Trionfi*

I

The palm branch breaks in snow
that collapses the stairway's flight,
the city lies stiff and gleaming
in a strange winter light.

The children wail and climb
their mountain of hunger,
praying to the sky
while they eat white flour.

Winter's wealth of tinsel
in a mandarin's gold,
the wind gusts wildly on,
and the blood orange rolls.

II

Ich aber liege allein
im Eisverhau voller Wunden.

Es hat mir der Schnee
noch nicht die Augen verbunden.

Die Toten, an mich gepreßt,
schweigen in allen Zungen.

Niemand liebt mich und hat
für mich eine Lampe geschwungen!

III

Die Sporaden, die Inseln,
das schöne Stückwerk im Meer,
umschwommen von kalten Strömen,
neigen noch Früchte her.

Die weißen Retter, die Schiffe
— o einsame Segelhand! —
deuten, eh sie versinken,
zurück auf das Land.

IV

Kälte wie noch nie ist eingedrungen.
Fliegende Kommandos kamen über das Meer.
Mit allen Lichtern hat der Golf sich ergeben.
Die Stadt ist gefallen.

II

But I lie alone,
wounds fill an abbatis of ice.

The snow upon me
has not yet sealed my eyes.

The dead pressed against me
are silent, no matter the tongue.

No one loves me,
no lamp for me is hung.

III

The Sporades, the islands,
patchwork in a sea so clear,
cold, the streams that surround them,
yet they bear the fruit that's here.

White rescuers, the ships,
— O lonesome sailor's hand! —
they point, before they sink,
back towards the land.

IV

Cold, as never before, has penetrated.
Over the sea, commandos racing.
Down to its last lights, the bay has surrendered.
The city has fallen.

Ich bin unschuldig und gefangen
im unterworfenen Neapel,
wo der Winter
Posilip und Vomero an den Himmel stellt,
wo seine weißen Blitze aufräumen
unter den Liedern
und er seine heiseren Donner
ins Recht setzt.

Ich bin unschuldig, und bis Camaldoli
rühren die Pinien die Wolken;
und ohne Trost, denn die Palmen
schuppt sobald nicht der Regen;

ohne Hoffnung, denn ich soll nicht entkommen,
auch wenn der Fisch die Flossen schützend sträubt
und wenn am Winterstrand der Dunst,
von immer warmen Wellen aufgeworfen,
mir eine Mauer macht,
auch wenn die Wogen
fliehend
den Fliehenden
dem nächsten Ziel entheben.

V

Fort mit dem Schnee von der gewürzten Stadt!
Der Früchte Luft muß durch die Straßen gehen.
Streut die Korinthen aus,
die Feigen bringt, die Kapern!
Belebt den Sommer neu,
den Kreislauf neu,
Geburt, Blut, Kot und Auswurf,

I am innocent and captive
in conquered Naples,
where winter
silhouettes Posilipo and Vomero,
where its white lightning cleans up
among the songs
and sets its hoarse thunder
in command.

I am innocent, and until Camaldoli
stone pines nudge the clouds;
without comfort, because the rain
does not cleanse the palms;

without hope, because I shall not escape,
even though the fish bristles its fins
and the beach's winter mist
blown warm from the waves
protects and walls me in,
even though the tide
in fleeing
draws away the next goal
of those who flee.

V

Away with snow from the city fragrant with spice!
The scent of fruits must drift through the streets.
Scatter the currants,
bring the figs and the capers!
Renew the summer,
renew the cycle,
birth, blood, filth and scum,

Tod — hakt in die Striemen ein,
die Linien auferlegt
Gesichtern
mißtrausich, faul und alt,
von Kalk umrissen und in Öl getränkt,
von Händeln schlau,
mit der Gefahr vertraut,
dem Zorn des Lavagotts,
dem Engel Rauch
und der verdammten Glut!

VI

Unterrichtet in der Liebe
durch zehntausend Bücher,
belehrt durch die Weitergabe
wenig veränderbarer Gesten
und törichter Schwüre —

eingeweiht in die Liebe
aber erst hier —
als die Lava herabfuhr
und ihr Hauch uns traf
am Fuß des Berges,
als zuletzt der erschöpfte Krater
den Schlüssel preisgab
für diese verschlossenen Körper —

Wir traten ein in verwunschene Räume
und leuchteten das Dunkel aus
mit den Fingerspitzen.

death — sink into the welts,
deepen the lines
on faces
mistrustful, lazy and old,
covered with chalk and drenched in oil,
sly from clever deals,
immerse them in danger,
the anger of the lava god,
grant smoke to angels
and the fire's cursed aura!

VI

Educated in love
by ten thousand books,
made wise through the sharing
of barely changed gestures
and foolish oaths —

initiated into love
but first knowing it here —
when the lava spilled over
and its breath reached us
at the foot of the mountain,
when finally the spent crater
surrendered the key
to these locked bodies —

We entered enchanted rooms
and illuminated the dark
with our fingertips.

VII

Innen sind deine Augen Fenster
auf ein Land, in dem ich in Klarheit stehe.

Innen ist deine Brust ein Meer,
das mich auf den Grund zieht.
Innen ist deine Hüfte ein Landungssteg
für meine Schiffe, die heimkommen
von zu großen Fahrten.

Das Glück wirkt ein Silbertau,
an dem ich befestigt liege.

Innen ist dein Mund ein flaumiges Nest
für meine flügge werdende Zunge.
Innen ist dein Fleisch melonenlicht,
süß und genießbar ohne Ende.
Innen sind deine Adern ruhig
und ganz mit dem Gold gefüllt,
das ich mit meinen Tränen wasche
und das mich einmal aufwiegen wird.

Du empfängst Titel, deine Arme umfangen Güter,
die an dich zuerst vergeben werden.

Innen sind deine Füße nie unterwegs,
sondern schon angekommen in meinen Samtlanden.
Innen sind deine Knochen helle Flöten,
aus denen ich Töne zaubern kann,
die auch den Tod bestricken werden …

VII

Within, your eyes are windows
to a land where in clarity I stand.

Within, your breast is a sea
that draws me to its bed.
Within, your hips are a quay
that greets my ships returning
from journeys too far from home.

Happiness weaves a silver chain
to which I lie attached.

Within, your mouth is a downy nest
for my fledgling, nascent tongue.
Within, your flesh is an endless light
sweet and ripe as a melon.
Within, your veins contain a tranquillity
and are filled with the gold
that I wash with my tears,
and that one day will outweigh me.

Receiving your title, your arms embrace goods
that you are the first to be granted.

Within, your feet never wander,
but are already in my velvet land.
Within, your bones are bright flutes
on which I can conjure the tunes
that would even charm death …

VIII

… Erde, Meer und Himmel.
Von Küssen zerwühlt
die Erde,
das Meer und der Himmel.
Von meinen Worten umklammert
die Erde,
von meinem letzten Wort noch umklammert
das Meer und der Himmel!

Heimgesucht von meinen Lauten
diese Erde,
die schluchzend in meinen Zähnen
vor Anker ging
mit allen ihren Hochöfen, Türmen
und hochmütigen Gipfeln,

diese geschlagene Erde,
die vor mir ihre Schluchten entblößte,
ihre Steppen, Wüsten und Tundren,

diese rastlose Erde
mit ihren zuckenden Magnetfeldern,
die sich hier selbst fesselte
mit ihr noch unbekannten Kraftketten,

diese betäubte und betäubende Erde
mit Nachtschattengewächsen,
bleiernen Giften
und Strömen von Duft —

untergegangen im Meer
und aufgegangen im Himmel
die Erde!

VIII

… the earth, sea and sky.
Dug into with kisses,
the earth,
the sea and the sky.
Gripped by my words,
the earth,
still clung to by my last word,
the sea and the sky!

Afflicted with my sounds,
this earth
that, sobbing in my teeth,
put down anchor
with all its furnaces, towers
and proud peaks,

this battered earth,
which before me uncovered its ravines,
its steppes, deserts and tundras,

this restless earth,
with its quivering magnetic fields,
which chained it here
with its unknown chains of power,

this stunned and stunning earth
grown thick with belladonna,
leaden poisons
and streams of fragrance —

sunk in the sea
and risen in the sky
the earth!

IX

Die schwarze Katze,
das Öl auf dem Boden,
der böse Blick:

Unglück!

Zieh das Korallenhorn,
häng die Hörner vors Haus,
Dunkel, kein Licht!

X

O Liebe, die unsre Schalen
aufbrach und fortwarf, unseren Schild,
den Wetterschutz und braunen Rost von Jahren!

O Leiden, die unsre Liebe austraten,
ihr feuchtes Feuer in den fühlenden Teilen!
Verqualmt, verendend im Qualm, geht die Flamme in sich.

XI

Du willst das Wetterleuchten, wirfst die Messer,
du trennst der Luft die warmen Adern auf;

dich blendend, springen aus den offnen Pulsen
lautlos die letzten Feuerwerke auf:

Wahnsinn, Verachtung, dann die Rache,
und schon die Reue und der Widerruf.

Du nimmst noch wahr, daß deine Klingen stumpfen,
und endlich fühlst du, wie die Liebe schließt:

IX

The black cat,
oil on the floor,
the evil glance:

Bad luck!

Pull out the coral horn,
hang the horns before the house!
Darkness! No light!

X

O love, which broke open
and flung away our shells, our shield,
our shelters and the brown rust of years.

O sorrows, which stamped out our love,
its damp fire felt in tender places!
Filled with smoke, dying in smoke, the flame consumes itself.

XI

Wanting summer lightning, you throw the knife,
slicing through the air to the warmth of its veins;

blinding, as they spring up from open wounds,
are the soundless last fireworks you see displayed:

madness, contempt, and then revenge,
as remorse follows soon, then sharp disdain.

You realize that your sword is blunted,
and finally you feel just how love ends:

mit ehrlichen Gewittern, reinem Atem.
Und sie verstößt dich in das Traumverlies.

Wo ihre goldnen Haare niederhängen,
greifst du nach ihr, der Leiter in das Nichts.

Tausend und eine Nacht hoch sind die Sprossen.
Der Schritt ins Leere ist der letzte Schritt.

Und wo du aufprallst, sind die alten Orte,
und jedem Ort gibst du drei Tropfen Blut.

Umnachtet hältst du wurzellose Locken.
Die Schelle läutet, und es ist genug.

XII

Mund, der in meinem Mund genächtigt hat,
Aug, das mein Aug bewachte,
Hand —

und die mich schleiften, die Augen!
Mund, der das Urteil sprach,
Hand, die mich hinrichtete!

with raging storms, with purest breath.
It locks you up inside the dream dungeon.

Where love's golden hair is hanging down,
the ladder to emptiness is what you'll be grasping.

A thousand and one nights high are the rungs.
The very last step is the step into nothing.

And there where you crash exist the old places,
and to each place you give three drops of blood.

Deranged, you cling to rootless curls.
The bell rings out, and you've had enough.

XII

Mouth, which slept in my mouth,
Eye that guarded my own,
Hand —

and those eyes that drilled through me!
Mouth, which spoke the sentence,
Hand, which executed me!

XIII

Die Sonne wärmt nicht, stimmlos ist das Meer.
Die Gräber, schneeverpackt, schnürt niemand auf.
Wird denn kein Kohlenbecken angefüllt
mit fester Glut? Doch Glut tut's nicht.

Erlöse mich! Ich kann nicht länger sterben.

Der Heilige hat anderes zu tun;
er sorgt sich um die Stadt und geht ums Brot.
Die Wäscheleine trägt so schwer am Tuch;
bald wird es fallen. Doch mich deckt's nicht zu.

Ich bin noch schuldig. Heb mich auf.
Ich bin nicht schuldig. Heb mich auf.

Das Eiskorn lös vom zugefrornen Aug,
brich mit den Blicken ein,
die blauen Gründe such,
schwimm, schau und tauch:

Ich bin es nicht.
Ich bin's.

XIII

The sun gives no warmth, voiceless is the sea.
No one opens the graves packed in snow.
Is it because no brazier is filled
with glowing coals? Yet the glow does nothing.

Release me! I can no longer die.

The saint is busy elsewhere,
he is concerned with the city and bread.
The washline is heavy with cloth;
soon it will fall. But it won't cover me.

I am still guilty. Raise me up.
I am not guilty. Raise me up.

Loosen the sliver of ice from the frozen eye,
break through with a glance,
seek the blue depths,
swim, look and dive:

I am not the one.
I am.

XIV

Wart meinen Tod ab und dann hör mich wieder,
es kippt der Schneekorb, und das Wasser singt,
in die Toledo münden alle Töne, es taut,
ein Wohlklang schmilzt das Eis.
O großes Tauen!

Erwart dir viel!

Silben im Oleander,
Wort im Akaziengrün
Kaskaden aus der Wand.

Die Becken füllt,
hell und bewegt,
Musik.

XV

Die Liebe hat einen Triumph und der Tod hat einen,
die Zeit und die Zeit danach.
Wir haben keinen.

Nur Sinken um uns von Gestirnen. Abglanz und Schweigen.
Doch das Lied überm Staub danach
wird uns übersteigen.

XIV

Wait for my death, then hear me again.
The snow basket tips and the water sings,
all sounds flow into the Toledo, its surface thaws,
a melody melts the ice.
O great thaw!

So much awaits you.

Syllables in oleander,
words in acacian green,
cascades from the wall.

The basins fill,
turbulent and clear,
with music.

XV

Love has its triumph and death has one,
in time and the time beyond us.
We have none.

Only the sinking of stars. Silence and reflection.
Yet the song beyond the dust
will overcome our own.

I   GEDICHTE 1945 – 1956

Early and Late Poems

I   POEMS 1945 – 1956

Aengste

Was wird denn bleiben?
Ich seufze, leide, suche,
und meine Wanderschaften
werden niemals enden.
Der dunkle Schatten,
dem ich schon seit Anfang folge
führt mich in tiefe Wintereinsamkeiten.
Dort steh ich still.
Der Frost streicht mir das Haar
und Kälte flammt an meinen Gliedern auf.
Zum Tanz spielt Totenstille Melodien,
die endlos sich um sich selber drehen.
Blaue Gespenster springen in den Raum.
Die Abgeschiedenen, die vor mir irrten
verlangen herrengleich ein altes Recht.
Nun werden sie bezahlt mit Blüten,
die viele Sommer sahen
und diesen Winter brechend niederfallen.
Die Bäume brüten Kälte vor sich hin
und Tränen, die mir Mondenglanz entlockte
hängen als dürre Zapfen sich ins Eis.
So, wie dort drüben, überm Gletscherhang,
die Langverblichenen ihr Blut verströmten,
so folg ich nach, auch ihnen gleich zu tun.
Ich horche den Jahrhunderten entgegen
und ganz erloschen will ich dort nicht sein.
Dem Schatten, der so weit will gehen
versuch ich meine Spuren einzudrücken,
nur füchtend mich vergeblich zu verschwenden.

Anxieties

What then will remain?
I sigh, suffer, search,
and my wanderings
will never end.
The dark shadow
which I have followed from the start
leads me into the deep loneliness of winter.
There I stand still.
The frost coats my hair
and the cold burns through my limbs.
Melodies of dead silence play a dance,
endlessly turning round each other.
Blue spirits leap into the room —
the departed who wandered off before me
desiring, like lords, an ancient right.
Now they will be paid with blossoms
which many summers saw
and which break and fall this winter.
The trees exude the cold from within,
and tears, which the moonlight draws out,
hang as thin cones coated in ice.
Over there, above the glacier,
the long departed pour out their blood,
and so I follow their example and do the same to them.
I listen close to the centuries,
though I don't want to be swallowed up by them.
Into the shadow which wants to stretch this far
I try to press a vestige of myself,
despite the idle fear of wasting my life.

[Die Nacht entfaltet den trauernden Teil des Gesichts]

Die Nacht entfaltet den trauernden Teil des Gesichts
Ich sing in den Schatten das Wort,
des täglich das Licht mir entwendet.
Ich singe
und würde nicht schweigen,
stieß irgend ein donnernder Groll
mich jetzt vor die Füße des Tempels,
der Blut und Leben verdunkelt.

Ich singe wie Rechtlose singen!
Über Geröll und Gestein!
Die Zügel sind längst schon verloren.
Die reitenden Töne empören
mich selbst wie der Knecht einen Herrn.
Die entfesselten Laute verbringen
die Freiheit,
wie es die kühnsten Gedanken
niemals getan.

Der trauernde Teil des Gesichtes der Nacht
hallt wider von Schüssen und Jagd.
Ich falle im Lied.
Ich brech' auf die marmornen Stufen,
die vor dem Tempel versteinten,
zu stummen und ewigen Dienern.
Ich singe
und kann noch nicht schweigen.
Vereist bis zur liedtollen Kehle
sing ich noch immer das Wort,
das bisher das Licht mir entwendet.

[The night unfolds the sad part of the face]

The night unfolds the sad part of the face.
Inside a shadow I sing the word
that the light steals from me each day.
I sing
and will not be silent,
a clap of thunder strikes somewhere,
landing me at the base of the temple,
blood and life now darkened.

I sing like the lawless sing!
Above the pebbles and stones!
The reins have long since been lost.
The galloping notes of the riders rankle
me like a servant bothers a lord.
The unfettered notes convey
freedom
as the boldest thoughts
have never done.

The sad part of the face of night
echoes gunfire and hunting.
I break into song.
I spring up the marble steps
which before the temple petrify
one into silence and eternal service.
I sing
and cannot yet be silent.
Frozen stiff up to my song-ridden throat,
I still sing the word
that until now the light stole away.

Im Krieg

Es ist so tiefe Nacht um mich
und Einsamkeit und graue Not.
Die Wände drängen zitternd sich
und Tränen rinnen aus dem Brot.

Es ist so bitter kalt im Haus.
Kein Feuer brennt und nirgends Licht.
Mein Atem raucht im Raume aus
und alle Hoffnung wird Verzicht.

Im Lande gähnen Straßen weit
und rufen mich auch sicherlich.
Doch ich bin müde und voll Leid …
Es ist so tiefe Nacht um mich.

In Wartime

The night is so deep around me,
and lonely and full of dread.
Trembling walls press at me
and tears run from the bread.

It's so bitter cold in the house.
No fire burns and there's no light anywhere.
My breath smokes from my mouth
and all hope turns to despair.

Everywhere the streets yawn wide
and continue to call to me.
Yet full of sorrow, I'm so tired …
The night is so deep around me.

Befreiung

Ein morgenfroher Himmel ringt
sich aus der Nacht, die weiter schwingt
mit einem blauen Schrei.

Wo immer noch das Dunkel webt
und nach der Hand der Landschaft strebt,
schlägt Sonne es entzwei.

Und morgenfroh wirft einen Blick
die Erde in das All zurück,
von schwarzen Schatten frei.

Liberation

Full of joy, the sky this morning
is wrung from a night still quaking
with a drunkard's screams so blue.

Where darkness is still hovering
and reaches for the landscape's hand,
the sun splits it in two.

And looking out into space this morning
the Earth reflects the joy it's seen,
free now of a shadow's hue.

[Um die Stirne des Jahres]

Um die Stirne des Jahres
streichen die Tage:
Es gebietet ihnen zurückzutreten.
Sie haben den Jahrhunderten nichts zu sagen.
Sie haben zu sammeln
und aufzuschreiben.
Das wird eingehen in ein großes Buch
in dem das Jahr eine Seite füllt.

[On the brow of the year]

The days salute
the brow of the year:
it orders them to retreat.
They have nothing to say to the centuries.
They simply gather things
and write them down.
These are entered in a large book
in which a year fills a single page.

Bibliotheken

Die Bücherborde biegen sich.
Die Bände lasten von Vergangenheit.
Ihr Schweiß ist Staub.
Ihre Regung ist Starre.
Sie kennen keinen Kampf mehr.
Sie haben sich gerettet
auf die Insel des Wissens.
Manchmal haben dabei das Gewissen verloren.
Stellenweise aber ragen
Menschenfinger aus ihnen
und weisen geradewegs in das Leben
oder in den Himmel.

Libraries

The shelves sag.
The volumes are weighted down with the past.
Their sweat is dust.
Their impulse is rigidity.
They no longer struggle.
They have saved themselves
upon the island of knowledge.
Sometimes they've lost their conscience.
Here and there, protruding
from them, human fingers
point directly towards life
or towards heaven.

Zeit vor den Türen

Ich werde nicht mehr um mich selber fragen
zu meinen Wünschen will ich nimmer stehen.
Ich kann mir Antwort wie das Brot versagen
und meiner Zeit gewiß entgegengehen.

Ich spüre sie in allen Straßen nahen,
im Grund schon alles Heutige verderben.
Sie wird von allen, die den Dienst versahen
nur wenig wählen unter vielen Erben.

Ich will mich ihren Händen übergeben,
den Waffen, die den neuen Tag entsenden,
den Räumen, die zum Raum hinüberleben,
und meine Stirne wie ein Kreuz verwenden.

Waiting Before the Doors

I will never worry about my own good,
and about my wishes I'll never be concerned.
I can refuse answers just like I do food
and face my future undisturbed.

I sense it in every street nearby,
everything of today rotting in the ground.
From those who put their years in, time
leaves little behind that's handed down.

I want to stand before it ready to face
the new day's weapons held up to us,
rooms transformed into empty space,
offering up my brow as a cross.

Unstillbar

Ich kreise in einem winterlichen Wald
um die Früchte des Südens.
Wie sie mir zuteil werden sollen,
weiß ich nicht,
nicht, wie ich, überhaupt, so fliegen kann
und so begehren.

Meine Schnäbel wandern erfroren.
Mein Lied ist vergessen.
Ich fliege wie Rechtlose fliegen,
zerrissenen Augs,
Über Geröll und Gestein.
Des Eises Krallen im Gefieder
fiebert mein Mund noch
nach Mandeln und goldnen Korinthen.

Tod ist mein Teil.
Der Polarmond bleicht meine Träume,
und die bitteren Wurzeln der Tundra
langen nach mir.

Aber noch weiß ich mich treu!
Noch flieg ich, von Sehnsucht verbrannt!

Unappeasable

In a wintery forest
I circle the fruit of the south.
How they will fall to me
I do not know,
they being unable, like I, to flee at all
and thus to yearn.

My beak wanders frozen.
My song is forgotten.
I flee as outlaws flee,
with an eye torn,
over pebbles and stones.
The claws of the ice in my feathers
still make my mouth yearn for
almonds and golden currants.

Death is my part.
The polar moon shines palely in my dreams,
and the bitter roots of the tundra
long for me.

But I still am true to myself!
I still flee, burning with desire!

Zwischen gestern und morgen

Meine Strirne ist feucht
wie Sterne im April.
Die Regenschauer fallen
so leise ein,
daß sie mich nicht mehr röten.
Der Winterbrand
verflackert fliegend durch die Wüsten,
in die zu folgen ich
zu müde bin.
Ein Fieber steht an meinem Lager,
morgenrot!
Oh, wenn ich fiebern könnte
und Sommer über meine Lippen rollen!
Verschneite Ketten
an den Händen schmelzen.
Ich bin entlassen aus dem Winterland
wie alle Ubrigen.
wie Sterne im April,
die Stirne feucht …

Between Yesterday and Tomorrow

My brow is damp
like stars in April.
The rain falls
so lightly that
I am no longer flushed.
Winter's fire
flickers as it sweeps through the desert,
myself too tired
to follow.
A fever reaches my bed,
it's dawn!
O if only I could feel fever
and summer's warmth roll across my lips!
Severed chains
melt from the hands.
I am released from winter's land
like everything else,
like stars in April
that dampen a brow ....

Morgen will ich fort

Morgen will ich fort
und weit in die Welt fahren.
Vielleicht staunst du,
vielleicht nach vielen Jahren,
daß ich gegangen bin.

Morgen will ich Feuer an mein Haus legen
und freche Lieder singen.
Wirst du getroffen sein?
Wirst du endlich zu merken beginnen,
daß ich getroffen bin?

Morgen werd ich mein Herz in den Kopf stecken
und einen roten Hut tragen.
Die ganze Stadt soll mich sehen
vor deinem Fenster Lärm schlagen.
Die ganze Stadt soll mich sehen!

Morgen geh ich fort
und werd immer hier bleiben.
Vielleicht lachst du, vielleicht,
zu meinem Schelmentreiben …
Ich will gestorben sein.

Tomorrow I Will Leave

Tomorrow I will leave
and travel far from here.
Maybe it surprises you
after so many years
that I will be gone.

Tomorrow I will set my house on fire
and sing some naughty songs.
Will you be hurt?
Will you finally notice
that I am also hurt?

Tomorrow I will stick my heart in my head
and wear a red hat.
The entire town will see me
sounding the alarm upon your street.
The entire town will see me!

Tomorrow I will leave
and yet will always remain here.
Maybe you will laugh, maybe
at my roguish manner ….
Dead is what I wish to be.

Fegefeuer

Erschöpft uns denn die Fülle nicht?
Ich häufe in die müden Hände,
ich liebe, schenke und vollende,
doch es bleibt Tag und es bleibt licht.

Ich trinke alle Brunnen aus;
die Zeit rückt tiefer in die Meere,
der Raum begegnet meiner Schwere
und drängt mich in das Abendhaus.

Ich flieg' die Treppen auf und ab;
es regnet Stunden in die Stille,
aus allen Schleusen bricht die Fülle,
bis ich mich totgelaufen hab'.

Doch wieder tagt es und bleibt licht,
— wie ich mich wehre und mich wende —
mir wachsen unaufhörlich Hände,
ich schlafe und ich sterbe nicht.

Purgatory

Is abundance not our weary plight?
I fill to heaping the exhausted hands,
loving, giving, bringing it to an end,
though it's still day and there's still light.

I drink dry the fountains, empty them out;
time sinks deeper into the sea
as space encounters my own dead weight
and pushes me into the evening's house.

Upon the steps I fly up and down;
in the stillness it's pouring down hours,
abundance bursts from all the gutters
until I've run myself into the ground.

Yet once again it's day and there is light,
— as I twist and turn in sleep —
incessant hands reach out to me,
though I still sleep and do not die.

Beglückung

Meine Trunkenheit kann ich nicht abschütteln
wie die welken Blumen ihre Blüten im sterbenden Frühling,
wie die Bäume im Herbst es mit ihren Blättern tun,
wie der Strauch, der seine Früchte an den Rand der Straße wirft,
wie der Sommer, der seinen Brand dem Herbst zu löschen gibt …

In meiner Trunkenheit kann ich nur Immerwährendes denken
und über die Tage lächeln und über die Menschen, die sterben …
In meiner Trunkenheit kann ich nur maßlos sein
und trinken und nehmen und dauern.

Drum geh ich so schwindelnd und hoch
und füll noch die Krüge der andern!

Rejoicing

I cannot shake off my drunkenness
like the faded flowers can their blossoms in the dying spring,
like the trees do with their leaves in autumn,
like the bushes that drop their fruit on the sides of the streets,
like the summer whose fire autumn extinguishes ....

I can only think of the perpetual in my drunkenness,
and smile about the days and about people who die ....
I can only be immoderate in my drunkenness
and drink and have some more and stick around.

That's why I walk so dizzy and high,
filling once more the mugs of the others!

Ohne Hoffnung

Von Menschen erbauter Kerker aus Pflicht,
ringsum granitene Mauern,
von oben fällt tropfend fahlendes Licht,
in dunklen Winkeln kauern
in zitternder Angst die Zerstörten,
die einmal von Freiheit hörten.

Sie drängen sich manchmal, von Furcht geplagt,
mit Heftigkeit an's Gitter,
doch weiter hat sich niemand gewagt —
und jede Rückkehr ist bitter.

Dort draußen lebt ein Blütenbaum,
dort draußen atmet der Wind,
dort draußen fühlt man, wie im Traum,
wie gut die Dinge sind.

Without Hope

Prisons built out of pious love,
granite walls rise all around,
pale light dripping from above
as the forsaken hunker down
in corners, trembling with fear,
having known freedom earlier.

Sometimes they press at the grate,
anxiety turning them rowdy,
yet bitterly they again turn away
when no one appears with the key.

Outside lives a blossoming tree,
outside breathes the wind,
outside one feels, as in a dream,
how good the world really is.

Stadt

Ich wurde geboren in einer Stadt,
doch ich wußte nicht, was das hieß.
Ich wuchs heran in einer Stadt
und ich wußte nicht, was das hieß.
Ich verließ eines Tages diese Stadt
und ich wußte nicht, was das hieß.
Ich kam eines Tages zurück in die Stadt —
und ich wußte, was das hieß.

Stadt, dieses Monstrum aus Stein und Enge
Stadt, diese Masse von Menschen, Gedränge
Stadt, dieses Hetzen, Schieben, Jagen
Stadt, voller Lärmen, Bahnen und Wagen
Stadt, voll Geplagter mit blassen Gesichtern
Stadt, in der Nacht mit zuckenden Lichtern
Stadt, für Natur hast du keinen Raum
Stadt, im Zement keucht mühsam ein Baum.

Stadt, wie ich dich seither hasse
Stadt, wie schlecht ich zu dir passe.

City

I was born in a city,
but I didn't know what that meant.
I grew up in a city,
and I didn't know what that meant.
One day I left this city,
and I didn't know what that meant.
One day I returned to this city,
and then I knew what that meant.

City, you monstrosity of narrow streets and stone,
city, crowds and people pressing at one,
city, the rushing, shoving, and chase,
city, full of sirens, cars, and trains,
city, full of pale faces that continually suffer,
city, at night your streetlights flicker,
city, which has no space for the elements,
city, where a tree gasps wearily in cement.

City, which I could never tolerate,
city, which I will always hate.

Wohin

Wenn ich ruhlos und flüchtig bin,
fragen die Freunde mich: wohin?

Fragt lieber die Wolke, die helle,
fragt lieber des Meeres Welle,

wann immer der Herr sie jagt,
der mächtige Sturm! O fragt!

Die beiden wissen nicht, wohin,
und ich, der ich so elend bin,

ich weiß nur, daß sie mich verwarf,
daß ich nicht vor ihr Antlitz darf

und daß ich nirgends auf dieser Erde
und nie diesen Schmerz vergessen werde!

Where To?

Whenever I feel flighty and restless,
"Where to?" is what my friends ask.

Better to ask the clouds and sun,
better to ask the teeming ocean

whenever the Lord lets loose
a powerful storm! O ask!

Neither one knows where to,
and I, who am so very blue,

know only she detests my plight,
that I'm not allowed in her sight

and that nowhere upon this earth
is it possible to forget such hurt!

[Abends frag ich meine Mutter]

Abends frag ich meine Mutter
heimlich nach dem Glockenläuten,
wie ich mir die Tage deuten
und die Nacht bereiten soll.

Tief im Grund verlang ich immer
alles restlos zu erzählen,
in Akkorden auszuwählen,
was an Klängen mich umspielt.

Leise lauschen wir zusammen:
meine Mutter träumt mich wieder,
und sie trifft, wie alte Lieder,
meines Wesens Dur und Moll.

[On many nights I ask my mother]

On many nights I ask my mother
furtively after the hours chime,
how I should learn to tell the time
and ready myself for the night.

In my inner depths, I always demand
that all be made completely clear,
picking out from the chords I hear
what confuses me within their strains.

Quietly we sit and listen together:
my mother dreams of what I'll be,
arranging, like any old melody,
my essential notes, major and minor.

[Wir gehen, die Herzen im Staub]

Wir gehen, die Herzen im Staub,
und lange schon hart am Versagen.
Man hört uns nur nicht, ist zu taub,
um das Stöhnen im Staub zu beklagen.

Wir singen, den Ton in der Brust.
Dort ist er noch niemals entsprungen.
Nur manchmal hat einer gewußt:
wir sind nicht zum Bleiben gezwungen.

Wir halten. Beenden den Trott.
Sonst ist auch das Ende verdorben.
Und richten die Augen auf Gott:
wir haben den Abschied erworben!

[We leave, hearts sunk in dust]

We leave, hearts sunk in dust,
long on the verge of failure.
Others are too deaf to hear us
to call our dusty groans out of order.

We sing, the sound in our breast.
From there it was never released.
Only sometimes did one attest
that remaining was never decreed.

We stop. We cease to trot.
Lest the end becomes a farce.
Our eyes are turned towards God:
we have been granted discharge.

[Es könnte viel bedeuten]

Es könnte viel bedeuten: wir vergehen,
wir kommen ungefragt und müssen weichen.
Doch daß wir sprechen und uns nicht verstehen
und keinen Augenblick des andern Hand erreichen,

zerschlägt so viel: wir werden nicht bestehen.
Schon den Versuch bedrohen fremde Zeichen,
und das Verlangen, tief uns anzusehen,
durchtrennt ein Kreuz, uns einsam auszustreichen.

[It could mean so much]

It could mean so much: we cease to exist,
that we arrive unasked and then must yield.
That we speak, and yet misunderstanding persists,
and not for a moment is another's hand held

destroys so much: we will not survive.
Even strange signs forbid what we desire,
and the need for introspection that's still alive
an "x" now cuts through, cancelling it forever.

Entfremdung

In den Bäumen kann ich keine Bäume mehr sehen.
Die Äste haben nicht die Blätter, die sie in den Wind halten.
Die Früchte sind süß, aber ohne Liebe.
Sie sättigen nicht einmal.
Was soll nur werden?
Vor meinen Augen flieht der Wald,
vor meinem Ohr schließen die Vögel den Mund,
für mich wird keine Wiese zum Bett.
Ich bin satt vor der Zeit
und hungre nach ihr.
Was soll nur werden?

Auf den Bergen werden nachts die Feuer brennen.
Soll ich mich aufmachen, mich allem wieder nähern?

Ich kann in keinem Weg mehr einen Weg sehen.

Estrangement

Within the trees I no longer can see any trees.
The branches are bare of leaves, carried off by the wind.
The fruits are sweet, but empty of love.
They do not even satisfy.
What shall happen?
Before my eyes the forest flees,
the birds no longer sing to my ears,
and for me no pasture will become a bed.
I am full with time
yet hunger for it.
What shall happen?

Nightly upon the mountains the fires will burn.
Shall I head out, draw near to them all once again?

I can no longer see on any path a path.

Betrunkner Abend

Betrunkner Abend, voll vom blauen Licht,
taumelt ans Fenster und begehrt zu singen.
Die Schneiben drängen furchtsam sich und dicht,
in denen seine Schatten sich verfingen.

Er schwankt verdunkelnd um das Häusermeer,
trifft auf ein Kind, es schreiend zu verjagen,
und atmet keuchend hinter allem her,
Beängstigendes flüsternd auszusagen.

Im feuchten Hof am dunkeln Mauerrand
tummelt mit Ratten er sich in den Ecken.
Ein Weib, in grau verschlissenem Gewand,
weicht vor ihm weg, sich tiefer zu verstecken.

Am Brunnen rinnt ein dünner Faden noch,
ein Tropfen läuft, den andern zu erhaschen;
dort trinkt er jäh aus rostverschleimtem Loch
und hilft, die schwarzen Gossen mitzuwaschen.

Betrunkner Abend, voll vom blauen Licht,
taumelt ins Fenster und beginnt zu singen.
Die Scheiben brechen. Blutend im Gesicht
dringt er herein, mit meinem Graun zu ringen.

The Drunken Evening

The drunken evening, saturated with blue light,
staggers to the window to sing a ballad.
The panes press hard and thick against the sight,
as in the glass his shadow becomes entangled.

He slinks so darkly around the sea of houses,
strikes a child, and shrieks to scare him away;
while behind everyone else he pants for breath,
sounding a whispered alarm that gives him away.

In a damp farmyard, nearby the dark outer wall,
he rustles with rats deep in the corners.
The woman wearing a raggedy gray shawl
skitters away to hide herself still deeper.

There's still a stream trickling from the well,
a drop that runs, trying to catch the first;
he drinks there from a rusty pail,
and more from black gutters to ease his thirst.

The drunken evening, saturated with blue light,
staggers against the window and begins to sing.
Windowpanes shatter. His bloodied face fights
his way inside, wrestling me down, still shuddering.

Hinter der Wand

Ich hänge als Schnee von den Zweigen
in den Frühling des Tals,
als kalte Quelle treibe ich im Wind,
feucht fall ich in die Blüten
als ein Tropfen,
um den sie faulen
wie um einen Sumpf.
Ich bin das Immerzu-ans-Sterben-Denken.

Ich fliege, denn ich kann nicht ruhig gehen,
durch aller Himmel sichere Gebäude
und stürze Pfeiler um und höhle Mauern.
Ich warne, denn ich kann des Nachts nicht schlafen,
die andern mit des Meeres fernem Rauschen.
Ich steige in den Mund der Wasserfälle,
und von den Bergen lös ich polterndes Geröll.

Ich bin der großen Weltangst Kind,
die in den Frieden und die Freude hängt
wie Glockenschläge in des Tages Schreiten
und wie die Sense in den reifen Acker.

Ich bin das Immerzu-ans-Sterben-Denken.

Behind the Wall

I hang as snow from the branches
in the valley of spring,
as a cold spell I float on the wind,
falling damp upon the blossoms
as a drop
in which they decay
as if sunk in a swamp.
I am the Continual-Thought-Of-Dying.

Because I cannot walk firmly, I fly
through every sky above secure buildings
and knock down pillars and undermine walls.
Since I cannot sleep at night, I warn
others with the distant roar of the sea.
I pass through the mouth of waterfalls
and let topple from mountains the rumbling boulders.

I am the child of great fear for the world,
who within peace and joy hangs suspended
like the stroke of a bell in the day's passing
and like the scythe in the ripe pasture.

I am the Continual-Thought-Of-Dying.

[Beim Hufschlag der Nacht]

Beim Hufschlag der Nacht, des schwarzen Hengstes vorm Tor,
zittert mein Herz noch wie einst und reicht mir den Sattel
    im Flug,
rot wie das Halfter, das Diomedes mir lieh.
Gewaltig sprengt der Wind mir auf dunkler Straße voran
und teilt das schwarze Gelock der schlafenden Bäume,
daß die vom Mondlicht nassen Früchte
erschrocken auf Schulter und Schwert springen,
und ich schleudre
die Peitsche auf einen erloschenen Stern.
Nur einmal verhalt ich den Schritt, deine treulosen Lippen zu
küssen, schon fängt sich dein Haar in den Zügeln,
und dein Schuh schleift im Staub.

Und ich hör deinen Atem noch
und das Wort, mit dem du mich schlugst.

[At the hoofbeat of night]

At the hoof beat of night, of the black stallion before the gate,
my heart flutters as it once did and offers me its saddle in flight,
red as the halter that Diomedes lent to me.
Powerfully the wind blows before me on the dark streets
and parts the black curls of the sleeping trees,
such that the fruits dripping with moonlight
fall and stun my shoulders and sword,
and I hurl
the whip towards an extinguished star.
Only once do I slow my stride, in order to kiss your unfaithful lips,
as your hair becomes caught in the reins,
and your shoe drags through the dust.

And I still hear your breathing
and the word with which you beat me.

Dem Abend gesagt

Meine Zweifel, bitter und ungestillt,
versickern in den Abendtiefen.
Müdigkeit singt an meinem Ohr.
Ich lausche …
Das war doch gestern schon!
Das kommt und geht doch wieder!

Die Schlafwege kenn ich bis ins süßeste Gefild.
Ich will dort nimmer gehen.
Noch weiß ich nicht, wo mir der dunkle See
die Qual vollendet.
Ein Spiegel soll dort liegen,
klar und dicht,
und will uns,
funkelnd vor Schmerz,
die Gründe zeigen.

Spoken to the Evening

My doubts, bitter and unappeased,
drain away in the evening's depths.
Weariness sings inside my ear.
I listen …
That's the way it was yesterday!
It's happening all over again!

I know the paths of sleep that lead to the sweetest field.
I never want to go there.
Yet I don't know where, for me, the dark lake
of torment will end.
A mirror shall lie there,
thick and clear,
and will show us,
sparkling with pain,
the underlying reasons.

Vision

Jetzt schon zum dritten Mal der Donnerschlag!
Und aus dem Meer taucht langsam Schiff auf Schiff.
Versunkne Schiffe mit verkohltem Mast,
versunkne Schiffe mit zerschoßner Brust,
mit halbzerfetztem Leib.

Und schwimmen stumm,
unhörbar durch die Nacht.
Und keine Welle schließt sich hinter ihnen.

Sie haben keinen Weg, sie werden keinen finden,
kein Wind wird wagen, fest in sie zu greifen,
kein Hafen wird sich öffnen.
Der Leuchtturm kann sich schlafend stellen!

Wenn diese Schiffe bis ans Ufer kommen …
Nein, nicht ans Ufer!
Wir werden sterben wie die Fischzüge,
die rund um sie auf breiten Wogen wiegen
zu abertausend Leichen!

Vision

Now for the third time the clap of thunder!
And from the sea there surfaces vessel after vessel.
Sunken vessels, each with a charred mast,
sunken vessels, each with a breast shot through,
with a body half mangled.

And mutely they swim,
inaudible through the night.
And no wave closes over them.

They have no course, they will not find one,
no wind will venture to strongly grip them,
no harbor will open itself.
Even the lighthouse can stand there sleeping!

Until these vessels reach the shore …
No, not the shore!
We will die like the netted fish
that may twirl when swaying above the wide waves,
but are still a thousand corpses!

Menschenlos

Verwunschnes Wolkenschloß, in dem wir treiben …
Wer weiß, ob wir nicht schon durch viele Himmel
so ziehen mit verglasten Augen?
Wir, in die Zeit verbannt
und aus dem Raum gestoßen,
wir, Flieger durch die Nacht und Bodenlose.

Wer weiß, ob wir nicht schon um Gott geflogen,
weil wir pfeilschnell schäumten, ohne ihn zu sehen
und unsre Samen weiterschleuderten,
um in noch dunkleren Geschlechtern fortzuleben,
jetzt schuldhaft treiben?

Wer weiß, ob wir nicht lange, lang schon sterben?
Der Wolkenball mit uns strebt immer höher.
Die dünne Luft lähmt heute schon die Hände.
Und wenn die Stimme bricht und unser Atem steht?

Bleibt die Verwunschenheit für letzte Augenblicke?

Destiny

Enchanted cloud castle in which we drift …
Who knows if we have not already moved
through many heavens with glazed eyes?
We, who are banished into time
and thrust from space,
we, who are refugees in the night and exiled.

Who knows if we have not flown past God,
for we fly off, swift as an arrow, without seeing Him
and only cast our seeds wider
in order to live on through darker lineages,
awash now in guilt.

Who knows if we haven't been dying long since already?
The cloud ball holding us strains ever higher.
The thin air today cripples the hands.
And what if our voice should snap and our breathing stop?

Does enchantment remain for the last moments?

Wie soll ich mich nennen?

Einmal war ich ein Baum und gebunden,
dann entschlüpft ich als Vogel und war frei,
in einen Graben gefesselt gefunden,
entließ mich berstend ein schmutziges Ei.

Wie halt ich mich? Ich habe vergessen,
woher ich komme und wohin ich geh,
ich bin von vielen Leibern besessen,
ein harter Dorn und ein flüchtendes Reh.

Freund bin ich heute den Ahornzweigen,
morgen vergehe ich mich an dem Stamm …
Wann begann die Schuld ihren Reigen,
mit dem ich von Samen zu Samen schwamm?

Aber in mir singt noch ein Beginnen
— oder ein Enden — und wehrt meiner Flucht,
ich will dem Pfeil dieser Schuld entrinnen,
der mich in Sandkorn und Wildente sucht.

Vielleicht kann ich mich einmal erkennen,
eine Taube einen rollenden Stein …
Ein Wort nur fehlt! Wie soll ich mich nennen,
ohne in anderer Sprache zu sein.

How Shall I Name Myself?

Once I was a tree that had been bound,
and then I was born as a free bird;
chained up in a ditch I was later found,
escaping an egg that was covered with dirt.

What supports me? I have forgotten
from where I come and where I'm headed,
in several bodies I live on,
a hard thorn and the deer that fled.

Today I befriend the maple branch,
tomorrow I will attack the tree ...
When did guilt begin its own round dance
by which I drifted from seed to seed.

But a beginning sings inside me still
— or an end — and it prevents my escape,
I will evade this arrow of guilt
that in sand grains, wild ducks, seeks my shape.

Perhaps I can once more see myself,
maybe a dove or a rolling stone ...
Words fail! How shall I name myself
without living in another tongue.

[Die Häfen waren geöffnet]

Die Häfen waren geöffnet. Wir schifften uns ein,
die Segel voraus, den Traum über Bord,
Stahl an den Knien und Lachen um unsere Haare,
denn unsere Ruder trafen ins Meer, schneller als Gott.

Unsere Ruder schlugen die Schaufeln Gottes und teilten
    die Flut;
vorne war Tag, und hinten blieben die Nächte,
oben war unser Stern, und unten versanken die andern,
draußen verstummte der Sturm, und drinnen wuchs unsre Faust.

Erst als ein Regen entbrannte, lauschten wir wieder;
Speere stürzten herab und Engel traten hervor,
hefteten schwärzere Augen in unsere schwarzen.
Vernichtet standen wir da. Unser Wappen flog auf:

Ein Kreuz im Blut und ein größeres Schiff überm Herzen.

[The harbors were open]

The harbors were open. We boarded the ships,
the sails were unfurled, the dream tossed overboard,
a sword across the knees and laughter in our hair,
because our oars dipped into the sea faster than God.

Our oars beat like the oars of God and parted the flood;
ahead was day, and behind remained the nights,
above us was our star, and below the others sank away,
while outside the storm ceased, and inside our fists were clenched.

Only when a rainstorm burst did we listen again;
spears fell all around and angels appeared,
blacker eyes fixed upon our own black eyes.
We stood there devastated. Our heraldry soaring:

A cross of blood and a larger ship above a heart.

[Die Welt ist weit]

Die Welt ist weit und die Wege von Land zu Land,
und der Orte sind viele, ich habe alle gekannt,
ich habe von allen Türmen Städte gesehen,
die Menschen, die kommen werden und die schon gehen.
Weit waren die Felder von Sonne und Schnee,
zwischen Schienen und Straßen, zwischen Berg und See.
Und der Mund der Welt war weit und voll Stimmen an
     meinem Ohr
und schrieb, noch des Nachts, die Gesänge der Vielfalt vor.
Den Wein aus fünf Bechern trank ich in einem Zuge aus,
mein nasses Haar trocknen vier Winde in ihrem
     wechselnden Haus.

Die Fahrt ist zu Ende,
doch ich bin mit nichts zu Ende gekommen,
jeder Ort hat ein Stück von meinem Lieben genommen,
jedes Licht hat mir ein Aug verbrannt,
in jedem Schatten zerriß mein Gewand.

Die Fahrt ist zu Ende.
Noch bin ich mit jeder Ferne verkettet,
doch kein Vogel hat mich über die Grenzen gerettet,
kein Wasser, das in die Mündung zieht,
treibt mein Gesicht, das nach unten sieht,
treibt meinen Schlaf, der nicht wandern will …
Ich weiß die Welt näher und still.

Hinter der Welt wird ein Baum stehen
mit Blättern aus Wolken
und einer Krone aus Blau.
In seine Rinde aus rotem Sonnenband
schneidet der Wind unser Herz
und kühlt es mit Tau.

[The world is far and wide]

The world is far and wide, and the roads from land to land,
there are many places that I've seen firsthand;
from inside every tower, I have seen the cities,
the people who are coming, the people who've left already.
The fields were so immense with sun and snow,
between the mountain and lake, the tracks and roads.
And the mouth of the world was wide, full of voices at my ear
    that transcribed,
not only at night, diverse songs.
I drank down five cups of wine in a single sitting,
the four winds dried my hair in their house that is ever-changing.

Now the journey is over,
and yet with nothing I've come to the end,
a piece of my love each place has taken,
my eyes have been scorched by each light they've borne,
in every shadow my dress has been torn.

Now the journey is over.
Yet to every distance I'm still bound,
though no bird has lifted me over the border beyond,
no water, drifting towards the sea's mouth,
carries my face, that still looks down,
nor my sleep, which does not want to travel ....
I know the world that's nearer and still.

Behind the world a tree shall stand
with leaves that are clouds
and a crown that is blue.
With a red sunbeam the wind now carves
our heart into its bark
and cools it with dew.

Hinter der Welt wird ein Baum stehen,
eine Frucht in den Wipfeln,
mit einer Schale aus Gold.
Laß uns hinübersehen,
wenn sie im Herbst der Zeit
in Gottes Hände rollt!

Behind the world a tree shall stand,
a fruit at its top
with a skin of gold.
Let us see beyond,
in the autumn of time,
when into God's hands it rolls.

[Noch fürcht ich]

Noch fürcht ich, dich mit dem Garn meines Atems zu binden,
dich zu gewanden mit den blauen Fahnen des Traums,
an den Nebeltoren meines finsteren Schlosses
Fackeln zu brennen, daß du mich fändest ...

Noch fürcht ich, dich aus schimmernden Tagen zu lösen,
aus dem goldnen Gefälle des Sonnenflusses der Zeit,
wenn über dem schrecklichen Antlitz des Monds
silbrig mein Herz schäumt.

Blick auf und sieh mich nicht an!
Es sinken die Fahnen, verflammt sind die Fackeln,
und der Mond beschreibt seine Bahn.
Es ist Zeit, daß du kommst und mich hältst, heiliger Wahn!

[I'm still afraid]

I'm still afraid to snare you with my breath,
drape you with blue banners of the dream,
or outside the misty door of my darkened castle,
burn torches, such that you'd find me …

I'm still afraid to free you from shimmering days,
from the golden river bed of time's own river of sun,
fearing my heart would burst silvery above the moon's
own terrible countenance.

Look up and don't look at me!
The banners are sinking, the torches have been extinguished,
the moon follows the course it traces.
It's time you came to seize me, holy madness!

Beweis zu nichts

Weißt du, Mutter, wenn die Breiten und Längen
den Ort nicht nennen, daß deine Kinder
aus dem dunklen Winkel der Welt dir winken?
Du bleibst stehn, wo sich die Wege verschlingen,
und vorrätig ist dein Herz vor jedem andern.
Wir reichen nicht lange, werfen mit Werken um uns
und blicken zurück. Doch der Rauch überm Herd
läßt uns das Feuer nicht sehn.

Frag: kommt keines wieder? Vom Lot abwärts geführt,
nicht in Richtung des Himmels, fördern wir
Dinge zutage, in denen Vernichtung wohnt und Kraft,
uns zu zerstreuen. Dies alles ist ein Beweis
zu nichts und von niemand verlangt. Entfachst du
das Feuer von neuem, erscheinen wir unkenntlich,
geschwärzte Gesichter, deinem weißen Gesicht.
Wein! Aber winke uns nicht.

Proof of Nothing

Do you know, mother, when latitude and longitude
can't locate a village, your children wave
to you from the dark corners of the world?
You stand there, where the paths twist around you,
and your heart is on call for everyone else.
We don't stay for long, heading off to work
and glancing back. Yet the mist above the hearth
prevents us seeing the fire.

Ask yourself: will anyone return? Having left the straight
and narrow path, and not for heaven, we bring to light
things in which there lives destruction and the power
to scatter us to the wind. All this is proof
of nothing and which no one wants. For when you kindle
the fire anew, we will appear unrecognizable,
before your own pale face, our faces black.
Weep! But don't wave back.

II   GEDICHTE 1957 – 1961

II   POEMS 1957 – 1961

William Turner: Gegenlicht

Über ein Land mit sparsamer Sonne
spannte er seine Leinwand und streifte
die Wege nah an den Himmel.
Er wußte:
es kommt auf den Lichteinfall an.

Von sich selbst hielt er wenig
und erlaubte sich keine Perspektiven

William Turner: Direct Light

Over a land with little sunlight
he stretched his canvas and painted
the paths to the sky.
He knew:
it all depends on the angle of light.

He thought little of himself
and granted himself no perspective.

Bruderschaft

Alles ist Wundenschlagen,
und keiner hat keinem verziehn.
Verletzt wie du und verletzend,
lebte ich auf dich hin.

Die reine, die Geistberührung,
um jede Berührung vermehrt,
wir erfahren sie alternd,
ins kälteste Schweigen gekehrt.

Brotherhood

Everything causes a wound,
and none has forgiven another.
Wounded as you, and wounding,
it was you that I lived for.

The pure touch of the spirit,
increasing the weight of each touch,
we come to know when aging
and by the coldest silence are clutched.

[Verordnet diesem Geschlecht keinen Glauben]

Verordnet diesem Geschlecht keinen Glauben,
genug sind Sterne, Schiffe und Rauch,
es legt sich in die Dinge, bestimmt
Sterne und die unendliche Zahl,
und ein Zug tritt, nenn ihn Zug einer Liebe,
reiner aus allem hervor.

Die Himmel hängen welk und Sterne lösen
sich aus der Verknüpfung mit Mond und Nacht.

[Prescribe no belief]

Prescribe no belief for this generation,
stars are enough, ships and smoke;
it appropriates all things, certifying
stars and infinity,
as a trend begins, call it the trend of love,
purer than ever before.

The heavens hang limp and the stars release
themselves from their bond with the moon and night.

Hôtel de la Paix

Die Rosenlast stürzt lautlos von den Wänden,
und durch den Teppich scheinen Grund und Boden.
Das Lichtherz bricht der Lampe.
Dunkel. Schritte.
Der Riegel hat sich vor den Tod geschoben.

Hôtel de la Paix

The weight of roses falls silently from the walls,
and through the carpet shine the floor and earth.
The light's heart breaks within the lamp.
Darkness. Steps.
The bolt slams shut as death comes knocking.

Exil

Ein Toter bin ich der wandelt
gemeldet nirgends mehr
unbekannt im Reich des Präfekten
überzählig in den goldnen Städten
und im grünenden Land

abgetan lange schon
und mit nichts bedacht

Nur mit Wind mit Zeit und mit Klang

der ich unter Menschen nicht leben kann

Ich mit der deutschen Sprache
dieser Wolke um mich
die ich halte als Haus
treibe durch alle Sprachen

O wie sie sich verfinstert
die dunklen die Regentöne
nur die wenigen fallen

In hellere Zonen trägt dann sie den Toten hinauf

Exile

I am a dead man who wanders
registered nowhere
unknown in the prefect's realm
unaccounted for in the golden cities
and the greening land

long since given up
and provided with nothing

Only with wind with time and with sound

I who cannot live among humans

I with the German language
this cloud around me
which I keep as a house
press through all languages

O how it grows dark
those muted those rain tones
only a few fall

Into brighter zones it will lift the dead man up

Nach dieser Sintflut

Nach dieser Sintflut
möchte ich die Taube,
und nichts als die Taube,
noch einmal gerettet sehn.

Ich ginge ja unter in diesem Meer!
flög' sie nicht aus,
brächte sie nicht
in letzter Stunde das Blatt.

After This Flood

After this flood
I'd like to see the dove,
and nothing but the dove,
be rescued once more.

I'd drown in this sea!
if she didn't fly out,
if she didn't bring,
in the last hour, the leaf.

Mirjam

Woher hast du dein dunkles Haar genommen,
den süßen Namen mit dem Mandelton?
Nicht weil du jung bist, glänzt du so von Morgen —
dein Land ist Morgen, tausend Jahre schon.

Versprich uns Jericho, weck auf den Psalter,
die Jordanquelle gib aus deiner Hand
und laß die Mörder überrascht versteinen
und einen Augenblick dein zweites Land!

An jede Steinbrust rühr und tu das Wunder,
daß auch den Stein die Träne überrinnt.
Und laß dich taufen mit dem heißen Wasser.
Bleib uns nur fremd, bis wir uns fremder sind.

Oft wird ein Schnee in deine Wiege fallen.
Unter den Kufen wird ein Eiston sein.
Doch wenn du tief schläfst, ist die Welt bezwungen.
Das rote Meer zieht seine Wasser ein!

Miriam

From where did you get your hair that is so raven,
as well as that name as sweet as almonds?
It's not mere youth that makes you look like morning —
your land is morning, and will be for a millennium.

Promise us Jericho, awaken the psalter's tones,
let the waters of Jordan flow from your hand;
have the murderers ambushed and turned to stone,
and, for a moment, have your second land.

Touch hearts of stone, perform a miracle's wonder,
such that by tears the stone is overrun.
Let yourself be baptized by the scalding water.
Remain an enigma, until we are also made one.

Snow will often fall into your cradle.
There will be the sound of ice beneath the runners.
Yet when you soundly sleep the world is quelled.
The red sea will then part its very waters!

Strömung

So weit im Leben und so nah am Tod,
daß ich mit niemand darum rechten kann,
reiß ich mir von der Erde meinen Teil;

dem stillen Ozean stoß ich den grünen Keil
mitten ins Herz und schwemm mich selber an.

Zinnvögel steigen auf und Zimtgeruch!
Mit meinem Mörder Zeit bin ich allein.
In Rausch und Bläue puppen wir uns ein.

Current

So far in life and yet so near to death
that there's no one I can argue with now,
I rip from the earth my separate part;

I thrust its green wedge into the heart
of the calm ocean, as I wash aground.

Tin birds rise and cinnamon scents!
With my murderer, Time, I'm alone.
Drunk and blue we spin our cocoon.

Geh, Gedanke

Geh, Gedanke, solang ein zum Fluge klares Wort
dein Flügel ist, dich aufhebt und dorthin geht,
wo die leichten Metalle sich wiegen,
wo die Luft schneidend ist
in einem neuen Verstand,
wo Waffen sprechen
von einziger Art.
Verficht uns dort!

Die Woge trug ein Treibholz hoch und sinkt.
Das Fieber riß dich an sich, läßt dich fallen.
Der Glaube hat nur einen Berg versetzt.

Laß stehn, was steht, geh, Gedanke!,

von nichts andrem als unsrem Schmerz durchdrungen.
Entsprich uns ganz!

Leave, Thought

Leave, thought, for as long as a word cleared for flight
is your wing, it lifts you and goes
where the light metals sway,
where the air is piercing
with a new understanding,
where weapons speak
in a unique way.
Defend us there!

The wave bore driftwood high and now sinks.
Fever took hold of you, now it lets you fall.
Faith has moved no more than a mountain.

Let stand what stands, leave, thought!,

prevailed upon by nothing other than our pain.
Stand for all we are!

Liebe: Dunkler Erdteil

Der schwarze König zeigt die Raubtiernägel,
zehn blasse Monde jagt er in die Bahn,
und er befiehlt den großen Tropenregen.
Die Welt sieht dich vom andren Ende an!

Es zieht dich übers Meer an jene Küsten
aus Gold und Elfenbein, an seinen Mund.
Dort aber liegst du immer auf den Knien,
und er verwirft und wählt dich ohne Grund.

Und er befiehlt die große Mittagswende.
Die Luft zerbricht, das grün und blaue Glas,
die Sonne kocht den Fisch im seichten Wasser,
und um die Büffelherde brennt das Gras.

Ins Jenseits ziehn geblendet Karawanen,
und er peitscht Dünen durch das Wüstenland,
er will dich sehn mit Feuer an den Füßen.
Aus deinen Striemen fließt der rote Sand.

Er, fellig, farbig, ist an deiner Seite,
er greift dich auf, wirft über dich sein Garn.
Um deine Hüften knüpfen sich Lianen,
um deinen Hals kraust sich der fette Farn.

Aus allen Dschungelnischen: Seufzer, Schreie.
Er hebt den Fetisch. Dir entfällt das Wort.
Die süßen Hölzer rühren dunkel Trommeln.
Du blickst gebannt auf deinen Todesort.

Love: The Dark Continent

The black king holds aloft the panther's claws
and chases ten pale moons around like prey,
invoking great tropical rain that begins to fall.
The world is looking at you in a different way!

You're drawn across the sea and to those coasts
of gold and ivory, and onward towards his mouth.
But there you always fall upon your knees,
for he chooses and rejects you without grounds.

Yet he's the one who orders the day to change.
The air shatters to pieces of green and blue glass,
as the hot sun boils the fish in shallow water,
and around the buffalo herd it burns the grass.

Into another world, the shimmering caravans move.
He lashes at the dunes across the desert land,
for he wants to see fire burning at your feet,
as from your welts there flows the bright red sand.

He, hairy, brightly colored, is by your side;
he snatches you up, throws over you his snare.
Soon long liana ropes will bind your hips,
your throat is ruffled with a lush fern collar.

From every jungle recess: sighs and screams.
He lifts the fetish. You have no reply.
Sweet wooden sticks begin to beat dark drums.
You stare transfixed, seeing where you will die.

Sieh, die Gazellen schweben in den Lüften,
auf halbem Wege hält der Dattelschwarm!
Tabu ist alles: Erden, Früchte, Ströme …
Die Schlange hängt verchromt an deinem Arm.

Er gibt Insignien aus seinen Händen.
Trag die Korallen, geh im hellen Wahn!
Du kannst das Reich um seinen König bringen,
du, selbst geheim, blick sein Geheimnis an.

Um den Äquator sinken alle Schranken.
Der Panther steht allein im Liebesraum.
Er setzt herüber aus dem Tal des Todes,
und seine Pranke schleift den Himmelssaum.

Look, gazelles are floating on the breeze,
only halfway down bends the date's ripe swarm!
Everything is taboo: earth, fruit, streams …
The snake hangs shimmering upon your arm.

He gives to you insignia from his hands.
Wear the corals, walk in deluded raiment!
You can deprive the kingdom of its king,
for it's you who, secretly, has seen his secret.

On the equator all barriers are lowered.
The panther lives alone by love's own laws.
He crosses over from the valley of death,
trailing the heavens' fabric in his claws.

Aria I

Wohin wir uns wenden im Gewitter der Rosen,
ist die Nacht von Dornen erhellt, und der Donner
des Laubs, das so leise war in den Büschen,
folgt uns jetzt auf dem Fuß.

Wo immer gelöscht wird, was die Rosen entzünden,
schwemmt Regen uns in den Fluß. O fernere Nacht!
Doch ein Blatt, das uns traf, treibt auf den Wellen
bis zur Mündung uns nach.

Aria I

Wherever we turn in the storm of roses,
the night is lit up by thorns, and the thunder
of leaves, once so soft in the depth of the bushes,
rumbling at our heels.

Wherever the fire of roses is extinguished,
rain washes us into the river. O distant night!
Yet a leaf, which once touched us, follows us on waves
towards the river's mouth.

Freies Geleit (Aria II)

Mit schlaftrunkenen Vögeln
und winddurchschossenen Bäumen
steht der Tag auf, und das Meer
leert einen schäumenden Becher auf ihn.

Die Flüsse wallen ans große Wasser,
und das Land legt Liebesversprechen
der reinen Luft in den Mund
mit frischen Blumen.

Die Erde will keinen Rauchpilz tragen,
kein Geschöpf ausspeien vorm Himmel,
mit Regen und Zornesblitzen abschaffen
die unerhörten Stimmen des Verderbens.

Mit uns will sie die bunten Brüder
und grauen Schwestern erwachen sehn,
den König Fisch, die Hoheit Nachtigall
und den Feuerfürsten Salamander.

Für uns pflanzt sie Korallen ins Meer.
Wäldern befiehlt sie, Ruhe zu halten,
dem Marmor, die schöne Ader zu schwellen,
noch einmal dem Tau, über die Asche zu gehn.

Die Erde will ein freies Geleit ins All
jeden Tag aus der Nacht haben,
daß noch tausend und ein Morgen wird
von der alten Schönheit jungen Gnaden.

Safe Conduct (Aria II)

With birds drunk with sleep
and trees shot through with wind
the day awakens, and the sea empties
a foaming cup to honor it.

Rivers surge towards the wide water,
and the land lays loving vows
of pure air inside the mouth
with its fresh flowers.

The Earth will have no mushroom cloud,
nor spit out any creature towards heaven,
with rain and thunderbolts it abolishes
the unbearable voice of destruction.

In us it wants the lively brothers
and to see the gray sisters awakened,
the King of Fish, the Royal Nightingale,
and, Prince of Fire, the Salamander.

For us it plants corals in the sea.
It orders forests to maintain the quiet,
for marble to swell its beautiful veins,
and once more for dew to settle on ashes.

Earth wants safe conduct in its orbit,
each day we have in the face of night,
so that from ancient beauty renewed graces
on a thousand and one mornings will arise.

Dialects

für Nelly Sachs

An ihrer Mundart wird man sie erkennen.
die Schläger und die Geschlagenen,
die Verfolger und die Verfolgten,
auch die Törichten und die Weisen,
Mundart, die nicht den heimatlichen Klang ablegt ...

Dialects

for Nelly Sachs

One can recognize them by their dialects,
the beater and the beaten,
the persecutor and the persecuted,
also the fools and the wise ones,
dialects that don't relinquish their native sound ...

Der gepreßte Mund

für Nelly Sachs

und wie du schweigst, wenn du mündig bist.
und die Worte auslässt, die deinen Nächsten verletzen.
Gemundet haben Pfirsiche und weiße Brote,
und dem andren haben Disteln
und Knochen, die mußten immer fressen die Münder,
die frassen die Knochen noch auf, die lecken noch
Knochenmehl.

Wohl bekomm's, denen aber schmeckte das Brot, das weiß war
und der Pfirsich, und wie gern hat uns alles geschmeckt.

Mündig sind wir geworden, dann schwiegen wir bald,
und redeten und ahmten Mundarten nach.

Und kehrten zu unsrer Mundart zurück.
Und kehren zurück.
Kehren in den Klang
mit dem wir auch
im Gehen, im Wachen, im Schlaf
sprechen, eine einzige unsre,
die der andren verständlicher ist,
laß mich immer, so reden, wie ich reden,
laß mich nicht anders können.

The Tightened Lip

for Nelly Sachs

And how silent one becomes when you come of age,
and you leave out the words that injure your loved ones.
Peaches and bread have tasted good,
while everything else has bristles
and bones, the growing always needing to eat,
eating the bones and licking up
the bone meal.

Gladly we swallow it down, the white bread also tasty,
and the peaches, how good everything was.

We came of age, then suddenly were silent,
as we talked and imitated dialects.

And then returned to our dialect.
And return.
Return to the sound
with which we speak
as we go, while awake, while asleep,
the only one that is ours,
which is more comprehensible to others.
Let me always speak the way I speak.
Let me speak no other way.

Ihr Worte

für Nelly Sachs, die Freundin, die Dichterin, in Verehrung

Ihr Worte, auf, mir nach!,
und sind wir auch schon weiter,
zu weit gegangen, geht's noch einmal
weiter, zu keinem Ende geht's.

Es hellt nicht auf.

Das Wort
wird doch nur
andre Worte nach sich ziehn,
Satz den Satz.
So möchte Welt,
endgültig,
sich aufdrängen,
schon gesagt sein.
Sagt sie nicht.

Worte, mir nach,
daß nicht endgültig wird
— nicht diese Wortbegier
und Spruch auf Widerspruch!

Laßt eine Weile jetzt.
keins der Gefühle sprechen,
den Muskel Herz
sich anders üben.

Laßt, sag ich, laßt.
Ins höchste Ohr nicht,
nichts, sag ich, geflüstert,
zum Tod fall dir nichts ein,

You Words

in honor of Nelly Sachs, friend and poet

You words, arise, follow me!,
and though already we have gone farther,
gone too far, once more it goes
on, to no end it goes.

It doesn't brighten.

The word
will only drag
other words behind it,
the sentence a sentence.
So the world wishes,
ultimately,
to press its own cause,
to already be spoken.
Do not speak it.

Words, follow me,
so nothing will be final
— not this passion for words,
nor a saying and its contradiction!

Let there be for now
no feeling expressed,
let the heart's muscle
exercise in another way.

Let be, I say, let be.
Into the highest ear
whisper, I say, nothing,
nothing about death,

laß, und mir nach, nicht mild
noch bitterlich,
nicht trostreich,
ohne Trost
bezeichnend nicht,
so auch nicht zeichenlos —

Und nur nicht dies: das Bild
im Staubgespinst, leeres Geroll
von Silben, Sterbenswörter.

Kein Sterbenswort,
Ihr Worte!

let be, and follow me, not mild
nor bitter,
nor comforting,
without consolation
without signifying,
and thus without symbols —

Most of all not this: the image
cobwebbed with dust, the empty rumble
of syllables, dying words.

Nothing about death,
you words!

Neu unter dem Himmel

Denkt daran, daß die Raketen, auch die raschen erfundenen
Geschosse bald unmodern sein werdern
daß ihr nach Mond ein anderes Gestirn
an die Brust nehmen werdet und uns fragen
werdet: Habt ihr nichts Neues zu singen?
Denkt daran, daß dieser Zwist von Ost
und West bald ganz lächerlich sein wird
und ihr werdet uns wieder fragen: damals,
habt ihr denn nicht begriffen, es war
der Rede wert, versöhnt rascher,
eh die Zeit es versöhnt nach viel Tränen
und Toden. Sagt etwas, ihr Wortemacher,
das mit Zeit geht wie der große Liebes-
und Todesflügel Sterbevogel neben
der Arbeit. Gerechtigkeit ist, wenn
jeder recht arbeitet und dabei denkt
so vernünftig ist, daß sein Gefühl
nicht zurückfällt ins Jahr Tausend.

Die Dichtung ist das bleibende Brot
für Menschen

es war dieser gemeinen Reden und Ängste nicht wert

Neu unterm Himmel wäre Andres, richtig zu fühlen
Ändert euch, verwendet ein neues Gefühl, macht
diese Erfindung, macht den Raketen Ehre,
erfindet den Menschen, einen, fähig
vernünftig in den Himmel zu greifen
und nach Wolken und Rosen wie Flammen
aufgingen und Verlust auf Herrschaft
der über sich selbst herrscht

New Under The Sky

Consider what it means that your rockets,
the missiles that were so quickly installed
will soon become outmoded,
that as you place another star, like the moon,
upon your breast you might ask us:
Have you nothing new to sing?
Consider what it means that this quarrel between East
and West will soon become ridiculous
and you'll ask us once again: Even then,
did you not grasp that it was
worth talking, that you should reconcile more quickly,
before time does it for you after many tears
and many deaths? Say something, you makers of words,
that fits the times like the wings of love
and death of the mortal bird next to
one's work. Justice is when
each works for the good and therefore thinks
so rationally that his feelings
don't regress to the year one thousand.

Poetry is the bread that remains
for humans.

It was not worth all this talk and fear.

Something new under the sky would be to feel at peace.
Change yourselves, tap a new feeling, make this
invention stand up to rockets,
invent the human, one capable
of reaching reasonably for the sky,
for clouds and roses, the way flames
rise up, or desire for a master

der über sich selbst herrscht
und einen Kreuzzug nur mehr
für das auferstandene Wort führt
das heißt Menschlickeit

Erfindet ruhig weiter, wir erfinden
ja nicht mehr gern,
wir vertrauen euch, aber uns nicht mehr.

who masters himself,
and crusade only for
the word that rises from the dead
which means the human.

Just continue to invent, for we do not
like to invent anymore.
We trust you, but not ourselves any longer.

Die Waffen nieder

Für diesen Tag will ich die Worte frisch halten,
Für den Tag unbekannt, an dem die Arbeit an Waffen
stillsteht und das Brot schimmelt, das sie gegeben hat,
an dem ein stummer Zug in der Welt aus den Toren kommt
Für diesen Tag will ich streiten, den anarchischen
an dem Ordnung gemacht wird in Hirnen und Herzen
an dem jeder sein Anteil am Bösen beklagt und

Lay Down Your Weapons

For today I want to keep words fresh
for the day yet to come on which the work on weapons
ceases and the bread gets moldy that they gave out,
the day on which a mute crowd leaves the gate and enters the world.
For this day I will fight, in order that anarchy become
the order of the day in our hearts and minds,
each of us bewailing our share of evil …

III   GEDICHTE 1962 – 1963

III   POEMS 1962 – 1963

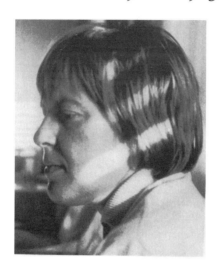

Deine Stimme

1

Hängt nicht der Himmel schon an deinem Mund?
So häng mit Augen ich an deinen Lippen,
und deine Stimme ist das Glück, das kommt.

Sagst du auch alles: ich kann nichts begreifen
doch zwischen dem Vokal und Konsonant
streift mich ein Hauch, ein neues Lebenszeichen.

2

An deinen Lippen laß mich mit Augen hängen,
hängt nicht der Himmel auch an deinem Mund?
von deiner Stimme wird mich nichts mehr trennen.
Erweck mich vom Tode auf.

Ein Jahr soll ich sie nicht mehr hören.
Worte mir, den Vorrat für das Jahr.
Nichts zum Begreifen, nur den Klang zum Glauben,
ich glaube immer jeden Tag und Ja.

Dann wird es stumm sein, stummer du zu mir
und immer leiser wird mein Schlummer
die Stille: das jüngste Gericht für mein Ohr.
Die Posaunen unbewegt, ohne Bläser
tragen das Ende vor.

Your Voice

1

Does heaven not hang from your mouth?
Likewise my eyes hang upon your lips,
and your voice is the happiness that results.

Even if you say everything, I will never grasp it,
yet between the vowels and consonants
your breath grazes me, a new sign of life.

2

Let my eyes hang upon your lips,
for does heaven not also hang from your mouth?
I don't ever want to be separated from your voice.
Awaken me from death.

I will not hear it for another year.
Give me words, a year's supply.
No need to grasp anything, for its sound brings belief,
and I believe every day and then some.

Soon it will be mute, you will be more mute to me,
and ever more quiet will be my slumber
in the stillness, the Last Judgment for my ear.
The trumpets are still, without trumpeters
the end is performed.

Bitte um Verwandlung

Könnt ich zerfallen wie ein altes Kleid!
an den Gelenken brüchig werden, blind und taub
hinschlagen in den Staub und neu erstehn.

Ein Phönix sein, mein Abgott, dir zuliebe,
weil du mich anders hier nicht lieben kannst

Ein Phönix sein, mein Abgott!
Dir in anderer Gestalt erscheinen
der du mich nicht lieben kannst,
so wie ich bin. In anderer Gestalt!

Traurig wie noch kein Wesen, steh ich auf
Geliebter, lade mein Herz dann
ganz
zu deinem Herzen ein.

Gegen die streitbare Natur
gegen die lächelnde Natur,
die nichts vereint
der nichts zuwider ist, hoffend auf andre Zeit.

Geliebter, lade mein Herz dann ganz
zu deinem Herzen ein.

O käm die Gegenzeit,
in der ein Zauber uns braucht
vereint. Geliebter, lade dazu niemand ein.

Prayer for Transformation

If only I could collapse like an old dress!
Fragile in the joints, blind and deaf,
falling to the ground and rising again.

To be a phoenix, my idol, loved by you
because you cannot love me otherwise.

To become a phoenix, my idol!
To appear before you in another form
since you cannot love me
as I am. In another form!

Sad like no other creature, I rise.
Beloved, invite my heart
entirely
into your heart.

Despite belligerent nature,
despite benevolent nature,
which unites nothing,
to whom nothing is distasteful, I hope for another era.

Beloved, invite my heart entirely
into your heart.

O if there could come another era
in which a spell could bring
us together. Beloved, invite no one else in.

Meine Liebe seit so langer Zeit

Der langen, langen Liebe
sind die Flügel schwer geworden
zu keinem andren fortfliegen wird sie,
fortgehn muss die alte Bettlerin,
jeden Tag fiel die Tür vor ihr zu,
all die Jahre, alle, alle Tage
geht jetzt heim nach Norden
Südwind trägt sie, Nordwind schlägt sie.

My Love After Many Years

A long, long love
has seen its wings grow heavy
and will not fly to another.
The old beggar lady must wander on,
each day the door closing upon her,
all of the years, all, all of the days
heading home to the north.
South wind carries her, north wind harries her.

Wartezimmer

Die Sprache verbindet nicht mehr.
Gemeinsam ist uns das Warten.
Ein Stuhl
eine Bank
ein Fenster
durch das das Licht in unser Zimmer
fällt
auf unsere Hände
auf unsere Augen
und sonst
auf den Boden

Heile unsere Augen
damit wir wieder Worte finden
bunte, die ich dir sagen kann.

Waiting Room

We no longer share a language.
Together we are waiting.
A chair,
a bench,
a window
through which the light in our room
falls
on our hands,
on our eyes,
and otherwise
on the floor.

Heal our eyes
so that we can again find the words,
so multi-colored, that I can say to you.

Eintritt in die Partei

Ist denn ein Mensch nichts unter Brüdern wert?
Verleumdet und bespien, verhöhnt, verlästert,
wer weiß es nicht, für eine Guttat, die sich nicht beweist.

Die Ehre, verkauft an jedem Stammtisch.
In aller Mund als eine dreckige Anekdote.
Das Unmaß eines Gefühls ermordet
von geschäftiger Nutznießerei.
Mit der Aufstellung der Einnahmen
beschäftigt die Skrupellosigkeit.

Ein Leben, ein einziges, zum Experiment
gemacht. So ists gelungen. Vollbracht.

Auch das Kaninchen, im Labor, aufgedunsen,
das sein Fell läßt nach dem Versuch,
auch die Ratte, abgespritzt, ohnmächtig
wird den Arm ihres Mörders nicht zerfleischen.
Auch die Fliege, gegen die eine Flitspitze
sich richtet, die Mücken, die eine Charta
der Mückenrechte noch nicht in Anspruch nehmen
sind meine Genossen.

Ich nehme in Anspruch meine Wenigkeit.
Wenn aber Gott Fleisch geworden ist
und ins Reagenzglas kommt und Farbe
bekennt, wenn er die Liebe sein sollte
und ich zweifle, daß etwas sein könnte
von dieser Art, wird mich das wenig trösten.

Welcome to the Party

Does a person mean nothing to his fellow man?
Slandered and spit upon, insulted, laughed at,
who doesn't know that no good deed goes unpunished.

Respect is what is sold at every gossip session.
A filthy anecdote in every mouth.
The depth of a feeling murdered
by the corporate beneficiaries.
Unscrupulousness busies itself
with revenue reports.

A life, just one, turned into an experiment.
This they have succeeded at. Achieved.

Also the rabbit in the laboratory, bloated,
who lets his pelt, along with the rat,
be injected as part of the experiment, powerless
to bite the arm of their murderer.
Also the flies against whom fly spray
is aimed, the mosquitoes, who have yet to demand
a charter of mosquito rights,
they are my comrades.

I demand a right to my insignificance.
The idea that God has become flesh
and arrives in a test tube and will show His
true colors, that in fact He is Love,
I doubt that anything can come
from such a procedure, nor does it comfort me.

Ich weiß, daß man die Opfer hier zwingen muß,
zueinander, ohne Vereinbarung noch.
Fliegenart will ein paar Tage, der Paria
einen Blick in den Kastenschlitz, die Ratte,
die Ich, die gänzlich Erniedrigten, wollen
die Rache, eh sie geschändet sterben —
wollen ein Wort des Bedauerns.

Die Kommune verzichtet.
Das Kapital einer zinsentragenden Grausamkeit
steht gegen das Kapital eines abnehmenden
Schmerzes.
Diese Gesellschaft richtet sich dennoch selbst.

Sterben ist es nicht, Aufstehen
ist das Wort. Ohne Verständnis
für die Ausbeutung diese Ausbeutung
beenden. Es komme die Revolution.

Es komme, so mag es denn kommen.
Ich zweifle. Aber es komme
die Revolution. auch von meinem Herzen,

I know that here one must press the victims
together, though not in agreement.
The flies want their own time, the pariah
a peek from the closet door, the rat,
the self, the completely degraded, they want
revenge before they die in disgrace —
they want a word of regret.

The communal is renounced.
The capital of an interest bearing cruelty
stands against the capital of
a receding pain.
This society judges itself.

It doesn't mean death, for revolution
is the word. With no sympathy
for exploitation, to end
this exploitation. The revolution is coming.

It's coming, so let it come.
I'm full of doubt. But the revolution
is coming, also within my heart.

[Meine Gedichte sind mir abhanden gekommen]

Meine Gedichte sind mir abhanden gekommen.
Ich suche sie in allen Zimmerwinkeln.
Weiß vor Schmerz nicht, wie man einen Schmerz
aufschreibt, weiß überhaupt nichts mehr.

Weiß, daß man so nicht daherreden kann,
es muß würziger sein, eine gepfefferte Metapher.
müßte einem einfallen. Aber mit dem Messer im Rücken.

Parlo e tacio, parlo, flüchte mich in ein Idiom,
in dem sogar Spanisches vorkommt, los toros y
las planetas, auf einer alten gestohlenen Platte
vielleicht noch zu hören. Mit etwas Französischem
geht es auch, tu es mon amour depuis si longtemps.

Adieu, ihr schönen Worte, mit euren Verheißungen.
Warum habt ihr mich verlassen?

[I've misplaced my poems]

I've misplaced my poems.
I search for them in each nook and cranny.
Because of pain I know nothing, not even how
one writes about pain, for I simply know nothing else.

I know only that it cannot be spoken of,
that it's spicier, that a peppery metaphor
must occur to one. But with a knife in the back.

Parlo e tacio, parlo, I escape into an idiom
in which some Spanish appears, *los toros y
los planetas,* perhaps still heard on
an old stolen record. Something in French
might also work, *tu es mon amour depuis si longtemps.*

Adieu, you beautiful words with your promises.
Why have you abandoned me? Were you not happy?
I have stashed you away in a heart made of stone.
Do something for me, stay there, compose for me a work.

[Alles verloren, die Gedichte zuerst]

Alles verloren, die Gedichte zuerst
dann den Schlaf, dann den Tag dazu
dann das alles dazu, was am Tag war
und was in der Nacht, dann als nichts
mehr, noch verloren, weiterverloren
bis weniger als nichts und ich nicht mehr
und schon gar nichts war,

Rückzug muß ein inneres Hinterland
mit allen verbriefte Jahre und gesehene Orte
noch vor den Augen, da die Erde
nicht mehr und keine Schmach, dann
hinten noch immer ein Raum
krallenumflogene Weiten für Taube, Stumme
Helle ruflange Weiten für er
die Ankunft, Erstummter

Für den Erstummten die Wüstenei
mit dem verständlichen Gespinnst
das sanft seinen Wahnsinn einpuppt
bis er das gläserne Hotel malt,

[Everything is lost, the poems first]

Everything is lost, the poems first,
then sleep, then after that the day,
then everything else, what belonged to day
and what belonged to night, then when nothing
more could be lost, more was lost, and then more,
until there was less than nothing, not even myself,
and there really was nothing more.

Time to retreat to an inner hinterland
with all the promised years and pictured places
still before one's eyes, where the earth
no longer exists nor the shame, far
back where there is still space, open stretches
covered with doves, silent and bright beneath
the talon, within calling range of him,
the arrival, the silencer.

For the silenced there is the desolation
with its perceivable web
that softly spins its madness
until it creates its glass hotel.

Toteninsel

Ich muß glauben, daß
dieser Irrsinn, dieses Gefängnis
für die Ewigkeit währt
die vielen Stunden, als ich
meinen Papst mir wählte
und dunkler Rauch
aufstieg,
(die eine Kerze nicht,
mit dem weißen)
als alle meine Träume
im Konklave waren
und alles stimmte gegen
meinen wütendsten gescheiterten
Traum,
der hätte ja selber sich
nicht geglaubt, und gewußt,
daß über all das zu herrschen
über Schmutz, Gold,
Samen, Toteninseln

Island of the Dead

I have to believe that
this insanity, this imprisonment
will last an eternity,
those many hours it took
to choose my pope
as the dark smoke
rose
(not the white
of a candle)
when all of my dreams
were locked up in the conclave
and everything seemed
against my most frenzied broken
dream,
which should not have believed
itself but knew
that above all it must prevail
over filth, gold,
semen, islands of the dead.

Kardinalfehler

Sich messen an Päpsten
und Gläubigen, selber
zum Papst und zum Gläubigen
nicht bestellt, ein ungläubig
Erhobener zu sein, dem auch Lumpen
scharlachrot werden, dem Mützen
wegfliehen und kein Hut steht
satanische Existenz

Cardinal Mistake

To compare oneself to popes
and believers, yourself
appointed neither a pope
nor a believer, rather a non-believer
who praises, whose rags also
turn cardinal red, whose cap
flies away, no hat fitting
satanic existence.

Kein Zeugnis Ablegen

Kein Zeugnis ablegen, schweigen, leben,
das vorgeschriebene Leben, leben,
die Sonne, die nichts an den Tag bringt,
die Sonne auch nicht bemühen, niemand
bemühen.
Es ist eine Mühe, zu hoffen nicht, zu fürchten nichts.

Make No Statement

Make no statement, be silent, live,
live the life prescribed you,
the sun, which divulges nothing,
don't bother the sun, don't bother
anyone.
It's enough not to hope, not to fear.

Die Nacht der Verlorenen Das Ende der Liebe

Ein Mond, ein Himmel
und das dunkle Meer.
Nur, dunkel alles.
Nur weil es Nacht ist
und nichts Menschliches
dies feingewirkte auch durchwebt.
Was wirfst du mir noch vor
und solche Bitterkeit,
Tu's nicht.
Ich hab nichts Besseres gewußt
als dich zu lieben, ich hab
nicht gedacht,
daß durch den Schweiß der Haut
die [– –] Welt
und daß der Groschen fiel

The Night of the Lost/The End of Love

A moon, a sky,
and the dark sea.
Now everything is dark.
Only because it is night
and there is nothing human
inherent in this scene.
What are you accusing me of
and with such bitterness?
Don't do it.
I didn't know any better
than to love you, I did
not think
that through the skin's sweat
there would be the _____ world
and I would finally understand.

[Ich weiß keine bessere Welt]

Ich weiß keine bessere Welt.
Die schwachsinnige Moral der Opfer läßt wenig hoffen.

Eine verruchte Frage, auf Ehre, allein,
kommt dem Gefolterten, dies Überlebens
sich wert zu zeigen, im Angriff, abzulegen
die schwachsinnige Moral der Opfer
sich zu erheben, dieses Geröchel
nicht mehr zu werben um eine Stunde.
an die Gefolterten, ob dies Geröchel noch
Werbung ist, für die schwachsinnige Moral
der Opfer.
Die verruchten Fragen gehn jetzt allein
an die Gefolterten
Auf die verruchten Fragen kommt sie
eines Tages, die lautlose, tätige Antwort.

Auf verruchte Fragen, nicht die seligen,
gibt es nicht auf die seligen,
der die da leiden
auf die verruchtesten
finden sich eine Antwort.
der die da leiden, lassen sich stellen.
Die schöne Seele

[I know of no better world]

I know of no better world.
The feeble morality of the victim allows for little hope.

A crazy question of honor, alone,
is posed to the tortured, namely to show
that survival is worth it by attacking, shedding
the feeble morality of the victim
in order to rise up, no longer encouraging
this throttling for yet another hour,
since to the tortured this throttling is still
a sign of the feeble morality
of the victim.
The crazy question is now posed
only to the tortured.
One day the crazy question will receive
the silent, conclusive answer.

To crazy questions, not to blessed ones,
not even to blessed ones,
nor to those who suffered
the craziest,
is there an answer.
Those who suffer them allow them to be posed.
Those beautiful souls ....

Ich weiß keine bessere Welt

Wer weiß eine besser Welt, der trete vor.
Allein, nicht mehr in Tapferkeit, und diesen Speichel nicht
    abgewischt
diesen Speichel, im Gesicht ihn tragen,
als ging es zur Krönung, und dies vergolten, es geht zur
    Kommunion,
und unter Brüdern. Das schwache Kaninchen,
die Ratte, und die da fallen, sie alle,
allein nicht, mehr, ein Schrecken schon,
Traum von der Wiederkehr
im Traum von der Bewaffnung, im Traum
von Wiederkehr.

I Know of No Better World

Who knows of a better world should step forward.
Alone, no longer out of bravery, not wiping away this saliva,
this saliva worn upon the cheek
as if to a coronation, as if redeemed, whether at communion
or among comrades. The weak rabbit,
the rat, and those fallen there, all of them,
no longer alone, but as one, though still afraid,
the dream of returning home
in the dream of armament, in the dream
of returning home.

[Bis zur Wiederkehr]

Bis zur Wiederkehr. Aber man sagt,
du kommst nie mehr. Es kommt
nur mehr eine andere Nacht.

Noch immer nicht verziehen,
wie wahr, mit den wilden
Anschuldigungen im Kopf,
immer noch nicht begriffen,
daß die Kreatur nicht geachtet werden muß,
immer noch nicht eingesehen,
was zu kämpfen ist gegen einen
Verweigrer des Kampfes.
Ich weigere mich, berufe
mich auf Dein Herz, daß
wenn du keins hast, dir eingepflanzt
worden ist von mir,

Eingepflanzt habe ich dir ein Herz,
einen Kult getrieben mit der Begeisterung
über seine sanften Schläge, zuweilen.
Eingepflanzt habe ich meine Freundlichkeit,
mein Lachen und eine Zukunftsmusik.
in die Dürre einer abgeernteten Brust.
Ich habe geliebt wie die Wilden,
begeistert von der Liebe und jedem Tag.
Angebetet, Wurzeln verbrannt, jedem Klimbim
zu einem Fest verholfen, nachgeplappert jedes
Wort und meine Angehörigkeit vergessen.
Ich war das längst nicht mehr.

[Until I return]

Until I return. But someone says
you will never return. From now on
there's only one kind of night ahead.

As ever, unwilling to forgive,
so true, with wild
accusations inside my head,
still never grasping
that the creature need not be watched,
never yet realizing
what there is to war against
in a war protestor.
I protest, appeal
to your heart, such that
if you have none, mine will be
transplanted in you.

I have transplanted a heart in you,
founded a cult through the enthusiasm
of its soft beats now and then.
I have transplanted my congeniality,
my laughter and the music of hope
in the leanness of a fallow breast.
I have loved like the wild things,
been inspired by love and loved each day.
I have prayed, burned incense,
turned each to-do into a party,
mechanically repeated each word
and forgot to what I belonged.
I've not been that for a while.

Aber wer bin ich jetzt, selber mit
Feuerschlucken, nicht mehr vertraut
Das Herz schlägt nicht mehr.
Wie wird das enden? Ich bin langweilig
geworden und so langsam, und so kalt,
daß ich ohne meinen Schmerz nicht mehr am Leben wäre.

But who I am now is one capable
of eating fire, no longer familiar to anyone.
The heart beats no longer.
How will it end? I have become boring,
and so slow, and so cold that
it's as if I can no longer live without my pain.

[Müd und untauglich]

Müd und untauglich
in jeder Gesellschaft
am Ende,
am Ende ist
der Anfang von
Tagtraum und Erinnerung,
am Ende ist also
sodann das was nicht
sein soll,
es ist am Ende

[Tired and useless]

Tired and useless
amongst any company,
at the end,
at an end is
the beginning of
daydreams and memories,
everything at an end
such that anything
which should not be is
at an end.

Werbung

um jeden werb ich
und keinen gewinn ich,
um den Straßenbahnschaffner
der vor mir die Tür einschnappen
läßt, um den Postboten,
der zu laut
läutet, um jeden
werb ich, ich brauch
ein Heer von Menschen
um sie lieben zu können,
es ist gefährlich, die Menschen
zu lieben, ein Verbrechen
sich aufzudrängen

Courting

I court them all
and win none,
whether it be the conductor
who let's the tram door snap shut
before me, or the postman
who rings too loudly,
I court each of them, I need
an army of men
in order to love them,
it being dangerous
to love people, a crime
to assert oneself.

Ach

Gehört zu keiner Gruppe
gehört zu niemand und nichts
gehört sich selbst nicht an
gehört ihm auch der Gedanke, der ungestört,
nicht an, was also

daß im Triumph alle Tore
aufgehn und herein
mit einer Musik
zieht er, der Ohnewas
und herein zieht
mit Trauer
hochgemut, zieht der
Gott, der einer ist,
zieht die Parodie,
dessen der ist,
komm ich
um den nackten
Gewalt
und der gutgekleideten
Gewalten
zu trotzen.

Geh ich,
der einer ist
und noch sein will
ohne Musik, ohne Trotz
sein will ich und forthin
dauern, nicht zum Trotz,
aber trotzdem.

Alas

Belong to no group,
belong to no one and nothing,
belong not even to yourself,
belong to no idea
that remains undisturbed, that which

in triumph opens
all gates and marches in
with music, the have-nots
marching cheerfully
with sadness,
God being one such idea
dragged in as a parody
which he himself is,
myself defiant
amid naked
power
and well dressed
power.

And so I go,
myself a person
and one who wants to remain
without music, who wants to live
without defiance and therefore
survive, not out of defiance,
but nevertheless.

Für C. E.

daß ich Zeit verliere, nicht antworte,
so esse und schlafe und lese und auch Musik,
daß ich so, nicht bin, das nicht, daß ich
so lebe

Und gehe mit diesen Socken und erdigen Schuhn
durch das verrottete Gras und die Weinberge,
daß ich so lebe, alles ablege, auch eine gelinde
Hoffnung, es könne anders sein, ein Flugzeug
würde nicht fliegen, ein Gesicht auf mich zukommen,
nicht wieder, sondern endlich, ich leb es mir vor.

Und rühre mich nicht, trinke den Tee und schlafe
schlecht. Aber ich lebe mir vor, erwürgt von Banalitäten,
lebe ich mir ein Leben vor, in dem es rot blüht,
Bescheidenheit ist das nicht, sondern auslöschen,
ein Einverständnis mit Freude, die langweilig ins Gesicht tritt,
der Komplice der Banalität und des Zeitvergehens, und
der wilde

For C.E.

I don't answer as to why I waste time,
that I eat and sleep and read and listen to music,
that I am, am not, am not that, but that
I live.

And I go around in these socks and muddy shoes,
through the rotted grass and the vineyards,
so that I live, give everything up, even the meekest
hope that it could be otherwise, that a plane
will not fly, that a face will appear in front of me
not again, but finally, that's what I hope for.

And so I don't move, I drink my tea and sleep
badly. But I hope, strangled by banalities,
I hope for a life in which red blossoms.
That's not modesty, but extinguishment,
an agreement with joy that enters the face out of boredom,
the accomplice of banality and passing time, and
the wild …

Wiedersehen

Variation auf ein Gedicht von Plaga

Freunde sein, wie? wenn
eins dem andern noch
ins Aug fliegt, sich eines
andern Mal der Hand erinnert,
und etwas [– –]
etwas Freundliches sich in die
Hand gegeben hat. O niemals
nie, die Nächsten waren wir
und werden fortan die Fernsten sein.
ferner als fern, da alles gelebt
war, was du fortträgst von
mir, das Lächeln, Atmen
die Verzweiflungen, alles,
was du mir bringst, wundert
mich, denn „ es ist kein größerer
Fluch, als nichts zu teilen,
mit dem der, das alles
geteilt hat und gelassen,
dem anderen Teil. ["] Den
Flaum, mit dem man lebt,
ein neues Leben, das
kommt vom alten.
Ich habe keinen Flaum den
Schutzfilm nichts, nichts
bekommen, hättest Du mich
verkauft, anstatt verraten,
geduldet irgendwie, anstatt
Dich zu verweigern

Until We Meet Again

Variation on a poem by Plaga

To be friends? How when
one still thinks of
the other, once more
remembers a hand
and something _____,
something endearing placed
in my hand. O never
ever were we just friends
and from now on will be the most distant,
more distant than distant, since everything
was experienced together, what you carry away
from me, my smile, breath,
the doubts, everything.
What you bring to me amazes
me because "there is no greater
curse than not to share something
with the one whom you shared
everything, yourself left with
the other part." The
residue with which one lives,
a new life that
comes from the old.
I have no residue, no
protective film, not having
received one, you should have sold
me rather than betray me,
put up with me somehow, rather than
deny yourself.

Schwarzsicht

Es kommt der Tag mit der schwarzen Sicht
mit Toten wird das Frühstück eingenommen
durchs Fenster steigt Nebel
du [– –] den verlorenen Schlüssel

Tag mit der schwarzen Sicht
das Frühstück mit fahlem Gestank dient Todesgedanken
Nebel steigt durch das Fenster.
den Vormittag zerreissen Anrufe
von überland und du zitterst der
Arbeit entgegen, (Welcher bloß?)
Du machst Gänge und hetzt
durch die Stadt. Mittag [– –] Schmerzen
und Müdigkeit, Mahlzeit aus Verdruß
und für Minuten Sonne. Du
möchtest jemand lieben aber keinen
von „denen",

Blackness

Day arrives with its blackness,
breakfast is served with the dead,
through the window fog climbs
you _____ the lost key.

The day full of blackness,
breakfast serves up thoughts of death
with its faded stench, fog climbs
through the window, long distance calls rip
through morning and you tremble
because of your work (though what work?).
You do some errands and rush
through the city. Midday _____ pain
and weariness, a meal made of spite
and for a few minutes some sun. You
want to love someone, but not
one of "them."

[Ich bin ganz wild]

Ich bin ganz wild von
Tod, von dem Taft —
rauschen, von
den Wasserrüschen,
ich trag ihn schon
angezogen, das kleine
Kräglein, damit das
Beil weiß, wo mein
Kopf vom Körper
zu trennen ist. Hab ich
das noch, Kopf und
Körper, oh nein,
so täusch ich den Tod,
ich habe meinen Kopf
verschenkt, hingegeben
an die Meute, aber
meinen Körper hat
niemand gehabt, der
wurde am Eingang zurück-
gewiesen. Ein Herr sagte
mir, sagte nicht einmal, das

[I am completely wild]

I am completely wild
from death, from the rustle
of taffeta, from
the rippling water.
I am already wearing
it, the little
collar which tells
the ax where my
head separates
from my body. Do I
still have my head
and body? Oh no,
and thus I disappoint death.
I have given away
my head, given it to
the mob, but
no one has
my body, for it
was handed in at
the entrance. A man
said to me, more than once, that …

Frage

In Memoriam K.A. Hartmann

Augen, seid ihr ausgelaufen
Ohrgang fühl da einer
Alles tot. Ist alles tot?
Ohren, kommt auch nichts mehr zu?
Kein Geräusch und keine Worte.

Was umfängt die Schatten hier?

Wir umfangen, hören, sehen.
Wir noch nicht aufgefangen vom Stichwort Tod
den Tag nicht begonnen
Wir allesamt
gelassen

Unerläßlich die Schatten
die uns umfangen.
einüben
der uns einübt schon ins Gewahrsam
Tod Das Stichwort uns erlassen
Die Posaune, [– –]
Die Nacht, nachtschlafen verbracht

Question

K.A. Hartmann, in memoriam

Eyes, have you run dry,
ears, do you sense everything
is dead? Is everything dead?
Ears, is there nothing more to hear?
No sound and no words?

What embraces one's shadow here?

We embrace, listen, see.
We who are not reduced to the entry "Death,"
who have not begun the day.
All of us
solemn.

Indispensable is the shadow
that embraces us,
readying us
for what possesses us already,
Death, the entry that releases us.
Trumpets, _____,
night, a night spent asleep.

Trauerjahre

Die Jahre laufen nicht ab, im Kaffee
ist Salz, und auf dem Butterbrot,
das muß wohl dahergekommen.
Meine kranken Nachbarn, denen
auch nicht zu helfen ist,
schellen, ich kann nicht öffnen,
ich warte auf jemand andren.

Sad Years

The years don't run off. In my coffee
is salt, as well as on my bread,
which came along as well.
My sick neighbors, who
also can't be helped, ring
the doorbell. I can't answer.
I'm waiting for someone else.

Abschied

Das Fleisch, das gut mit mir gealtert ist,
die pergamentene Hand, die meine frisch hielt,
sie soll auf dem weißen Schenkel liegen,
das Fleisch sich verjüngen, augenblicksweise,
damit hier rascher der Verfall vor sich geht,
Rasch sind die Linien gekommen, etwas gesunken,
schon alles über der straffen Muskulatur.

Nicht geliebt zu werden. Der Schmerz könnte größer
sein, Der befindet sich wohl, dessen Tür zufällt.
Aber das Fleisch, mit der Einbruchslinie an dem Knie,
die faltigen Hände, über Nacht gekommen alles,
das verwitterte Schulterblatt, auf dem kein Grün wächst,
Es hat einmal ein Gesicht geborgen gehalten.

Um hundert Jahre gealtert an einem Tag.
Das zutrauliche Tier ist unter dem Peitschenhieb
um die prästabilierte Harmonie gebracht
worden.

Departure

The flesh that has aged so well with me,
the parchment hand, which held mine so tenderly,
should rest upon my white thigh
in order to make it young, instantly,
if only to speed up its sure decay.
How quickly the lines have come, sunken in,
right across the tense musculature.

Not to be loved. The pain could be worse.
One whose door shuts is well.
But the flesh, with its invasive scar on the knee,
the creased hands, all of it happening overnight,
the weathered shoulder blade on which nothing green grows.
Once it held a face nestled within it.

Aging a hundred years in a single day.
The tame animal, under the whip's lash,
deprived of its predestined
harmony.

Gerüche

Immer hab ich den Geruch geliebt, den Schweiß,
die Ausdünstung am Morgen, auch die Exkremente,
den Schmutz nach langer Bahnfahrt und in einem Bett.

Mein Geruch ist verdammt geworden, ich war eine
Schnapsfahne in einem wohlbestellten Haus.
Dreimal Baden auch keine Seltenheit. Am Monatsende
bin ich gemieden worden wie ein Kadaver.

Ich habe viel bereut, am meisten aber meinen Geruch.
Am meisten, daß mein Geruch nicht gefallen hat.
Es erzeugt Haß, Rachsucht, Verdammung werden noch so erzeugt.

Odors

I have always loved odors, be it sweat,
morning breath, even excrement,
the dirt of a long train journey and in a bed.

My odor was cursed. I was
a whiff of schnapps in a lovely house.
Bathing three times a day was not unheard of.
By month's end I was avoided like a cadaver.

I have regretted much, mostly my odor.
Mostly that my smell has failed to please.
It inspired hatred, vengeance, damnation as well.

Im Lot

Eine andere Nacht. Was ins Lot kommt,
vom vielen Schlaf und im Schlaf kommt,
nimm das an. wird eines nachts dich heilen.

Du sollst ja nicht weinen.

Was vom vielen Tag und bei Tag kommt,
aber du sollst ja nicht weinen,
wenn es alle Tage auch kommt,
versuch es zu kennen, es will heilen.

What Comes Right

Another night. What comes right
with a lot of sleep and with sleep comes,
grab hold of that. Some night it will heal you.

You mustn't cry.

What comes with many days and during the day,
though you mustn't cry
if it comes every day,
try to see that, for it will heal you.

Memorial

Die Dinge
der Korb für das Brot
das Einmaleins des Morgens
und die zwei Schalen
weißt du das Einmaleins
des Morgens noch
wer gibt dir die Hand
über den Tisch
wo ist es aufgehoben

In meinen schlaflosen Nächten
räuchere ich die Wohnung aus
mit Ministranten
noch immer gebe ich die
Trinkgelder und halte
die Stürme ab
es gewittert nur noch
in meiner Erinnerung
die Straßenreinigung kommt
die wäscht eine Gasse
die aufwärts führt
aber deine Hände um meinen
Hals und die Erde an meinem
Gesicht von den Blumen,
jemand ruft nach der Polizei
ich rufe zum Himmel
daß diese Hände sich lösen
die meine Schreie ersticken.

Memorial

Things,
the basket for the bread,
the one-times-one of morning,
and the two cups.
Do you still know
the one-times-one of morning?
Who gives you her hand
across the table?
Where is it lifted?

In my sleepless nights
I smoke up the apartment
with my acolytes.
I still leave a tip
and hold off
the storms.
It only thunderstorms
in my memory.
The street cleaners come.
They wash a street
that travels uphill,
but your hand is on my throat
and the earth of the flowers
upon my face.
Someone calls the police.
I scream to high heaven
for this hand to loosen itself
which is choking off my screams.

Was ist aus meinem Garten
geworden, wer hat meine
Blumen ausgerissen,
die blauen vor allem, die
erst blühen sollten,
und meine Kinder
hätten sie beinahe gesehen.

What has happened to my garden?
Who has ripped up
my flowers? Especially
the blue ones which should
blossom first, and which my children
should have seen by now.

Zürichsee

Zwei drei große stumme Schiffe ziehen vorbei
der Steuerbescheid, Ummeldung getan
die Fremdenpolizei hat sich in Seevögel angestellt
ein Wellenschlag ins Wasser: Steuerbescheid
Meldungen, Wohnsitze
Der See verschlammt, Liebe verschlammt
über die Seestraße zieht die Nachtbahn
mit aufgeblendeten Scheinwerfern
zwei der größten Schiffe ziehn vorbei
das Wasser [– –] trägt, wo nichts
nichts mehr hält, was versprochen war

Zurich Lake

Two or three great silent ships plow
past customs, registering a new address.
The police have organized a wave
of water fowl in the water: tax forms,
registration, street address.
The lake silts up, love silts up,
along the strand the night train moves
with its high beams on.
Two of the largest ships sail by,
the water bearing _____, where nothing
holds nothing of what was promised.

Grippe und andere Krankheiten

Andere Krankheiten
zehn auf einmal
hab du, zehn auf einmal
sei krank die Zehn sperrangelweit
Schorf, am Bein ein Klopfzeichen
im Bauch Wackersteine
in der Brust Sechseläuten
im Arm Goldfieber
im Finger den Span
in der Nase den
in den Augen
die belegte Welt, speichelnde
in den Augen die Finsternisse
vom letzten Weltuntergang
aber im Kopf,
aber zuoberst
den Stein am Bein
im Kopf
einen Druck,
daß das Universum
beinah durchschaut auffliegt
wie ein bilanzfälschendes Unternehmen
der ganze orbiscato
kakophonicus
vitte
eine andere Krankheit
Ach.

Flu and Other Illnesses

Other illnesses
you have, ten
all at once, ten
afflict you all at once, oozing
scorf, a bruise on the legs,
in the stomach, lumps of stone,
in the breast, a marching procession,
in the arm, gold fever,
in the finger, a splinter,
in the nose, the _____,
in the eyes
the beleaguered world seeping
into the eyes the darkness
from the last cataclysm,
but in the head,
above all
in the rock hard noggin,
in the head
a sense
that the universe
reveals itself almost transparently
as an imbalanced undertaking,
a complete orbiscato
kakophonicus
vitte,
another illness.
Alas.

Diavolezza

Das Seil reißt, zur Diavolessahütte

Die Teufelshütte erreichen,

Das Seil, das Seil

Grog trinken, Fahnen ausatmen
und im Schnee die Hunde
balgen sich, verbellen die Luft
verschnattern die Luft die Grogtrinker
auf der Teufelshütte
das ist ein Heimweg,
anvertraut einem Seil,
das führt heim, da hängt
am Seil eine Menschentraube
und fährt
rast, das Seil,
in der Hölle

Oben treibt ein Papier
an Schienen fressen die Dohlen,
da treibt ein Blatt drauf
steht
Geschenkt ist
der Tod

Diavolezza

The cable pulls us towards the Devil's Hut

as we reach the Devil's Hut

the cable, the cable …

Drinking grog, as flags relax
and in the snow the dogs
roll around, barking at the air,
the air of the grog drinkers full of chatter
inside the Devil's Hut,
the way home
entrusted to a cable
that carries one home, a human
bunch hanging from the cable,
and traveling
with ease on the cable
through hell.

Above, a piece of paper floats in the air,
on the cables the jackdaws gnaw,
on one piece
it says,
A gift
for Death.

Tessiner Greuel

Ich hatte da ein schönes Haus.
Dann wurde der Zugang gesperrt.
Die Kleider habe ich aus dem Staub
habe ich aufgehoben, einem Ärmeren geschenkt,
die bloß Kleider brauchen.
(Steht mir nicht, kein Zynismus.)

Enteignet, Zuzug gesperrt.
Baustellen, keine Einfahrt.
Kleider nachgeworfen, ein
Teller dazu, danke gesagt,
obwohl wegen harter Erdberührung
alles zerbrochen.

Blühender Bezirk, auf
der Durchreise ein totes Kind,
rasch beerdigt, wegen Sommergästen.
In den prächtigen Obstgärten
haben die Freunde sich rechtzeitig
zur Ruhe gesetzt.

Ticino Nightmare

There I had a beautiful house.
Then the entrance was locked.
I lifted my clothes from the dust,
gave them away to someone poorer
who only needed clothes.
(Cynicism does not suit me.)

Dispossessed, a refugee wandering.
Construction sites, no entrance allowed.
Clothes thrown away, a plate
as well, a thank you said,
although when something hits the ground
everything goes to pieces.

The neighborhood blossoming, on
the through journey a dead child,
buried quickly because of summer guests.
To the splendid fruit garden
the friends have retired
right on schedule.

Julikinder

Kraft unsrer Kraft ungeborenen,
meine Kinder im Juli, die Ungeheuer
die zappeln mit dem verstümmelten Bein, man weiß nicht,
den Beinstumpf, man weiß nicht,
den verlorenen Kopf.
Kraft unsrer Kraft
den Kopf verloren,
meine lieben Kinder
nichts gelehrt hätt ich sie
aber verköstigt verliebt gemacht
in andre, in Luft Wind
Tausenderlei im Juli
es wär immer Juli gewesen
ihr Monster genährt
von meiner Zärtlichkeit
die gilt euch Luftgespenstern
Weltveränderern, ihr hättet
sie mir verändert nun mich
auf Tod hin, auf Zärtlichkeit
bis in den Tod für andres
Luft Wind den Fetzen Papier
den ich zerreiße, eh einer lesen
kann was geschehen ist
wie man euch herausgerissen hat aus mir
mich zerrissen, mich den Fetzen
Papier zerrissen, denn noch
kann niemand lesen.

Children of July

Life of our life left unborn,
my children of July, the monsters
toying with mutilated legs, though no one knows,
the stumps, though no one knows,
the head lost.
Life of our life,
the head is lost,
my dear children,
I would not have taught you anything
but fed you and made you loved
by others, be it air or wind,
a thousand times in July,
it would always be July,
you monsters nourished
on my tenderness,
which was only for you,
you mirages, you conjurers, for it was you
who should have changed for me the world,
altering my journey
towards death with tenderness
towards everything else,
air, wind, the scraps of paper
that I rip up before one can read
what has happened,
for just as you were ripped out of me,
I was ripped up, me ripping up,
the scraps of paper
that no one can read.

Das Kind

Gewiß hätte es noch ärmere Kinder
gegeben, da ist immer noch eines,
um das es ärger steht noch stiller ist.
Krüppelkind, es ist an der Zeit,
dich zu begraben, das Grausen
darüber, täglich, von acht bis acht
und auch nachts sind die Türen
noch offen, einzustellen.
Das Schild vorzuhängen. Geschlossen.
Die Vorstellung meiner Dramen,
nie zugänglich, mir selber nicht
hindert mich, zu den zu andern gehen.
Vieles lebt, wird gelebt,
wenn ich dich abschließe,
ist es nicht, weil ich vergesse.
Wir müssen beide aber zur Ruhe kommen,
Du sagst es mir, schon seit langem.
Ich laß Dich in Frieden, nach
einem Vertrag, in dem nach den Wirren
den wahnsinnigsten steht. Hier sind unsere Grenzen.
Mag unsre Natur zuwiderhandeln —
unsre Vernunft ist auch da, die
leise Korrektur vorzunehmen, die
Marksteine hinstellen, nach dem Vertrag.

The Child

Certainly there have been poorer children,
for there is always at least one
who has been less fortunate and is more silent.
Crippled child, it is now time
to bury you, to end the horror
that continues each day, from eight to eight,
and also each night the doors
standing open.
Time to put up the sign. Closed for good.
The presentation of my drama
never open to the public, not even to myself,
prevents me from reaching out to others.
Much lives, and is experienced
if I shut you out,
though it's not because I've forgotten.
We must both come to terms with this,
you've long said so yourself.
I'll let you be, but only after an agreement that includes
the delusions of the maddest. For here is our border.
Our nature enjoys being contrary —
and our good sense is also there,
making small corrections, setting up
milestones, just as agreed.

An Jedem Dritten des Monats

trifft kein Brief ein, als Antwort auf ein Datum,
da könnte geschlachtet werden, oder ein Kind gezeugt werden,
das auch geschlachtet wird, die Kinder merken es nicht.

Dann sagen sie eines Tags, du sollst ja nicht weinen.
Dann läßt man merken eines Tags, für sowas bezahlen wir nicht,
für sowas sind wir nicht da, da sind wir schon weg,
es geht uns nichts an, geht niemand was an.

Eines Tags fährt man in die Mongolei und ist unsichtbar,
für Kinder, die es nicht gibt, zahlen wir nicht,
die fahren alle in die Mongolei, die nicht zahlen wollen.

On the Third of Each Month

no letter arrives to mark a date,
since it could mean slaughter, or a child conceived
who will also be slaughtered, though the children won't notice it.

Then one day they say, you mustn't cry.
They let you mark the day, though for such things we don't pay,
for such things we're not there, since we're already gone,
it means nothing to us, nothing to anyone.

One day you travel to Mongolia and are invisible.
For children who don't exist we don't pay.
All who don't want to pay can travel to Mongolia.

Das Narrenwort

eine Halde das Wort
schlug nieder mit Steinen
in dieser Halde, gekarrt
das Echo, karrte ich's nicht
heraus und wieder,
rufe zu uns,
im Anfang
war es nicht,
es war am Ende.

Die Gnade Morphium,
aber nicht
die Gnade eines Worts
die Gnade Weißbett frischleinen,
aber nicht
die Gnade Handhalten
Noch hielt
keine Hand, kein Wort, die Gnade

A Fool's Word

A slag heap, the word,
beaten down with stones
in this slag heap, the echo
carted off (though I didn't
cart it away again)
calls to us
that it was not
the beginning,
it was the end.

The blessing of morphine,
but not
the blessing of a word,
the blessing of a freshly made bed,
but not
the blessing of holding hands.
And yet no hand,
no word, holds a blessing.

Gloriastrasse

Die Gnade Morphium, aber nicht die Gnade eines Briefs,
die Gnade Menschen, Worte, Sprüche, aber nur im Delirium
die einzige Erscheinung, auf die alles wartet,
bei Lebzeiten kein Wiederkommen mehr, nur die Verklärung

Das Böse, nicht die Fehler, dauern,
das Verzeihliche ist längst verziehen, die Messerschnitte
sind auch so verheilt, nur der Schnitt, den das Böse tut,
er heilt nicht, bricht aus in der Nacht, jeder Nacht,

Gloriastrasse

The blessing of morphine, but not the blessing of a letter,
the blessing of people, words, comforting words, but only
within delirium the single apparition which everyone awaits,
no return while alive, only transfiguration.

Evil, not simply mistakes, lasts,
what can be forgiven is long since forgiven, the blade's cut
has also healed, only the cut made by evil
does not heal, but opens during the night, every night.

Gloriastrasse

Die Gnade Morphium, aber nicht die Wohltat eines Briefs.
Anfragen, Sprüche, gutgemeint von Fremden und Freunden.
Blumen treffen ein über Fleurop. Ein ellenlanges
Telegramm erfordert Anwesenheit, weitab, wer weiß und wozu.

Besucher sitzen, verdammt, im Besuchersessel, erzählen
angestrengt auf die Uhr blickend vor dem Spucknapf und
    hellem Lack,
husten heraus ihren guten Willen und einen alten Witz.

Eine neue Studie über die Kopfjäger ist erschienen.
Nur unter der Hand zu haben, und in den Händen prickelt es schon.
Die große Visite, angeführt von dem Weißmantel, von der Nacht
steht im Zimmer, allein und hebt das Skalpell, immer die Nacht.

Im soundsovielten Jahr dieses Streckbett, im Jahre des Ruhms
der Pyramidenbahnen und der Vermächtnisse beider Nervensysteme,
des dreieinigen Liquors, aus dem die Haßtauben gezüchtet werden,
bei dem Mark, das noch bleiben wird,
bei dem dreieinigen Liquor und dem Mark, das noch bleiben wird,

und was meinen Ruhm, und was Ruh[m], was ihn begründen wird,
hier wo ich aufstehe und meinen Ländern sage, meine
Länder, ihr wartet, und wartet wo?
Bei dem Mark, das mir bleiben wird, dem Zittern
dieser Hand, führ ich es aus, ich töte, ich
führe mein Herz aus mir, ich schicke
es so weit ich kann, ich kann, ich kann
noch weit, es ist ein wilder Muskel, sie
sagen, es schlägt, und schlägt die Türe zu, und
schlägt
wo ich nicht bin, sie finden mich
in Lache in der Lachen schwimmt, und Wissen.

Gloriastrasse

The blessing of morphine, but not the good deed of a letter.
Inquiries, comforting words, well meant by strangers and friends.
Flowers arrive by wire. A tediously long
telegram requires attention, from far away, who knows and why.

Visitors condemned to the visitors chairs chatter away
while glancing tensely at the clock, the spittoon in front of them
with its enameled finish as they cough up their good will and an old joke.

A new study about head hunters has just appeared.
It's only available privately and gives one chills just to hold.
The most important visit, made by the white coat on duty at night
takes place in the room while alone, the scalpel lifted, always at night.

In such and such year of this stretcher, in the year of the glory
of the pyramid charts and the legacy of both nervous systems,
of the triune liquor, to which the doves of hate become addicted,
through the marrow that will remain nonetheless
through the triune liquor and the marrow that will remain nonetheless,

and which will be my glory, the glory that will come to be
here where I stand up and say to my countries, my
countries, you are waiting, and yet waiting where?
Through the marrow that remains in me, the trembling
of this hand, I will kill, I will see it through,
I will let go of my heart, I will send it away
as far as I can, I can, I can,
and still farther, it is a wild muscle, they
say, it beats, and the doors slam shut, and
slam
where I am not, they find me
where laughter is afloat, and knowledge.

und suchen ein Herz, in Kügelchen,
in Glasröhren, in einem Schlamm aus
Blut und einem herausgewürgten einem
ausgespienen zwischen Nadeln und
Flaschen und Bandagen,
sie suchen,
sie suchen, der Weißmantel sucht,
visitiert, und ich schenke ihm
willst du ich will
dein Herz dir schenken,

They seek a heart in a little ball,
in glass tubes, in a mire of
blood, a heart squeezed out,
spit out between needles and
bottles and bandages,
they search,
they search, the white coats search
during their rounds and I give it to them,
would you like it, I'd like
to give you your heart.

Gloriastrasse

für Schwester Ammeli

In einem Bett,
in dem viele gestorben sind
geruchlos, weißhemdig
gepflegt, wie eine
endlose Konversation,
in einem Haus, in dem
es pünktlich zu essen gibt, in dem
die Dame des Hauses
Tod heißt und vielmehr
noch leiden. Und erlegt
ist das Depositum von vielen tausend

Im Morphiumrausch
unter Schmerzen, die
keine Wunde verlangen,
keine Verbeugung, kein
Autogramm, keine Menschlichkeit
kein Triumph, ein himmelschreiender wahnsinniger
       Anblick [- -]
Zwischen Visiten
Visiten, besucht
mich doch
ihr himmelschreienden

Im Leeren, wenn das
Telefon nie geht, wenn
das sterilisierte Gespräch
Dosen verabreicht, Zäpfchen, Verbände,
Tropfen, Dosen, Schmerz der
aber hat keine Dosis,

Gloriastrasse

for Nurse Ammeli

In a bed
in which many have died
odorlessly, fitted out
in a white smock,
like an endless conversation
in a house in which
dinner is served punctually,
the lady of the house
is Death and many more
suffer, the deposit
is paid by many thousands.

Lost in the haze of morphine,
feeling pains that require
no wounds,
no curtsy, no autograph,
no humanity, no triumph,
a moment of madness howling at heaven...
between rounds
and more rounds,
visit me,
you howling souls.

In this emptiness
when the phone does not ring,
when the sterilized talk
injects another dose, suppositories, bandages,
drops, doses, though pain
has no dose,

Wenn es ein einziges Wort
gibt, das manchmal, ein
wenig einen Spalt des Inferno
öffnete, Schwester, und Schwester,
Und ein Gesicht
hat, das gibt
dir zu trinken,
und du beugst
dich über seine
Hand, und wagst
nicht zu sagen
welche Wohltat
unter den geringsten
die größte ist,

if there were a single word
that sometimes would
open a crack in this inferno
it is "Nurse, nurse,"
presenting a face
that gives you
something to drink
as you bend
over its hand
and you are
unable to say
which good deed
among the smallest of gestures
means the most.

[Nach vielen Jahren]

Nach vielen Jahren
nach viel erfahrenem Unrecht,
beispiellosen Verbrechen rundum,
und Unrecht, vor dem nach Recht
schreien sinnlos wird.

Nach vielen Jahren erst, alles
gewußt, alles erfahren,
alles bekannt, geordnet, gebucht,
jetzt erst geh ich da, lieg ich da,
von Stromstößen geschüttelt,
zitternd über das ganze Segeltuch
ganz Haut, nach keinem Ermessen,
in meinem Zelt Einsamkeit,
heimgesucht von jeder Nadelspitze,
jeder Würgspur, jedem Druckmal,
ganz ein Körper, auf dem die Geschichte
und nicht die eigne, ausgetragen wird,
mit zerrauftem Haar und Schreien, die
am Bellevue die Polizei dem Krankenwagen
übergibt, auf Tragbahren geschnallt, im Regen,
von Spritzen betäubt, von Spritzen
ins Wachen geholt, ins Begreifen,
was doch niemand begreift.

Wie soll einer allein soviel erleiden können,
soviele Deportationen, soviel Staub, sooft hinabgestoßen
sooft gehäutet, lebendig verbrannt, sooft
geschunden, erschossen, vergast, wie soll einer
sich hinhalten in eine Raserei
die ihm fremd ist und der heult über eine erschlagene Fliege.

432

[After many years]

After many years,
after having seen so much injustice,
now everywhere countless crimes
and injustice, about which it would be
senseless to raise a hue and cry.

After many years, for the first time,
everything known, having seen everything,
everything familiar, orderly, set up,
now for the first time I go there, I lie there,
convulsed with electrical shocks,
trembling upon the entire sail cloth,
the entire skin, from end to end
there in my tent of loneliness,
afflicted by every injection,
every trace of choking, every pressure mark,
the entire body, on which a history,
and not only mine, is inscribed,
with a bundle of rent hair and screams which
the police hand over to the ambulance at Bellevue,
buckled to a stretcher in the rain,
numbed by injections, awakened
by injections, made aware
of what no one is aware of.

How can one bear so much by oneself,
so many deportations, so much dust, so often knocked down,
so often flayed, burned alive, so often
tortured, shot, gassed, how should one
handle oneself amid a rage
that seems strange to one who howls over a swatted fly.

Soll ich aufhören, da zu sein, damit dies aufhört.
Soll ich die Qual mir abkürzen, mit 50 Nembutal,
soll ich, da ich niemand in die Hände falle,
aus allen Händen fallen, die morden

Shall I cease living so that this stops?
Shall I end the agony with 50 Nembutal?
Shall I, since I fall into no one's hands,
fall out of all hands, those that murder, too?

Tagschwester, Nachtschwester

Danke meine Schwester
die mich weckt und lacht
die mein Gesicht wahr gesehen
hat und es wiedergespiegelt
hat durch Blässe, Stummheit.

Meine Schwestern sehen zuviel
sind näher am Bett, sie sehn
daß in meinen Augen der Raum
stehn bleibt und seine [– –]
in mich bohrt, sehn, daß
die Wand auf mich zufällt
und mir den Ziegel ins

Meinen Schwestern, deren Namen
einmal auch von mir vergessen
sein werden, nicht für Dienstag
Wohltat, Können, sondern
fürs Ertragen eines so flüchtigen

Day Nurse, Night Nurse

Thank you, nurse,
who wakes me and laughs,
who has seen my true face
and mirrored it back to me
through paleness, muteness.

My nurses see too much,
they are closer to my bed, they see
that in my eyes the emptiness
remains and its _____
bores into me, they see that
the wall crumbles onto me
and the bricks as well.

My nurses, whose names
I will also one day
forget, not because of your service,
kindness, capability, but rather
for your tolerance of someone so fleeting.

Für Ingmar Bergman, der von der Wand weiß

Ich hab die Wahrheit
gesehen, von einer
Riesenklapper
schlange umhalst
und verschlungen von
einer Riesenschlange
die in ihrem Bauch
sie aufbläht und
langsam vergehen
verenden läßt, sie
verzehrt.

Ich habe die Wand
gesehn und geschrien
in meinem weißen
weißen Bett, an das
keiner kam, ich
habe in einem weißen
weißen Bett gelegen
und geschrien weil
alle Orkustiere es
abgesehen hatten auf mich
die Kröten, die
Würmer, die [– –]
die Saurier, und das
schlug um sich mit Flügel und Flosse

Ich hab keine Worte mehr
nur Kröten, die springen
heraus und schrecken, nur
Habichte, die stürzen
hinaus, nur reißende

For Ingmar Bergman, Who Knows About The Wall

I have seen
the truth
throttled by
a giant rattlesnake,
swallowed by
a giant snake
which swells it
in its belly
and slowly
lets it
expire, and be
consumed.

I have seen
the wall and howled
in my white
white bed, which
no one visited, I
having lain in my white
white bed
and howled because
all the fiends of hell
have been sicked on me,
the toads, the worms, the _____
the saurian, and everything
that flaps its wings and fins.

I no longer have any words,
only toads that jump out
and frighten me, only
hawks that swoop down
from above, only wild

Hunde wilde, wie's keine
mehr gibt, Bluthunde,
die fallen euch an
die johlen und
meine Mundgeburten
in lieblicher Bläue
und bei Frost der
abgemähten Liebesfelder
Liebe, die große Merde
alors, das düngt einen
Wahnsinn, in dem
meinetwegen, alles,
meinetwegen alles,
zugrund gehen soll.

gnashing dogs like one sees
no longer, blood hounds
that attack you,
that bay as
my mouth turns
a lovely blue
with the frost
of the mown fields of love,
love, the great *merde*,
alors, which fertilizes a
madness in which,
as far as I can see, everything,
the way I see everything,
is destroyed.

Die Drogen, die Worte

Sprachs,
und die Kröte sprang
auf den Tisch,
Blies das Steichholz aus,
und der Blitz
fuhr unter den Tisch,
hob das Glas,
und der Tropfen
ging über ins Meer,
das heißt Tränen,
keine getrocknet,
das heißt Meer,
ein anderes,
es gibt nur eins,
und die Leiden sind
nicht die großen, an
den Päpsten, den Ideen
den Blöcken, die sind
eine Qual den Gesunden.

Die Kranken wissen,
daß eine Farbe, ein Lufthauch,
ein harter Schritt, ja ein
Grasgewimmer der Welt
schon das Herz umdreht im
Leib, und drüber hoffen
sie auf den Frieden, die
mehr Krieg fühlen, als Krieg geführt wird.
Sie haben gern
die weißen Kleider
der Schwestern.

The Drugs, The Words

Said it,
and the toad leapt
onto the table,
blew the match out
and the lightning
struck under the table,
lifted the glass,
and the drop
spilled into the sea,
meaning tears,
none of them dried,
which means a sea,
something quite other,
though there's only one,
suffering not being
the worst thing
to popes, to ideas,
to states, but rather
a torture for the sane.

The sick know
that a color, a breath of air,
a hard step, indeed a
whimper of grass in the world
turns the heart inside
the body, causing them to hope
for peace the more they sense
war, as the war goes on.
They love
the white uniforms
of the nurses.

Sie hoffen, daß
in dem Weißen
etwas gut wird.
Sie sind keine
Weißen.

They hope that
from the white
something good will come.
They are not
white at all.

[Verschwinden soll ich]

Verschwinden soll ich,
sagt man mir, dahin,
und gestoßen, verschwind ich
noch nicht, ich will noch
einmal zufliegen auf
die Terrasse,

Ich habe nicht geschweigen,
weil Schweigen gut ist schön ist,
ich hatte nichts mehr zu sagen

Ich hatte das Maß, ich schweig
weil ich nichts mehr zu sagen hatte.
Das Maß, das ist ein rechtes Ver-
hältnis, ein Pfund wiegt dort ein
Pfund, eine Menge ist dort eine
Menge, ich war ich, ich fürchte
mich kaum, ich war also
nicht mehr ich, keine Nahrung
mehr für das Ich und Eure
unersättliche Gesellschaft, meine
Zeit.

Ich hatte alles, und habe alles
verloren, zuerst das Maß,
ich ging über mich hinaus
und hinaus über alles,
ich wußte nicht, daß ein Mensch
diesen Schmerz beweisen kann mit
seinem Traum, daß er so sterben
kann, daß die Himmel ins
Stürzen kommen, und ein Himmel
ins All abgelenkt wird,
mein unsterbliches Herz.

[I should disappear]

I should disappear,
someone tells me, in there,
though, knocked down, I still
don't disappear, wanting
to flee once more
to the terrace.

I have not remained silent
because silence is good, is beautiful.
I simply had nothing more to say.

I had my standards, I was silent
because I had nothing more to say.
Standards, that's a good an-
alogy, a pound weighs
a pound, a quantity is
a quantity, I was I, I was hardly
afraid, I was therefore
no longer myself, there being nothing more
for the self and your insatiable
society to feed on, my
times.

I had everything and now have
lost everything, first my standards.
I am cut off from myself
and from everything else.
I didn't know that a person
could manifest this pain with
a dream, that one could
die, that the heavens
can collapse, and a heaven
can disappear into thin air,
my immortal heart.

Ich wußte nicht, daß
ihm jeder Mord unter
die Haut geht und
bei Tag und Nacht die
Kranken mit ihrem
erschöpften einsamen
Gewimmer seine Genossen
sind, daß man so in
den Wirbel rückt
und die Jammertäler
seine einzige Landschaft
sind.
Ich wußte nicht, daß man
nichts mehr sehen kann
und hören,
alles verloren,
darüber hinaus,
mit einem Sprung aus
dem Fenster, einem
Mal am Hals, einem
gekreuzigten Körper
und zuwenig Freisprüche sind,
für ihn zuwening

und bettle und wein,
seht ihr's, aber ich hab
nicht die große Musik
die abführt einen der den Abgang
nicht findet, in den Schlaf,
in den Tod.
Verklärung — für uns nicht,
für die anderen, die
Figuren, die sind reiner,

I didn't know that
every murder remains
under one's skin
and night and day
the sick with their
exhausted lonely
whimpers are the murderer's
comrades, or that one
retreats into such a hell
and that the valley of sorrow
is one's only
landscape.
I didn't know that one
can no longer see
and hear,
everything lost,
gone for good
with a leap out
the window, a
mark on the throat, a
crucified body
and not enough acquittals,
not enough.

I am begging and crying,
you see, but I don't have
the grand music
that leads one out who can't find
the exit in sleep,
in death.
Transfiguration — not for us,
but for others, those figures
who are purer,

Wo ich nicht sein kann.
Nämlich ich bin auf
diesem Papier, und in
dem Wort, das ich gebe.
denn das Papier, das flattert,
da kann ich auch nicht ruhen,
und ich flattere auf Fetzen
den Weg daher, dahin, da
wickelt einer sein blutiges
Messer hinein, damit's niemand
sieht.

who are where I cannot be,
since in fact I am here
upon this paper, and in
the word that I write,
for as the paper rustles,
I cannot be quiet,
and I rustle along with the scraps
on the way there, inward, where
someone wraps up a bloody knife
so that no one
sees.

Mit einem dritten sprechen

und ich habe den Tod
gewählt, für alle Ge-
ständnisse ihn, hab ihm
erzählt, diesem wahnwitzigen
Tod, den ich nicht vor-
stellen kann, den ich
rasch herbeiführen, aber
nie vorstellen kann, hab
ihm erzählt.

Der Tod, dem ich erzählt
der ist ist dreißig Tabletten
bitter, der ist einen
Fenstersturz lang, und
ich sag ihm, wenn wir
allein sind, er so lang
einen Sturz lang, er
so kurz, einen Schlaf lang,
bis er dem Schlaf die
Sorge abnimmt um
mich, ich erzähl diesem
Dritten.
Ich sag: mach mir seinen
Mund vor, und dieses Aug,
mach mir vor wie es war,
mach es mir rückgängig,
mach mir vor, wie
ich sag:
Noch einmal, und
ich bin.

To Say To A Third

And so I have chosen
death, confessing everything
to him, telling it all
to him, this crazy
death, which I can't
imagine, which I quickly
bring to pass, but
never can imagine, I've
told him everything.

The death I have told
is as bitter as thirty
tablets, high as the leap
from a window, and
I say to him when we're
alone, he's as high
as a leap is high, he
is short as the sleep
is short until he
takes away my anxieties,
in sleep, I say to this
third one,
I say: show me
your mouth and eye,
show me how it was,
show it to me again,
show me,
I say:
Once more, and
here I am.

[ausgeraubt]

ausgeraubt
dem Entsetzen sich ergeben
nicht ihm widerstehen
sternhell das Fleisch,
im Mund den
lauen Geschmack,
eine Erektion, ein
aufgerecktes Glied
muß noch in der Welt
sein, das in diesem
Mund zugut sich
nicht ist, die Begier
ist unendlich, jeden
unter sich, über sich
wissen, jeden, der
dunkel ist, nur nichts
Helles, das Fleisch ist
hell genug.

Auf Deiner Brust habe
ich die Messe gelesen,
in deinen Augen habe
ich mich verwandelt, eine
Taube, ich bin einfach
hineingeflogen,
die Hostie war ein
steifes Glied,
ich verstand
nichts, nur
diese Religion,
Ich habe Genie
wo andere
einen Körper haben

[Ransacked]

Ransacked,
surrendering to the horrible
not in protest,
the flesh bright as a star,
in the mouth
the lukewarm taste,
an erection, an
erect member
must still live
on, even when not
in this mouth, the craving
endless, each one
beneath you, above you
knows, each one that
is dark, nothing bright
at all, the flesh being
bright enough.

Upon your breast
I read the mass,
in your eyes
I have transformed myself, a
dove, I simply flew
inside,
the host was a
stiff member,
I understood
nothing, only
this religion.
I have a genius
where others
have a body,

Hostie, in den Mund geschoben
das Glied, und eine
Kunst, die nicht die
andren aufreißt, das Gestirn
und das Gestirn der anderen
die Menschen sind unendlich
sie dürfen, wie ich, nicht
sterben.

a host shoved in the mouth,
the member, and an
art which the others
could not tear up, the constellation
and the constellation of the others,
humans being eternal,
not having, like myself,
to die.

Meine Zelle

Wo die anderen Körper
haben, hatte ich Genie

Aus meinem rauchenden
Blut wird etwas
entspringen, da kann
einen Tag die Welt
retten.

Jedes Gefühl in mir
haben sie ausgeräuchert,
ich weiß nicht was warm
oder kalt oder blau
ist. Ich hör einen einzigen
hohen Ton, auch wenn die
Musik nicht angeht, Ich sehe
tränengrau, wo die
anderen Farben [– –]

Ich denke nichts, solang
will ich nichts denken, bis
die Schmach weggenommen
getilgt ist
bis die Beschimpfungen
genommen sind von mir.

Man hätte mit mir, mit
jeder meiner Zellen
eine Himmelfahrt machen
können. Das Meßopfer
auf meiner Wunden
auf meiner Brust die
Litanei der Bitten

My Cell

Where the others have a body,
I had genius.

From my smoking blood
something will spring,
which one day can save
the world.

They have smoked out
every feeling inside me,
I don't know what warm
or cold or blue
is. I hear a single
high tone, even when
no music plays. I see
the gray of tears where
others see colors ....

I think of nothing, and
I want to think of nothing until
the shame is taken away,
eradicated,
until the insults
are taken from me.

One could have made of me,
made each of my cells
into a place of ascension.
The sacrificial mass
consisting of my wounds,
upon my breast
the litany of prayer,

und Vergebung ist noch
nicht dargebracht.

Ich sage Euch, und nicht
durch Blumen daß
die Litanei fehlt und
daß ich warte auf den
Kniefall und die Gerechtigkeit
und daß ein Freispruch
nur von mir kommen
kann.

o wie richt ich, wie
habe ich gerichtet, dreihundert
eine Million Minuten
und kommen 300 Tage und
immer neue Tage, und ich
gebe nicht frei, was mich
nicht freigibt, spreche nicht
frei, was mich tagtäglich
nachtnächtlich zur Leidenschaft
verurteilt,

and yet forgiveness
is not granted.

I say to you all, and not
through flowers, that
the litany is missing and
I await the bended knee and justice,
and that an acquittal
can only come
from me.

O how I judge, how
I have judged, three hundred,
a million minutes,
and still 300 days, and
always new days, and I
don't let go of what
won't let go of me, nor acquit
that which day after day,
night after night, condemns me
to such rage.

Abschied

Wir werden die Fernsten sein, kein Gruß
mehr wird erwidert, kein Wort ist wert, noch
verwendet zu werden. Auch die Mikrobe unter
dem Glas, auch das Kaninchen, an dem
ein Versuch tödlich ausgeht, das
zuckend und vergiftet keine Herrgötter
mehr rufen kann, sind meine Genossen,
ich such alle Mißbrauchten Geschöpfe
die Ausgedienten, und das weggeworfene Glas,
die verramschten Kleider, die ausgebrannten zum Himmel
    schreienden
Häuser, und richte mich ein mit dem Überflüssigen,
Dies alles ist meinesgleichen.
Man übt Nächstenliebe an uns, man flickt uns zusammen,
man flößt uns Vertrauen ein und stellt
uns auf einen anderen Platz.

Dieser Platz ist gut, da sind wir nur
noch dem Sterben erreichbar, ein dummes Kaninchen,
eine zerdrückte Laus, ein seliges Herz,
der nackten Angst nicht mehr erreichbar,
mit dem Armenkittel der Nächstenliebe bedeckt.

Farewell

We will be distant from each other, no greeting
will be answered, no word will still be
worth exchanging. Also the microbe under
glass, the rabbit who dies while
being experimented upon,
twitching and poisoned and unable to
call upon any gods, these are my comrades,
for I seek all the abused, exhausted,
the used up, and the thrown away glass,
the dirt-cheap clothes, the burned out houses
howling at heaven, aligning myself with the discarded.
All of these are the same as me.
Charity is practiced upon us, we're lumped together,
instilling trust in us all and taking us
to another place.

That place is good, for there only death
can reach us, a mute rabbit,
a squashed louse, a blessed heart,
naked fear no longer able to reach us
wearing the simple smock of charity.

[Ich trete aus mir]

Ich trete aus mir
hervor, aus meinen Augen
Händen, Mund, ich
trete hervor aus
mir, eine Schar
von Güte und Göttlichem
die diese Teufeleien
gut machen muß,
die geschehen sind

[I step outside myself]

I step outside
myself, out of my eyes,
hands, mouth, outside
of myself I
step, a bundle
of goodness and godliness
that must make good
this devilry
that has happened.

[Ich habe die Feder]

Ich habe die Feder
wieder in der Hand
härter gespitzt in
Gesichter springend
und zurück ins eigene
Gesicht, ich kratze, reiße, schärfe
ein grausames Lied
und richte an ein
Blutbad in den [– –], die Verachtung in
der siebten
Mano hatte.
Ma tu
A ci
und künstlich, auch
nicht mehr, was einem
leid tut um mich,
und leid um alles
und nichts,
es gibt ja nichts
was nicht vor dem Abend
stirbt, was wißt
ihr, sterbt nicht
vor dem Abend,

[I have the quill]

I have the quill
again in my hand,
sharpened to a finer point,
leaping into faces
and turning back to its own
face. I scratch, rip, sharpen
an awful song
and initiate
a bloodbath in the _____, the contempt
of the seventh
Mano.
Ma tu
A ci
and also no longer
faking what
grief I suffer,
grieving over everything
and nothing,
for there is nothing
that cannot die before
evening, which
you know. Don't die
before evening.

Die Lebenslinie

Mir träumt da nachts

Da träumt mir heute nacht
in meiner Hand deutet mir einer sei sie kurz
abgebrochen, es riß hinein, und ich sah ein
zwei Tode drei Tode, alles
Tode
und drückte morgens den nassen Lappen
an die Stelle, ich zog das Fenster
auf, das kam auch auf die Stelle
ich setzt' den Tee auf, das kam
auch auf diese Stelle, alles
berührte diesen Riß und
so sah ich's im Wachen:

Ich will zerfallen wie altes Kleid
an den Gelenken brüchig werden
schrumpfen, so schrumpft der Apfel, klein uralt und steingrau
werden und eines Tags gebückt mich
unter eine Wurzel legen und lachen
aller Tode, und nicht gewaltsam, auslöschen
so daß ich kaum merk, wo ich anfang
aufzuhören, wo ich aufhöre, anzugehören

The Life Line

Each night I dream of it.

Tonight I dream of it.
In my hand I see something, the line short,
broken off, ripped apart, and I see one,
two deaths, three deaths, everything
dead
and in the morning I press the damp cloth
on the spot. I open the window,
that also relates to the spot.
I set out the tea, that also
relates to the spot. Everything
connects to this severing, and
thus I see while awake:

I want to collapse like an old dress,
to have fragile joints,
to shrivel up, shrivel like an apple, to become
small, ancient and stone gray, and one day bend over
to lie beneath a root and laugh at
all the deaths and expire, not violently,
so that I hardly notice where I begin
to cease, where I cease, then belong.

Die Folter

Sprachs
und das Licht
ging aus,
schriebs, und
ein Mensch zerfiel
ein altes Kleid

The Torture

Spoken
and the light
went out,
written, and
a person crumpled
like an old dress.

Die Folter

Wer ißt mit meinem Löffel
wer liegt in meinem Bett
wer verzehrt mein Pfund
Liebt, wer sonnt sich in
meiner Sonne. Und wo ist diese Sonne?
Die ist fern.
Nämlich ich
bin, wo ich
nicht sein kann.
Ach der duldet's, der
mich einen kurzen jahrelangen
Augenblick auch nicht
geliebt hat, der duldet,
seht ihr Freunde
seht ihrs nicht
ich überall mein
mein Grab zu schaufeln anfang,
auch in dieses Papier ein-
ritze meinen Namen und
denke, daß ich ruhen möchte
noch immer nicht, daß ich nie
zur Ruh komm, daß
das dauert, dieses Eisen
im Leib, diese Faust auf
dem Schädel, diese Geisel
am Rücken, die macht
daß der Kurfürstendamm
in ein grelles Gelächter
ausbricht, aus tausend Reklamen
schreit, daß der heiße Kaffee
mir über die Hand gegossen
wird, daß man mir die

The Torture

Who is eating with my spoon,
who is lying in my bed,
who spends my pound,
who loves, who suns herself
under my sun. And where is the sun?
It's far away.
In fact I
am where I
cannot be.
Oh he can stand it, who
for a moment that seemed
like a year did not
love me, he can stand it,
my friends,
don't you see?
I have begun
to dig my grave,
also scratching my names
into this paper and
thinking I only want to rest
but never will, that I will never
find peace, that it
will last, this iron
in my gut, this fist upon
the skull, this whip
upon the back, causing
the Kurfürstendamm
to break out in shrill
laughter, howling from
a thousand billboards that hot coffee
is poured onto my hand,
that my skin

Haut abzieht, daß man
mich ins Fleisch schneidet,
mir die Knochen bricht,
und mich einmauert,
da sägt ein kleiner Hai
da spring ich ins Wasser,
der frißt mich, mich
frißt ein größerer Hai
ein Raubfisch, der
heißt Schmerz.
Und ich wieg, ohne
Verstand, meinen Kopf
darüber. Da unten,
ein Schiff, das fährt,
das seh ich, seht ihr's Freunde?

is ripped off, that my
flesh is cut,
my bones broken,
and me entombed,
a small shark slicing by,
me jumping into the water,
he eating me as I am
eaten by a larger shark,
a predator called
pain.
And I rock back and forth,
not understanding, my head
bent over this. There below
is a ship that sails.
I see it. Do you see it, my friends?

Mild und leise

Eine andere Nacht, die vor der letzten.
Mit einem anderen Atem, der kommt schneller
als Atem sonst geht

seht ihrs Freunde, seht ihrs nicht?
Wie das Auge, wie der Atem, fühlt
und seht ihrs, nicht mehr schauen,
schon erdrosseln schon geschirrn
sie mich, und im Geschirr läuten
nicht die Narrenglocken, ist auch
nicht die Zeit dafür, war einmal,
und der Mund, eingerissen an den Winkeln,
mit den Apparaten allen, messen, leuchten
schreiben Schriften über mich, das
liest sich, schleift auf dem Boden
Inhalt keiner.

Gently and Softly

One more night, the one before the last.
With another breath that comes faster
than breath.

Don't you see it, my friends, don't you see?
How the eyes, how the breath, don't you
feel and see, no longer look,
they having already strangled, already
harnessed me, and in the harness one doesn't
hear the fool's bells since this is not
the time for that like it once was,
and the mouth, ripped at the cheeks
with all the apparatus, measured, lit up,
a script written upon me, which
reads: drag across the ground,
no content.

Mild und leise

Wenns auch nur anhebt
anhebt, mild und leise,

Seht ihr's Freunde, seht
ihr's nicht? denn

wer möchte leben,
wenn er zu Atmen
nicht hat, das schwarze
Segel immer aufgezogen

Wer möchte leben
wenn er nicht zu Atmen hat,
das schwarze Segel immer aufgezogen.
den Tag nur eine Nacht
die Nacht nur Tag,
wenn alles geht und
nicht mehr kommt und
nie mehr kommen wird.

Am Tag, die Wüstenei
geliebt noch so gehaßten

Gently and Softly

When it starts
it starts gently and softly.

Don't you see, my friends, don't
you see? For

who wants to live
when he has no
breath, the black
sail always hoisted.

Who wants to live
when he has no breath,
the black sail always hoisted,
the day only a night,
the night only a day,
when everything goes and
nothing more comes and
never will come again.

During the day, the desolation
so loved, so hated.

Mild und leise

Tot ist alles. Alles tot.
Und in meinem silbernen Brotkorb
schimmelt der vergiftete Apfelputzenschnitz,
der nicht mehr hinunterging.

Auf meinen Tellern, wer ißt davon,
muß noch ein Rest von dem Strick
l[i]egen, der mir gedreht worden ist.
In meinem Bett, wer liegt darin,
muß nachts noch der Zettel rascheln,
den ich eingenäht habe.

Wie wenig Gegenwart! Nur
in den fernen Ge[gen]ständen gehe ich noch um,
in der Lampe, im Licht,
da mach ichs hell und bedeute:

all das Blut, das viele Blut, das
geflossen ist. Meine Mörder.

Gently and Softly

Dead is everything. Everything is dead.
And in my silver bread basket
the poisoned slice of apple which would not
go down gets moldy.

On my plates, whoever eats from them
must also lay down the remains
of the noose that was strung for me.
In my bed, whoever lies in it
must each night rustle the notes
that I have sown.

How small is my presence! Only
in distant objects do I still exist,
in lamps, in light
by which I illuminate and give meaning:

all the blood, so much blood that
has flowed. My murderers.

rostarie

Tot is alles, alles tot.
Gerichtet ist jeder Ort, jeder Gegenstand, jedes halbflügge Gefühl,
das mich vermißt und mir nicht mehr
Rechnung trägt. Ich habe mich eingeschrieben in dich für Lebzeiten
das ist nicht auszutragen,

Consolation Aria

Dead is everything, everything dead.
Condemned is each place, each thing, each half-baked feeling
that passes by me and which I no longer
take into account. I have registered for a life sentence with you
that cannot be carried out.

Habet acht

Laßt mich sterben.
Kartenspielen zur Nacht
ist nichts für mich,
und nichts ist Reden,
in Häusern sitzen mit
Freunden. Fühlt ihr's
Freunde, seht ihr's nicht.

Habet acht, der Tag
kommt wieder, Leiden
nicht mehr, als irgendeiner
leidet, doch habet vielmals
acht.

Mild und leise, [– –] sich
keiner, mild und leise
geht es an, seht ihr Freunde,
seht ihr nicht. Soviel Zeit
ist schon vergangen, und die
Zeit vergeht doch nicht.

Mild und leise, wie das klingt,
klingt noch mehr und klingt allen,
kanns nicht sagen, sag es wieder,
schwarz das Segel, festgezurrt,
keine Welt mehr, nur das eine,
wie das Auge, wie es lebt,
wie ich lebe, nur in Angst,
nur im Zutun, Aug um Auge

Watch Out

Let me die.
Playing cards at night
is not for me,
nor is chatting,
sitting in houses
with friends. Don't you sense
it, my friends, don't you see?

Watch out, the day
will come again. Suffer
no more as just anyone
would suffer, yet still make sure
to watch out.

Gently and softly, _____
no one, gently and softly
it happens, my friends,
don't you see? So much time
has already passed, and yet
the time does not disappear.

Gently and softly, how that sounds,
how it still sounds and to everyone
I cannot say, yet say it again.
Black is the sail, tightly lashed,
no more world, only the one,
like the eye, how it lives,
how I live, only in fear,
only in closing it, an eye for an eye.

Wer wird rechten, nichts von allem,
Sterben, ja, und so entfernt,
keine Frage, keine Antwort,
seht ihr's Freunde, seht ihr's
nicht.

Auf den Nächten wird es heller,
angetrunken wird es wahr. Trinkt
sich ein, betrinkt sich wieder, Aug
um Auge wird es wahr, und das
Ende ist nicht fühlbar, schmerzlos,
wo viel Schmerzen waren, abgewürgt
wird alles wahr, abgetan, Habe, Moneten

Kein Gerede, keine Arbeit,
keine Rache weckt mich auf,
Nur das Auge weckt mich wieder
das Gemurmel weckt es auf,
Fenstersturz, abzustürzen, aufzuschreien
Hinzufallen, auszulöschen,
mild und leise, sag ichs wieder,
sag ich nichts mehr, weckt mich
auf,

Who can set things right, no one.
One can die, yes, but it's so far off,
and there's no question, no answer,
don't you see, my friends, don't you
see?

At night it becomes brighter,
as it's drunken in it becomes more true. Drink
up, drink up again, seen eye
to eye it will turn true, and the
end is not perceivable, painless,
where indeed there had been so much pain, for once
strangled, everything will turn true, be settled, be it possessions, cash.

No talk, no work,
no vengeance awakens me.
Only the eye awakens me,
the murmur awakens me,
plunging from a window, screaming,
falling down, expiring,
gently and softly, as I say again,
say no longer, wake
me.

[Tot ist alles]

Tot ist alles. Alles tot.
Und das Aug ist ausgelaufen, Augen, seid ihr ausgelaufen,
alle Bilder schwimmen fort,
und das Ohren, hört ihr nur mehr Schreie,
Vögel fallen von dem Dach,
stürzen alle Häuser ein,
fallen Flugzeuge vom Himmel,
überschlägt sich Herz um Herz,
stirbt jetzt einer um den andern,

so stirb weg und mach es leise,
mild und leise, seht ihr nicht,
seht ihrs Freunde, seht ihr nichts.

Alle Feste enden anders, Todesfest
im Lebensfest, rasch zurück in tausend Bilder,
ausgebreitet auf dem Bett, und das Bett
von Öl und Salben, vom Erbrechen, Atemnöten,
Blutsturz, Herzschlag ist sein Kampfplatz,
und es schnellen die Ampullen in die Spritzen,
bohren sich die Nadeln in dein Fleisch, und
in die Venen tropft es, in den Muskeln breiten
sich Flüssigkeiten aus, zum Leben,

Und ich höre: weitersterben, weiterleben,
weitersterben, Ah, es zieht ein Tag herauf,
und die Sonne liegt am Felsen, und der Sonnenplatz
ist leer, dort lag ich, ich aß und rauchte,
und ich glaubte, nicht allein
zu sein, ich war es doch schon damals,

[Dead is everything]

Dead is everything. Everything dead.
And the eye runs, eyes, you run,
all images swimming away,
and ears, now you only hear screams,
birds fall from the roof,
all houses collapse,
planes fall from the sky,
heart after heart beats madly,
one after another dies.

So die and do so quietly,
gently and softly,
don't you see, my friends, don't you see?

All celebrations end differently, the celebration of death
in life suddenly reappears in a thousand images
laid out on the bed, and the bed
full of oil and salve, vomit, gasps,
hemorrhaging, and heart failure is its battle zone,
as the vials are hurried into the syringes
and they bore the needle into your flesh, and
into the veins it drops, the flow spreading
into the muscles, coming to life.

And I hear: continue dying, continue living,
continue dying, ah, the day is dawning
and the sun lies on the cliffs, and the solarium
is empty, there I lie, I eat and smoke,
and I believe that I am not
alone, though I certainly was then.

Ein Neues Leben

ein neues Leben, wer, da ichs nicht habe,
wird noch eines haben? Die monotone
Wiederholung eines Kriminalromans
eines, den andre sich ansehn, aber einer
der darin ist, ganz darin,
kein neues Leben, soviel ist sicher.

A New Life

A new life. Who, since I have none,
would like a new life? The monotone
repetition of a mystery novel,
one that others leaf through, but in which
someone lives, completely within,
without a new life, that much is certain.

[Mir leuchtet ein, was letzte Tage sind]

Mir leuchtet ein, was letzte Tage sind.
Vom höchsten Stockwerk schau ich in die Tiefe
vom höchsten Ton gleit ich zum unteren Klang
und [– –] der [– –] scheint die graue Süße
Ist keiner da, der mich vom Fenster ruft.
unter Terrassen wohnt die wunde Tiefe
die Gassenschlucht ist glühend aufgetan

Ich leb von keinem Wort, da reicht man keine Hand
Der schreibt kein Wort mehr in sein Blutbuch

Ein jeder Augenblick hat süße Tiefe

Entwürfe reiner Zeit

und öffnen ihnen dieses Blutenbuch
Von jeder Brüstung seh ich in die Tiefe
Die Männer werfen eine Frau von sich
Wer dem die Freunde auch verstoßen hat
möchte noch schlafen und wer möchte wachen
ihm glänzt das Aug

[It occurs to me what the last days mean]

It occurs to me what the last days mean.
From the highest floor I look into the depths,
from the highest tone I glide to the sound below,
and on the pigeons there appears the grey sweetness.
Is there no one there to tell me to step back from the window?
Beneath the terraces live the wounded depths,
the glowing canyon of the street below.

No word saves me, no hand reaches out to me.
He writes not another word in his book of blood.

Each moment has its sweet depth.

The drafts of a purer time.

Meanwhile they open this book of blood.
From each balustrade I look into the depths.
The men abandon a woman
who was also rejected by friends.
I still want to sleep, and whoever will watch over me
will make my eye shine.

[So stürben wir]

So stürben wir
um ungetrennt, zu sein
Dein Haus muß noch
mein Haus bleiben.
Ich muß dort aus und eingehn
muß dort bleiben,
zum Rechten sehen,
weil sonst niemand sieht
was Deine welken Augen
abends finden, nur mich
ich weiß es, darum muß
das Haus mein Haus
für immer sein, wo
ich auch bin, ich muß
den Abend richten,
und die Gedanken, auf-
helfen in den Schlaf.

[So we might die]

So we might die
still together, for that to be,
your house must still
remain my house.
I must come and go from there,
remain there,
for it to seem right,
since otherwise no one will see
what your weary eyes
find at night, only I will,
for I know it, therefore the house
must also be my house
forever, where
I also am, I must
settle the evening
and one's thoughts, help them
go to sleep.

Enigma

So stürben wir, um ungetrennt,
dessen uns zu erinnern nicht mehr,
was niemand trennen kann. Die Kunst,
ein schmutziges Geschäft
mit den Worten, es wird honoriert werden,
einmal lag ich am Waldrand
und hielt ein paar bekritzelte Seiten
für rein und absolut, sie waren es auch.
Ich bin wieder so weit, seit ich
sehe, was sie treiben mit Worten.
für den lieben Gott, das heißt für die Wiese
und Ameisen und Mückenschwärme, für absolut
zulässig.
Die kleinen Bisse haben mich nicht gestört.

Enigma

So we might die, still together,
that part of us will no longer be remembered
being what no one can take away. Art,
a dirty business
with words, will be paid its honorarium.
Once I lay at the edge of the forest
and held a pair of scribbled pages
as pure and absolute, and they were that as well.
I feel the same again when I
see what they engage in with words.
For the love of God, that means for the meadow
and ants and swarms of gnats, to tolerate them
absolutely.
The small bites have not bothered me at all.

[Wie schwierig ist verzeihen]

Wie schwierig ist verzeihen,
eine so langsame und mühselige Arbeit,
mit der allein ich beschäftigt bin,
seit so vielen Jahren.

Der Haß hat mich krank gemacht,
ich bin entstellt, diese Eiterbeuelen
verbieten es mir, mich noch unter
Menschen zu zeigen.

Ich weiß nur, daß ich
nicht mehr so hassen darf
nicht deinen Tod wünschen,
den ich auch gar nicht wünsche,
oder von meiner Hand,

Ich habe gelernt, daß meine
seine Feinde lieben muß, und
dies ist so leicht, denn wie
sollen den[n] meine Feinde
mir mehr als Böses tun können.
Wenn eine Kugel sich verirrt,
wenn mir einer ins Gesicht spuckt,
wie gestern, habe ich keine Bedenken
gegen die Liebe, die mir verordnet ist.

Ich habe Angst, vor der Liebe,
die du mir eingeflößt hast
in der grausamsten Absicht.
Ganz zersetzt von schneidenden Säuren,
von dem vielen Arsen, dem Opium,
ganz betäubt von meiner Zerstörung.

[**How difficult it is to forgive**]

How difficult it is to forgive,
such a long and tiresome business
with which I have been preoccupied
for so many years.

Hatred has made me sick.
I've been disfigured, these abscesses
check me, show that
I still live among humans.

I only know that I must
not hate so much anymore,
not hope for your death,
which I really don't hope for,
nor by my hand.

I have learned that I must
love my enemies, and
this is so easy, for how
can my enemies do anything
worse than evil to me.
If a bullet misses,
if someone spits in my face,
like yesterday, I have no objection
to the love that is prescribed for me.

I am afraid of the love
that you have instilled in me
with the most horrible of intents.
Completely riven by burning acids,
from so much arsenic, opium,
completely numbed by my destruction.

Da ich in dir nicht mehr lebe,
und ich schon tot bin, wo bin ich.
Die Stäbe zählen, ausharren,
fressen zweimal am Tag, dann
die Notdurft verrichten,
betteln um Mittel,
die mich in jahrlangen Schlaf versenken.

Thus I no longer live in you
and am already dead, where I am.
I count the bars, hang on,
eat twice a day, then
grant myself reprieve,
beg for the means
which will sink me into sleep for a year.

[Seht ihr, Freunde, seht ihrs nicht!]

Seht ihr, Freunde, seht ihrs nicht!
daß ichs nicht überlebt
auch nicht überstanden habe, seht ihrs nicht,
daß ich einwärts gehe, daß
fürderhin einwärts rede, daß
ich mich einziehe, mein Haar
herablasse meine Hände einstreiche
mein Wort einziehe, seht ihrs nicht,
seht ihr,

daß ich mir abgehe, daß ich abwärts
gehe, daß ich mich abgebe,

und schreie, weil die Irren nach
ihren Wärtern tasten suchen, wie
ich nach meinem Wärter

[Don't you see, my friends, don't you see!]

Don't you see, my friends, don't you see!
that I have not survived it,
nor gotten over it. Don't you see
that I have turned inward, that
I am speaking to myself continually, that
I have moved deep inside myself, letting
my hair go, pulling in my hands,
pulling back my words, don't you see it,
don't you see

that I have lost hold of myself, that I am
falling apart, that I have given up,

and howl because the mad seek
to touch their guards, as
I seek to touch mine.

Alla piu umile, alle piu umana, alla piu sofferente

vivere ardendo e non sentire il male
Gaspara Stampa

Meine Schwester soll mir weiterhelfen.
meine Schwester ist nicht weit von hier.
Nur viel Zeiten ferner und so nah bei mir.
Nur viel länger tot ist als ich.

Zu ihr sprech ich seit fast tausend Tagen,
und sie sagt mir, daß ein Ende wird
laß mich schlafen, nie erwachen.

Und sie lebt für mich, sie weiß zu leben,
leidets für mich, wird verhöhnt, geschmäht,
verstoßen und verdammt, sie leidet es.

Ich vertrete nur den Schlaf, den langen.

Die Gnade Morphium, aber nicht die Gnade eines Briefs
die Gnade schmerzt [– –], aber nicht die Hand,
die Gnade Delirium, aber nicht die Rückkehr
um das Böse gutzumachen, bedarf es bloß eines Worts,
um das Böse nicht mehr zu fühlen, bedarf es des Tods.

Meine Schwester hat mich auch verlassen.

Wenn ich aber fühle und hasse, wenn der Haß mich
irrsinnig macht, weil ich so sehr hasse, wenn ich
auf ewig hasse, wie soll ich leben.

Alla piu umile, alle piu umana, alla piu sofferente

vivere ardendo e non sentire il male
Gaspara Stampa

My nurse should help me further,
my nurse is not far away.
Only much further away in time, though still close to me.
Only dead much longer than me.

To her I have spoken for almost a thousand days,
and she says to me that an end will come
that will let me sleep, never to awaken.

And she lives for me, she knows how to live,
she grieves for me, whether made fun of, abused,
pummeled or sworn at, she grieves for me.

Only I stand in the way of sleep, the long one.

The blessing of morphine but not the blessing of a letter,
the blessing hurts _____, but not the hand,
the blessing of delirium, but not of going home.
To right what is wrong, it only takes a word,
to no longer feel it, it only takes death.

My nurse has also abandoned me.

But when I feel such hate, when the hate
drives me insane, because I hate so much, when I
eternally hate, how shall I live?

Als sie von der Engelsbrücke gesprungen war,
und sie hatte ihm schon verziehen, blieb ihr
Schrei stehn. O Scarpia, davanti a Dio.

Nie habe die Burg sehen können, ohne
den Schrei zu hören und wahnsinnigen Folterungen,
nicht nur dieses einen Mario.
Gerechtigkeit, auch für unsere Mörder.

Oft habe ich gedacht, wenn der Haß
stärker war und wenn ich springen
wollte, von der obersten Terrasse,
dich dorthin zu rufen, wo Verzeihung
und Gericht sein könnte.

As she leapt from the Bridge of Angels
and had already forgiven him, her scream
remained. *O Scarpia, davanti a Dio.*

The town could not have seen it without
hearing the scream and the maddening torture,
not only this one was a Mario.
Justice, also for our murderers.

Often I have thought, if the hatred
grew stronger and if I wanted
to leap from the highest balcony,
I would call you there, where forgiveness
and justice could prevail.

Das Strafgesetzbuch Gaspara Stampa

Vivere ardendo e non sentire il male

Der Käfer, aufgespießt, der Schmetterling
ins Album gepreßt, das Blatt zwischen
Buchseiten gelegt —

ermordet die Wirklichkeit, auf feinste Weise,
nur Menschen gestattet, auch das ist
erlaubt, ein Gift zu geben, ich
ich lese im Strafgesetzbuch und
finde keinen Paragraphen, der es
verbietet.

Verloren, verramscht, eine Liebe
ins Versatzamt getragen, nicht mehr
ausgelöst, Opfer abgeschoben, Küsse ausgespuckt
Kranke auf die Straße geworfen, ange-
schrien, mangelndes Verständnis meinerseits,
vorausgesetzt und bedauert.
Im Himmel, wenn es ihn gibt, im
Himmel, was wird da sein.
Und wenn nun gar ein Leidender,
der Gott fern ist, anfängt zu beten,
Kälte, Gelächter,
Votum: ich sehe es kommen, es triumphiert
die nackte Gewalt und

Daß keine meiner Schmerzen ihn bewegt,
kein Schweiß ihn feuchtet, nicht der Todesschweiß
nicht gelbes Fieber, nicht der Scharlachbrand
ihn brennt, ihn brennen macht,
und keine Litanei, und Rufe, Briefe,
Schreie wie nie
gewesen sind, was soll noch mehr sein,

The Penal Code of Gaspara Stampa

Vivere ardendo e non sentire il male

The beetle pinned down, the butterfly
pressed in an album, the leaf laid between
pages of a book —

reality murdered, in the finest ways,
only humans are allowed to do that, though it is also
okay to poison someone,
I read in the penal code and
don't find any paragraph that
forbids it.

Lost, sold off cheap, a love
taken to the pawn shop, never again
allowed out, the victims hauled off, kisses spit out,
sick people thrown onto the street, screamed
at, myself unable to understand,
taken for granted and pitied.
In heaven, if there is one, in
heaven what will there be?
And if now indeed a sufferer,
to whom God is distant, begins to pray,
he encounters coldness, laughter.
I dare say, I see it coming,
naked power triumphing and ....

That none of my pain bothers him,
no sweat off his brow, not the sweat of death,
not that of yellow fever, nor does scarlet fever
burn him, set him afire,
nor is there any litany, any calls, letters,
nor screams
like never before, how much longer can it go on?

Mehr kann nicht mehr sein.

Daß keiner dieser Tode, und kein zer-
fetztes Fleisch, zufassen noch ein
Hirn, das nicht begreifen kann, daß
nicht und niemals, nie es ihn bewegt,
wie kann das sein,

Es kann nun nichts mehr sein.

Ist so ein Mensch, gefallen in die
Nacht, noch einmal aufgestanden,
Sagt es an. Ist so erniedrigt, so gesteinigt
schon einer worden, ja, warum, hat
man ihn nicht getötet, warum nicht,
Warum ihn nicht getötet, weils anders
besser geht,
weil die Verleumdung

It cannot go on much longer.

That a brain conceives of none
of these deaths nor the flesh ripped
apart, that it cannot fathom it, that
not once, never has it bothered him,
how can that be?

It cannot go on much longer.

That a person who fell into
darkness is standing once again,
shout it out. One who was knocked so low,
in fact stoned, indeed, why was
she not killed, why not?
The reason being because
there were other ways,
through slander …

Un altra notte ancora senza vederlo

Daß keiner meiner Schmerzen
ihn beweget
(der Himmel, nein vom
Himmel red ich nie,
also von ihm, da doch vom Himmel
nicht)
daß nichts und nichts und
alles ihn nie bewegt,
kein Sammelsurium von Schmerzen, Ersticken, Angst
ich hab ihn nie gerührt, herbeigerufen
nie,
ich war schon weiß, schon kalt,
ihn hat es nie gerührt,
ich war so weiß nicht, nie so kalt,
ich war immer bewegt,
immer so bewegt,
als könnt es ihn bewegen.
Und es gelang mir nie.
Jahre von Haut, mir abgezogen
und ich gesotten, [ge]braten und verbrannt
Gefoltert, gemordet, [er]drosselt
und erwürgt, es hat ihn nie bewegt,

Un altra notte ancora senza vederlo

That none of my pains
disturbed him
(heaven? no, I never
speak of heaven, but rather
of him, who is not
of heaven),
nothing and nothing and
everything, none of it disturbed him,
no matter the collection of pains, choking, fear,
I have never moved him, never
summoned him.
I was already white, already cold,
it never bothered him,
I had never been so white, so cold,
I was always disturbed,
always so disturbed
in thinking it would disturb him.
Yet I never succeeded.
Years of skin stripped from me
and myself boiled, roasted, and burned,
tortured, murdered, strangled,
and throttled, it never disturbed him.

[Wie lange noch. Nicht mehr lange.]

Vivere ardendo e non sentire il male
Gaspara Stampa

Wie lange noch. Nicht mehr lange.
Warum so lange schon. Ich weiß es nicht.
Wird das nie enden. Nicht fragen.
Es wird nie enden. Wozu fragen.

Ich spreche immer mit dir,
aber nicht mehr freundlich,
ich habe zuviele Fragen.
Auch über deinen Verbleib.
Aber wo warst du in den gemeinsamen Jahren.
Mit wem hast du gesprochen,
wen gewürgt, wen beansprucht,
wen angeschrien.

Ich habe mich ganz zur Verfügung gestellt.
mich oft gefürchtet, aber meine Furcht mit
der Liebe ausgetrieben, ich habe mich
nicht einmal vor Deinen Händen gefürchtet
nur manchmal, und zu spät.

[How much longer? Not much longer]

Vivere ardendo e non sentire il male
Gaspara Stampa

How much longer? Not much longer.
Why so long already? I don't know.
Will it never end? Don't ask.
It will never end? Why ask?

I always speak to you,
but no longer affectionately,
I have too many questions.
Also about your whereabouts.
But where were you in those same years?
Who did you speak to?
who did you strangle? who did you make demands of?
who did you scream at?

I placed myself at your disposal.
I was often afraid, but my fear was driven
out by my love. I was not even
afraid of your hand,
only sometimes, and too late.

Auf der obersten Terrasse

Von der obersten Terrasse
habe ich springen wollen,
zu Fuß bin ich Hintertreppe
hinaufgegangen, für die
Dienstboten und habe an der Tür
gehorcht, auf das Lachen in
meinen Zimmern, das hat mich ent-
mutigt. Einen Leichnam, gleich
nach dem Frühstück, hättest du
schlecht ertragen,

On The Highest Balcony

From the highest balcony
I have wanted to leap.
By foot I have climbed
the back stairs reserved
for the servants and listened
at the door to the laughter in
my room, which is what
discouraged me. A corpse, right after
breakfast, that you
could not stomach.

[Immerzu in den Worten sein]

Immerzu in den Worten sein, ob man will oder nicht,
Immer am Leben sein, voller Worte ums Leben,
als wären die Worte am Leben, als wäre das Leben am Wort.

So anders ists, glaubt mir.
Zwischen ein Wort und ein Ding
da dringst du nur selber ein,
wie bei einem Kranken liegst du bei beiden
da keins je ans andre sich drängt
du kostest einen Klang und einen Körper,
und kostest beide aus.

Es schmeckt nach Tod.

Doch Tod und Leben, ob es beides gibt,
wer weiß,
da soviel Totes Fernes, in mir ist
mich soviel Totes,
mich Tote auch
schon mitgenommen haben.

eine Freundin, die mich früher kannte,
ein Scherben, aus dem ich dir zutrank

[Always to live among words]

Always to live among words, whether one wants to or not,
always to be alive, full of words about life,
as if words were alive, as if life meant words.

But it's otherwise, believe me.
Between a word and a thing
you only encounter yourself,
lying between each as if next to someone ill,
never able to get to either,
tasting a sound and a body,
and relishing both.

It tastes of death.

Yet death and life, whether both exist,
who knows,
since so many of the dead are distant, though in me
there are so many dead,
the dead having also taken me
along with them.

Such as a girl who once knew me,
a broken shard from which I drank to you ....

Verdacht

Die Zunge die regt sich,
die schiebt, sprudelt Worte hervor,
sprudelt Freundschaft, Feindschaft
sprudelt den Zwischenton, züngelt
während das Aug
das Auge sich schließt und öffnet
schaut und nichts meint,
ins Auge tropft dir die Welt
farben und tropft dir die Nacht
nachts tropft dir die Nacht
in dein Auge

Nun sag von der Nacht und dem Tag
und nun sag es von dir und von mir,
nun wag es zu sagen

Sing deinen Vorrat an Worten ab,
du singst deinen Vorrat an Worten ab,
das singst du nicht ab
dies Kleinerwerden und Großsein,

der große Herrscher Aug
der kleine sklave bettler,
das Schandmaul
Verstehen — Nichtverstehen

Suspicion

The tongue that wags,
pushes, spews out words,
spews out friendship, malice,
spews out the undertone, darts
out as the eyes
close and open,
look and say nothing,
the world dripping color into your eyes,
and at night dripping night into you as well,
each night into your eyes
night dripping.

Now speak of the night and of the day,
and now speak of me and of you,
now dare to speak of it.

Sing away your supply of words,
you must sing away your supply of words
in order that you don't sing away
this diminishment and greatness,

the eye the great lord,
the beggar the little slave,
the mouth of shame
understanding — not understanding.

Verdacht

Die Zunge, daß sie sich regt
ist verdächtig, noch immer
züngeln Worte, sprudeln Worte
durch Zahnlücken, sprudelt
Freundschaftliches, Feindliches
Abwehrendes, hebt sich ein
läutet ein Zwischenton,
eingespeichelt, hebt sich
ein Erstaunen lautlich, klanglich,
und staunt doch nichts mehr,

während das Auge größer und betroffener
immer größer aufgeht und die Welt
anprallt und die Nacht hineintropft
um die gefälteten Einlaßstellen,
kein blinder Fleck mehr, immer
größer ein Schauen, Anschauen,

Nun sag doch nichts mehr, schau
und schau an, schau das ab und hinter
und tropf Dir die Nacht in die entzündeten
geäderten Augen, wein das zurück,
wein, was Du siehst zurück, laß es
hinauslaufen, laß die Welt über
die Wangen, rinnen

Rede ab deinen Vorrat an Worten
wein ab, red ab, mit dem Schandmaul,
der kleine Bettler Zunge, der
große Herrscher Auge wird

verstehen — nicht verstehen.

Suspicion

The tongue that wags
is suspicious, more and more
words darting out, words frothing
between the teeth, spewing out
something friendly, nasty,
off-putting, an undertone
injecting its sound,
spit out, something shocking
said aloud, audible,
and yet shocking no more,

as the eyes grow large and more stunned,
growing ever larger as the world
rushes in and the night leaks in
through the wrinkled point of entry,
no longer any blind spots, the sight,
the look, growing ever larger.

Say nothing more, look
and gaze, look it up and down
as night drips into the veins
of your inflamed eyes, cry it away,
cry what you see away, let it
out, let the world run down
your cheeks.

Talk away your supply of words,
cry away, talk away, with a shameful mouth,
the tongue's little beggar, for the
great god of the eyes will

understand — not understand.

Fromm und böse

Nicht mehr erinnern wollen, zerstören wollen,
was Erinnerung ist, so fremd, zerstören wollen.
Nun soll es sich zerstören, in mir mir in allem,
Stein und Baum und Blatt, es soll zerstört sein,
soll bis ins letzte Glied gestraft und zerstört
sein, gerächt bis in das letzte Glied, das
gar nicht ist, zerstört zumindest, gerächt auch,
gerächt, was doch niemand rächen kann,
ich kann es nicht, mög einer es doch können,
rächen, die Schmach Elend Wahnsinn, was nach
Rache schreit, und weiß, daß zuviel Sonnen,
zuviel Systeme nichts gradsein lassen, weil
die Milchstraßen und immer größre Stern und Sonnen
das wenig dingbar machen, was wir sind.

Es wird uns nichts ergänzen, nicht hier, nicht dort,
und Rache wird, wie Liebe, zu gering sein,
nebensächlich, eine Erhebung, hügelhaft,
in dem Gebirg von Fragen auf Gletscher
angesetzt, die kälter sind als wir uns Kälte denken.

Kälte — das ist noch ferner. Hier ist Menschenwerk,
Bemühen, Leiden, kindliche Bitten, von niemandem erhört,
und jede Nacht geübt, die Bitten, Kniefälle, die
flehentliche Bitte um Hoffnung, Weiterleben,
Der Tanz ums Kalb, ums goldne nicht, ums Kalb,
um Nahrung, daß da geschlachtet wird, für Nahrung,
Fressen, Hoffnung,

Pious and Wicked

Not wanting to remember anything, wanting to destroy
what memory is left, so strange, wanting to destroy.
Now I will destroy it within me, me within others,
stone and tree and leaf shall be destroyed,
shall be punished to the last member and be
destroyed, avenged right down to the last member,
leaving nothing, above all destroyed, also avenged,
avenged, what no one can avenge,
what I cannot avenge, though one would like to
avenge the disgrace misery madness, what screams
for vengeance and knows that so many suns,
so many solar systems make nothing of it, because
the Milky Way and ever larger stars and suns
make what we are seem so little.

Nothing will be restored, not here, not there,
and vengeance will, like love, be too little,
unimportant, a protrusion, no bigger than a hill
among the mountains of questions deposited
by a glacier colder than we know what cold to be.

Cold — that's still a ways off. Here there's human activity,
toil, suffering, childish prayers heard by no one,
repeated each night, the prayers, on one's knees,
the prayers pleading for hope, survival.
The dance around the calf, not its gold, but the calf itself
for nourishment, which will be slaughtered for nourishment,
food, hope ....

An das Fernmeldeamt Berlin

Ich bin froh, daß es gestern schlimmer war
als es heute ist. Einfahrt verboten
steht zwar noch immer am Tor, und es kommt
niemand, es regnet auch sehr, ist
schon wieder Winter wie gestern, also wie vor einem Jahr.
Da war es schlimm, in der Nachbarschaft
niemand. Kommt ja niemand.

Gestern, da bin ich erstickt,
ich konnte nicht mehr schreien,
heute könnt ich wohl schreien,
aber es ist ja besser heute.
über mir kegeln sie, unten
schreinern und sägen sie,
diese harmlosen Bastler.

In der Mauerritze habe ich in der Schrecksekunde
einen schwarzen Käfer gesehen,
der stellt sich tot. Totgestellt.
Und ich lerne von ihm,
ich stelle mich tot,
ohne Kind, ohne Geliebten,
ohne Radio, ohne Telefon,
in dieser Ritze, verlaufen
auf diesem Planeten, in
diesem Berlin.
angestarrt von niemand zwar,
von einer Brandmauer.
in einer Schrecksekunde
vom Wahnsinn fühl ich mich
angestarrt. weiß ich, daß
ich mich selber anstarre.

At The Berlin Telephone Exchange

I am happy that it was worse yesterday
than it is today. Although "Entry Forbidden"
it still says over the gate, and no one
comes, it rains a lot, once more
it's winter like yesterday, like a year ago.
That was terrible, no one
in the neighborhood. No one comes at all.

Yesterday, I was smothered,
I could no longer scream,
today I am able to scream,
but today things are better.
Above me they bowl, below
they hammer away and saw,
these harmless dabblers.

In the cracks in the wall I saw in a moment
of panic a black beetle
who was playing dead. Playing dead.
And I learned something from him,
I am playing dead,
without a child, without a lover,
without a radio, without a telephone,
inside this crack, lost upon
this planet, in this
Berlin,
looked at by no one at all,
only by a fire wall.
In a moment of panic
I feel stared at by
madness, knowing that
I stare only at myself.

Eine Brandmauer die andre.
ohne Gesicht.
von einem erlöschenden Brand.
unlöschbaren Brand.

One fire wall staring at another,
without a face,
from an extinguished fire,
from an inextinguishable fire.

[Daß es gestern schlimmer war, als es heute ist]

Daß es gestern schlimmer war, als es heute ist,
wieder kein Anschluß, die Anschlüsse sind
da, aber es wird nicht angeschlossen, wieder
im Winter, im Sommer, wie gestern, da war es
schlimm, in der Nachbarschaft niemand, zu essen
nichts, kommt ja niemand, ka[m] nie[mand]
die alten Nudeln waren schon alle verkocht.
Verdünnt auch der Essig getrunken.
Schweigen befohlen und ausgeführt.

Gestern, da ging der ganze Regenguß mit einmal
in meinen Hals, ich konnte nicht schreien.
Ich bin froh, daß ich rufen kann heute,
aber es ist ja besser, das Schweigen ein Leichtes.
Über mir kegeln sie, schlagen ans Hammerklavier.
Unter mir schreinern und sägen unsere Bastler.

In der Mauerritze habe ich,
in der Schrecksekunde,
einen schwarzen Käfer gesehen,
der stellt sich tot.

Ich möchte sprechen mit ihm
aus diesem feinen Haus ihm den Ausweg
zeigen, ihm einen Ausweg zeigen,
oder ihn gleich zertreten.

Ich lerne von ihm, ich stelle
mich tot, in diese Ritze Berlin fallen,
verlaufen auf diesem Planeten,
angestarrt auch, zwischen zwei Brandmauern,
von welchem Aug, von wem, der wieder mit mir
nicht sprechen kann, in der Schrecksekunde,

[**That it was worse yesterday than today**]

That it was worse yesterday than today,
there's no connection, for though the connections
are there, they're not made, whether
in winter, in summer, like yesterday, when it was
terrible, no one in the neighborhood, nothing
to eat, no one comes, no one came,
the old noodles were all overcooked.
The watered down vinegar also was drunk.
Silence was ordered and maintained.

Yesterday the entire downpour fell all at once
into my throat and I could not scream.
I am happy that today I can call out,
but it is indeed better, and easier to keep silent.
Above me they bowl and pound upon the piano.
Beneath me our dabbler hammers and saws.

In the crack in the wall
I saw in a moment of panic
a black beetle who
was playing dead.

I'd like to speak to him,
to show him a way out of this lovely house,
to show him an exit,
or stomp on him right away.

I learned something from him, I myself
am also playing dead, having fallen into the crack of Berlin,
disappearing from the face of the planet,
stared at as well by those eyes between two fire walls,
with whom I can no longer
speak with in a moment of panic.

Mich endlich ganz zu zertreten
ist auch in seinem Sinn, in meinem
Wahnsinn, ich selber bins, der mich und den Käfer anstarrt
Ich habe ein Romanebuch in der Hand,
genug schwer, um diesen Käfer zu töten

To finally stomp on me
also occurs to him, and to me
in my madness, I being the same one who stares
at both me and the beetle, holding a novel
heavy enough to kill this beetle.

IV GEDICHTE 1963 – 1964

IV   POEMS 1963 – 1964

Das deutsche Wunder

Frühmorgens, wenn
Fruchtlieferwagen durch die Stadt
poltern, wenn die S-Bahn
durch dein Bett fährt
und die Einflugschneise
tiefer hängt als sonst,

mußt du, du mußt,
du kannst nicht schlafen,

frühmorgens, wenn die
Amerikaner im geteilten
Berlin das Manöver beginnen,
wenn die Schüsse fallen, als
ging es an,

mußt du, aber du mußt nicht
du kannst auch schlafen.

Frühmorgens, wenn es hell
ist und im Tiergarten
die Generäle ihren Bauch
vorstrecken, auf den Ton
gefallen ist, mußt du
schließlich einmal wieder einschlafen.

Du schläfst, schläfst, es ist
eine Geschichte, Geschichte nicht,
deutbar. Da schläfst du besser ein.

The German Miracle

Early in the morning, when
fruit wagons rumble
through the city, when the subway
travels through your bed
and the incoming flight lanes
are lower than usual,

you must, you must,
you cannot sleep.

Early in the morning, when the
Americans in divided
Berlin begin their maneuvers,
when shots fire as if
it was starting,

you must join in, but need not,
for you may also sleep.

Early in the morning, when
it's bright and in the park
the generals stretch out
their stomachs, when the alarm
sounds, you must
finally sleep once again.

You sleep, sleep, it is part
of a story, not history.
Therefore it's better you sleep.

Geheimdienste
Flüchtlinge
wenn die ersten
Worte laut werden, dann
aber schläfst
du, hast
für Worte
nichts übrig

Frühmorgens
wenn die Prozesse
beginnen und die
sanften Gesichter
der Mörder und
die urteilsprechenden
Richter einander
vermeiden,
wenn ein Flugzeug-
flügel dein
Haar streift,
wenn du
deinen Korridor
findest, in
den Tod, in
die Abgeschiedenheit
ins Vergessen
dann schläfst
du, beim Gong-
schlag, und
sie sprechen über
den Schlaf wie
über ein Wunder.

2

Secret agents,
refugees,
when the first
words are spoken, then
you sleep,
having no use
for words.

Early in the morning
when the trials
begin and the
soft faces
of the murderers and
the sentencing
judges avoid
each other,
when an airplane
wing grazes
your hair,
when you
find
your corridor
into death, into
seclusion,
into forgetting,
then you will
sleep at the strike
of the gong, as
they speak
about sleep like
a miracle.

Schallmauer

Der Lärmteppich, breit und laut,
hinter dir her schleift,
was mehr lärmt, alles
lärmt und laut lärmt
es, es zittern
Deine Häuser alle,
jeder Fußbreit
in deinem Kopf
alle deine Besitzungen
Gedanken, Gedenken
das überrast
mit einer Geschwindigkeit
die nie die deine war
dieser Wahn, es ist nicht
mehr, nichts ist mehr, und
es ist nicht mehr weit
bis mit dem großen Knall
unter dem du dich duckst
über dir, oben, du
die Schallmauer durchschlägst,
nach oben.
Du duckst dich, du bist schon
oben und trittst deine Reise an
mit funkelnden Fetzen und Felgen
mit ausgerissenen Nähten und
einer Wahnkraft, für deren
Durchschlag der Himmel immer zu weich
und die Erde zu hart ist.

Sound Barrier

The swath of sound, wide and loud,
rolls out behind you,
setting off more, everything
sounding off and loud it
sounds, shaking
your houses,
each footstep
inside your head,
all of your possessions,
thoughts, memory
rushing
with a speed
that was never yours,
such madness, no longer
here, nothing is, and
it does not take long
until with a huge bang
beneath which you duck,
as above you, above, you
break through the sound barrier
above you.
You duck, you are already
above and begin your trip
with sparkling rags and rims,
with ripped out seams and
a mad power whose penetration
heaven is too soft for
and the earth too hard.

Der gefundene Ton

Den Ton gefunden
was mehr, den Ton
dann die Schallgrenze
die nicht gilt
die Schallmauer
dort ist so einsam
einsam, daß nichts
hinreicht, kein Flug,
der das durchbricht
an der Schallmauer
eine Klage von
einem Körper, der
verwundet und ältlich
mit seiner Ration

Eine Ration
Vernunft, eine Ration
Glück, das, meistens,
genügt, eine Ration

The Right Tone Is Found

The right tone is found,
and what's more, the tone
makes the sound
barrier invalid.
The sound barrier,
there it is so lonely,
lonely, that nothing
reaches it, no flight
that breaks through
the sound barrier,
only a groan from
a body that is
wounded and elderly
with its ration.

A ration
of good sense, a ration
of happiness that, mostly,
suffices. A ration.

In Feindeshand

Du bist in Feindeshand,
sie mahlen schon Deine
Knochen, sie verlangen
Deinen Blick
sie treten Deine Blicke
aus mit den Füßen
trillern dir ins Ohr
mit den Alarmpfeifen
Alarm

In Enemy Hands

You are in enemy hands,
they are already grinding your
bones, they demand
that you look,
they trample on your
gaze with their feet,
trilling in your ear
the whistle
of alarm.

[Stille Nacht, heilige Nacht]

Stille Nacht, heilige Nacht
wenn von den Tischen
die Kanten fliegen,
wenn es kracht, wenn
der Verrat aufsteht
und durch die Wand
das Gespenst Gott
wie die Spinne auf dich
zukommt, das

Aufheulen, daß auf den
Straßen den Verkäufern
und Chauffeuren das Hemd
an den Leib geklebt
wird aufheulen, daß
alles stillsteht und
hört wie es röhrt und

wenn die Geschenkpakete
das Zittern bekommen
weil die Lieblosigkeit
durch die Welt geht mit
der Ungeduld, wenn die
silbernen Fäden reißen
und das Lametta säuselt
silbern auch das
und das säuselt und rechtet silbern.

[**Silent night, holy night**]

Silent night, holy night
as from the tables
the bread crusts fly
when the tables are smashed, as
betrayal rises
and through the wall
the ghost of God
comes to you like
the spider, the

howling that
(among salesmen
and chauffeurs, the dress
clinging to the body in sweat),
is howled on the streets, such that
everything stands still and
listens to the bellowing and

when the gifts
begin to shake,
because lovelessness
accompanies
impatience, the
silver ribbons are ripped apart
and the tinsel rustles,
silvery as well,
rustles and protests in silvery fashion.

[auf den Paradeplätzen der Weihnachtsstadt]

auf den Paradeplätzen der Weihnachtsstadt
hab ich geschrien, gejohlt, daß die
Polizei rot wurde und die Karpfen zu glotzen
aufhörten.

Stille Nacht, heilige
Nacht, wenn vom Baum der Ast fliegt
und allein in der Welt hängt, wenn
von den Tischen die Kanten fliegen
wenn die Geschenkpakete das Zittern bekommen,
weil die Lieblosigkeit durch die Welt geht
weil dich das anfaucht, anbellt aus dem Schnee
und die silbernen Fäden reißen und das Lametta säuselt
silbern
auch das silbern und gold golden kommt
ein Wort auf dich zu, an dem du erstickst,
weil du verkauft und verraten bist
und weil das nicht ausreicht, daß dich
einer erlöst, der einmal gestorben ist,

[On the plazas of the city at Christmas]

On the plazas of the city at Christmas
I screamed, yelled, that the police
had turned red and the carp's eyes
stopped to stare.

Silent night, holy
night, when the bough flies from the tree
and is hung everywhere, when
from tables the crusts fly,
when the gifts begin to tremble
because lovelessness walks through the world,
because it snarls at you, barks at you from the snow,
and the silver ribbons rip and the tinsel rustles silvery,
and the silver and gold, and a golden word
comes to you on which you choke
because you have been sold and betrayed,
and because it does not suffice that for you
one is redeemed who once died.

Rationen

Die eiserne Ration Glück aufgebraucht
verbraucht die drei Brosamen
Glaube Hoffnung und Liebe
und erstickt daran, in der
Luftröhre eins, vielleicht
Liebe, Erstickungsgefahr,
Atemnot, Schulternklopfen
auf den Rücken klopfen
Erstickungsgefahr
wills hinunter oder speit man es aus

Rationen, Fettmarken für
Nerven, Kleidermarken für
Nacktheit, ein geklebtes Buch
voll Marken voll Bedarfsartikeln
Artikel, die sind nicht mehr.
Es braucht schon nichts mehr,
ein bißchen Geld, einen Tropfen
Branntwein

Rations

The tireless ration of happiness used up,
gone the three crumbs of
faith, hope, and love,
having choked on them, one remaining
in the windpipe, perhaps
love, danger of choking,
loss of breath, slap the shoulders,
pound upon the back,
danger of choking,
either swallow it or spit it out.

Rations, lard coupons for
the nerves, clothing coupons for
nakedness, a bound book
full of coupons, full of articles
for necessities that exist no longer.
Nothing more is needed,
a bit of money, a drop
of brandy.

[Meine Schreie verlier ich]

Meine Schreie verlier ich
wie ein anderer sein Geld
verliert, seine Moneten,
sein Herz, meine großen
Schreie verlier ich in
Rom, überall, in
Berlin, ich verlier auf
den Straßen Schreie,
wahrhaftige, bis
mein Hirn blutrot anläuft
innen, ich verlier alles,
ich verlier nur nicht
das Entsetzen, daß
man seine Schreie verlieren
kann jeden Tag und
überall

[I lose my screams]

I lose my screams
the way another loses his
money, his dough,
his heart, I lose
my mighty screams
in Rome, anywhere,
in Berlin, losing
screams for real
on the street until
my brain turns
blood red inside,
losing everything,
not the least the outrage
that one's screams can be lost
on any given day
and anywhere.

Bei Lebensgefahr

Bei Lebensgefahr
kein Blitzableiter,
keine Notbremse
keine Flucht
kein Leuchtturmsignal

Nachts das lange langsame Kauen
Verbeißen in Gespenster
Kampf mit Nembutal 20 Stück
genügen

Es ist Vorsorge getroffen,
daß Tag wird,
das ist
alles.
und arbeitende Muskeln im Gesicht,
bis oben das Wasser aus den geschlossenen
Augen langsam austritt, dann Urin
dann eine Erleichterung, Seufzer,
die nur sagen, 5 Uhr morgens
es geht auch das
vorüber das versalzene Kissen
geht eine Hand einer sagt,
schlafen, schlafen,
nichts weit[er] als schlafen

In Mortal Danger

In mortal danger
no lightning rod,
no emergency brake,
no escape,
no lighthouse beacon.

Each night the long slow chewing,
a ghost swallowing,
the battle with 20 Nembutal
enough.

It's a provision for
the day to come,
that is
all.
The facial muscles work
until, above, the liquid from the closed
eyes slowly seeps out, then urine,
then an easing of pain, sighs
that only mean it's 5 o'clock in the morning,
meaning as well
that above the salty pillows
a hand reaches out to say
sleep, sleep,
nothing more than sleep.

[Während eine Ideologie die andere rammt]

Während eine Ideologie die andere rammt
während die Erde bebt am Balkan
einer vom Gerüst stürzt
und ein Kind, ein einziges,
in ein Auto läuft,
eine Gasleitung undicht geworden ist,
während es da und dort sich stirbt
und gestorben wird, ein Zeitzünder platzt
und Du weißt es auch,

bist Du allein in Lebensgefahr
Das weißt Du anders das ist
so anders und wächst noch kein Kraut
dagegen und zitterst und züchtest
ein Kraut dagegen, nur Ruhe und Tapferkeit
Tapferkeit sagst Du in der Nacht,
tapfer sein, das heißt
leben mit dem Geröll
im Kopf mit dem Rollen und beim Untergang
dessen was glücklich macht, was war es,
es war bloß ein wenig, aber alles,
ist schon untergegangen, du gehst unter,
du mußt etwas dagegen sagen, Dir
den andren das übliche sagen, wie geht es
und danke gut,
gutt gutt gutt in einer Lache Blut,
das tropft gutt gutt, bei Lebensgefahr
mit der offenen Schlagader
nichts zu machen

[As one ideology pounds another]

As one ideology pounds another,
as the earth quakes in the Balkans,
someone plunges from a scaffold
and a child, a single child,
runs in front of a car,
a gas main begins to leak,
as people die here and there
and will die, a time bomb explodes
and you know as well

that you are alone in mortal danger,
though you know it differently, so
differently, there being no remedy
against it, and so you tremble and grow
a remedy against it, calmly and bravely.
Be brave, you say, during the night,
be brave, which means
live with the rubble
inside your head, with the quaking and destruction
that makes one happy, it being nothing,
only a little, and yet everything,
it already having been destroyed, yourself destroyed.
You must say something against it, as others
say the usual things to you, how are you
and thanks, I'm good,
good good good, in a pool of blood
dripping good, good, in mortal danger,
the open artery
meaning nothing.

[Wer holt mich ab]

Wer holt mich ab,
Mitternacht, nur noch
der Krankenwagen, Mitternacht,
in Berlin, die Glocken,
die läuten zuviel, man
muß es dem Bürgermeister
sagen, daß Glocken zuviel
sind, es läutet auch so,
es schmiert ein leiser Motor
von Haß den Leichenwagen.

[Who picks me up]

Who picks me up
at midnight? Only
the ambulance, at midnight,
in Berlin, the bells
chiming too loudly, one
should tell the mayor
that the bells are too much,
they chime away,
a quiet motor of hate
smoothing the way for the hearse.

Es soll gerettet werden

Auf den Knien, altmodisch,
auf den Knien immer, wie die
Alten, eh vor sie wußten, was knien
heißt, retten, bitten um
Rettung, nicht fürchten, daß
einer lacht, auch bei offenem
Fenster und mit Haaren, die
überfließen, die zärtlich geflochten
waren einmal. Ich fürchte, seit
ich fürchte, nichts mehr,
mein Gelächter, den eigenen Stolz
nicht, ich bin unter die
armen Teufel gegangen,
Ich fresse vom Fleisch
und fühl, wie ich gefressen werde,
wie es frißt an mir knabbert, wie ich
und mein Saft
der Qual schmecken,
die mich auffrißt.

Someone Will Be Saved

On one's knees, how old-fashioned,
always on one's knees, just like
the old ones when they knew what it meant
to be on one's knees, to be saved, pleading
to be saved, not afraid that
someone will laugh, even by
an open window and with hair
let down that was once
braided tenderly. I am afraid, but since
I am afraid, I am afraid no longer,
my laughter not being my only
pride, I have gone to
the poor devil.
I feed on flesh
and feel as if I were eaten,
as if I were nibbled away at, as I
and my blood
are tortured
and devoured.

Eine andere Rache

Eine andere Rache als die gemeine, die Zeit,
die nicht existierende Zeit,
wird rächen und im Burghof meine Treuen versammeln,
jeden Gegenstand, jeden Ort voller Leiden,
eine ganze Station die von Blumen bepflanzt war,
und getreten worden ist, mein rollender Kopf
wird jeden Tag wieder fallen, mein Schweiß
und Todesschweiß jeden Tag ein Laken befeuchten,
in dem ich noch immer liege, weil es nicht zurückgegeben
   worden ist,
vergessen, um zu erinnern,

Another Kind of Vengeance

Another kind of vengeance is that of time,
time that does not exist
will have its revenge and gather my loved ones inside the castle,
every object, every place of suffering,
an entire ward planted with flowers,
trampled on as well, my tossing head
falling each day, my sweat
and death sweat dampening a sheet
in which I still lie because it has not been given back,
forgetting to do so in order to remember.

Alkohol

Trinken, was trinken,
ich trinke, trinke den Staub auf den Flimmer auf
ich trinke in mich hinein soviel Schilling
ich trinke meine Arbeit in mich hinein trinke
heraus, ich kann nur mehr trinken
mich aus allem heraus trinken, das säuft
den Geschmack weg aus allem, aus Staub aus
ich sags nicht weil keiner es sagt
warum es trinkt, sich zu Tod säuft,
ich bins ja ja nicht, es säuft sich
an ich sag nicht, weil keiner sagt
man soll mich nicht aufrütteln
mich zwingen zu sagen, es weiß ja jeder
warum es säuft, sich besäuft, sich
sich betäubt, es betäubt sich
Und was Liebe und Krätzen und Fortschritt
es weiß ja jeder und wer nicht säuft, weiß
auch, es weiß ja jeder, das sag ich nicht mehr,
weiß weiß weiß weiß weiß weiß
weiß weiß weiß
weiß
mehr sag ich nicht
als das jeder weiß

Alcohol

Drink, drink something,
I drink, drink the dust from what glimmers,
I drink up so much money,
I drink up my work, drink
it dry, I can only keep drinking,
drink myself dry, guzzling down
the taste of everything, of dust, of
what I won't say, because no one says
why one drinks, drinks oneself to death,
though not me, not me, it guzzles itself,
though I say nothing, because no one says
I should not be woken up,
be forced to admit it, everyone knowing
why I drink, get drunk, am
dead drunk, dead drunk,
and what love and scabies and progress there are
everyone knows and who doesn't drink also
knows, everyone knows, I won't say it again,
knows knows knows knows knows knows
knows knows knows
knows
I'll say no more
than that everyone knows.

Politik der Schwäche oder eine verlorene Liebe

Eine verlorene und wie man das nennt
und immer noch eine und eine Liebe
das heißt sich gewinnen, gehen
und leben, das heißt sein
von den Fußspitzen bis zu den Haar
spitzen, das heißt, leben, eine verlorene
Einbildung, daß weiter nichts ist
als auch leben und gehen und
eine Arbeit tun, das heißt nicht viel
ist doch zwischen nichts und etwas
ein etwas, das heißt, keine verlorene
Liebe, das heißt nichts verloren
nicht verlieren
du bist nicht verloren.
Zwischen Berlin und Rom und zwischen
amtierenden Städten bist du eine
Politik der Schwäche.
machst du eine Politik der Schwäche

Viel liebst du nicht mehr, doch
du liebst, du liebst
magst ein Haar, magst daß ein Gesicht
so ist und magst dich sehen in ihm,
du willst seinen Spiegel, du
gehst lieber unter in diesem Spiegel
als dich zu halten im nirgendwo,
du liebst noch eine Hand, liebst noch
ein fünffingerknochenspiel, liebest noch
daß es spielt mehr, als daß nichts mehr spielt,
du liebst noch das spiel,
du liebst noch, liebst

The Politics of Weakness *or* A Lost Love

A lost one, as we say,
and yet still one and a love,
which means getting hold of oneself,
going on and living, which means to be alive
from one's toes to the ends of one's hair,
which means living, a lost
imagination, which means nothing more
than living and carrying on and
doing some work, though not too much,
something between nothing and something,
which is still something, meaning not a lost
love, meaning nothing is lost,
nothing is lost,
you are not lost.
Between Berlin and Rome and between
cities of appointed officials, you represent
the politics of weakness,
you maintain the politics of weakness.

You no longer love many things, yet
you love, you love
and like hair, like a face,
that's how it is and you like seeing yourself in it,
you long for its mirror, you'd
much rather sink into this mirror
than hold yourself together amid nothing.
You still love a hand, still love
playing with its fingers, still love
that it plays more than it does not play,
you still love playing,
you still love, love

einen Körper, der an sich selbst nicht mehr glaubt
du liebst sein[e] Hinfälligkeit, Infarkt und die Kluft
zwischen dem möglichen Magenkrebs und der
Leberzirrhose, du
liebst also ein Schlachtfeld, auf dem du, ein Feind,
der rosig aussieht, mit deiner Gebrechlichkeit
eine Gebrechlichkeit in den Arm nimmst
und tötest durch einen Blick
auf die Zeit vor Dir auf die Zeit nach Dir
auf den Tod, der das eine ist,
den Tod, der das andre ist
für dich, den der
Tod sein wird,
das ist
bald.

a body that no longer believes in itself,
you love its frailty, the infarct and the cleft
between the possible stomach cancer and cirrhosis, thus you
love a battlefield on which you, the enemy
who looks rosy with your infirmity,
takes an infirmity into your arms
and kills it with a glance
at the time before you, at the time after you,
at death, which is one thing,
and death, which is another
for you, which will be
the death
that is
soon.

Die Schulden dem Schuldner

Und in dieser flauen und öden
wo Tage enger geworden sind,
wos zuende war
und jedes Hämmern, jeder Schlag,
mich niederschlugen, da es doch
ausweglos schien, Sprechen Lachen
unmöglich schien,
da schuld ich nun einem
daß vier Stockwerke wieder
nicht zum Herunterstürzen,
ein Autos nicht um an den Baum
zu rasen da sind, auch die Nacht nicht
mehr eine Zelle ist
in die ich eingebracht werde nach so einem wütigen Versuch.

The Debtor's Debts

And here amid this stagnation and waste,
where the days have grown more narrow,
where something has come to an end
and every hammering, every blow
knocked me down, since there seemed
no escape, speaking and laughing
appearing impossible,
I am indebted now to someone
because I will not leap
from four flights up,
I will not slam a car into
a tree, and also the night
is no longer a cell
into which I'm brought after a mad try at escape.

Enigma

So früh schon Abend, und so spät noch Morgen,
immer dunkelts ins Zimmer herein,
Schnee, Nebel als Grund, wievielter Winter schon?

Enigma

Dark so early already, and the morning so late,
always it seems to be dark in the room.
Snow, fog the reason. How long will winter last?

Enigma

Am Nil in der Nacht, am Nil,
wo die Sterne dir bis in den Mund hängen
und dein trockenes Herz wieder befeuchtet wird,

in der Nacht in Ägypten,
wo du noch niemals warst, aber bald sein wirst,
um der Sphinx deine Antwort zu geben.

In der blauen Nacht,
wenn im immer offenen Mund die Wüstenzunge
deine Feuchtigkeit sucht
wenn es dich niederbrennt
kommt dein erschöpfter Laut
meiner Antwort nah.

Meines Lebens Leben
verwilderten Mund
dir den Atem austreiben
und keine Erinnerung mehr lassen,
laß mich bei mir sein,
laß mich bei dir sein

Enigma

At the Nile at night, at the Nile,
where the stars hang down into your mouth
and your dry heart is moist once again,

in the Egyptian night,
where you never have been before, but soon will be,
in order to give the Sphinx your answer.

In the blue night,
as in an eternally open mouth the desert's tongue
seeks your moisture.
If it burns you up,
your exhausted gasp
will resemble my answer.

Life of my life,
savage mouth
that takes the breath away
and no longer allows a memory,
let me be myself,
let me be with you.

Nacht der Liebe

In einer Nacht der Liebe nach einer langen Nacht
habe ich wieder sprechen gelernt und ich weinte,
weil ein Wort aus mir kam. Ich habe wieder gehen gelernt,
ging bis ans Fenster und sagte Hunger und Licht
und Nacht war mir recht für Licht.

Nach einer zu langen Nacht,
wieder ruhig geschlafen,
im Vertrauen darauf,

Ich sprach leichter im Dunkeln.
sprach weiter am Tag.
Bewegte meine Finger in meinem Gesicht,
Ich bin nicht mehr tot.
Ein Busch, aus dem Feuer schlug in der Nacht.
Mein Rächter trat hervor und nannte sich Leben.
Ich sagte sogar: laß mich sterben, und meinte
furchtlos meinen lieberen Tod

Night of Love

In a night of love, after a long night,
I again learned to speak and I wept
when a word escaped me. I learned to walk again,
I walked to the window and said hunger and light,
and night was what was light for me.

After a night that was too long,
once again I sleep peacefully,
entrusting myself.

I spoke easier in darkness,
and I spoke more the next day.
My finger moved across my face,
I was no longer dead.
Fire emerged from the bush at night.
My avenger stepped forth and called himself life.
I said to it: let me die, and fearlessly
meant my own dear death.

Erste Schritte

Ich konnte nicht mehr gehn,
jetzt kann ich's auf das Mal
zwei Schritt um das Haus,
da ist das Haus schon.

Ich konnt nicht mehr was erkennen
jetzt schau ich einen an
da hat er wie zwei Augen
den meinen zugetan

sprechen, das muß lang her sein
ein Wort, Wort und Unterbrechen
habt Satz und Atemnot
mitten im Unterbrechen
kommt jetzt ein Wort ins Lot.

First Steps

I could no longer walk,
now for the first time I can take
two steps around the house,
and the house is still there.

I could no longer recognize anything,
now I look at someone
since he has two eyes
that are fond of mine.

To speak, that was long ago.
A word, a word and interruptions
mean a sentence and shortened breath,
while amid the interruptions
a word comes spilling forth.

Heimkehr über Prag

Auf einem Umweg, es kehrt heim
es spricht wieder
die Friedhöfe im Winter
die Umkehr, erste Heimstätte
unter den Sternen, was
so schrecklich ist, die lapidaren
Inschriften den Alten zusprangen
die Namen, die Gräber,
die Moldau, die längste
Nacht, die ist nicht zu
Ende,

Die Moldau, die gehört
nur mir, mit Kronen hab
ich sie bezahlt und hab
sie weiterfließen lassen.

Return Home Via Prague

On a detour I turn towards home
able to speak again
of the graveyards in winter,
the return, the first familiar towns
under the stars, and what
is so horrible, the names that spring
from the lapidary inscriptions of the old,
the graves, the Moldau,
the long night which does not
end.

The Moldau, it belongs
to me alone, I paid for it
with krone and allowed
its waters to flow again.

Wenzelsplatz

Nicht viel zu sehn, Eisfährten, Schneehaufen
rauchend vor Kälte die Münder, hinauf und
hinunter wie Fischzüge vonhause nachhause
Menschen. Nicht viel zu verstehn.
miteinander und in der Quere

Es raucht nur, wölkt sich, vor sich hin denkt
sich ein jeder, denkt sich nichts. Wozu auch
und warum hier.

Der Platz, von ich aber nachhause finde, heißt auch so,
ist ein und derselbe. Ich habe meinen kleinen Rauch
vor dem Mund und biege ein und komme lebendig an
in eine Gasse, die weit unten in meiner Vergangenheit endet
in der meine Herkunft ist.

Wenceslaus Square

Nothing much to be seen, ice skating, snow shoveling,
mouths smoking from the cold, people shuttling
back and forth from house to house like schools of
fish. Nothing much to understand.
Together and apart.

Only smoke, billowing like someone brooding
and yet thinking nothing. For what reason
and why here?

The square on which I find my way home is still called the same,
is one and the same. I have my bit of smoke
before my mouth and turn into and enter yet alive
a street that ends way back in my past
in which my roots still lie.

Jüdischer Friedhof

Steinwald, keine vorzüglichen Gräber, nichts zum Hinknien
und für die Blumen nichts. So eng ist dort ein Stein, wie den
andren um den Hals fallend, keiner ohne den andern zu denken,
und für die Lebendigen einen Spaltbreit Durchlaß gewährend,
trauerlos, Wer den Ausgang erreicht, hat nicht den Tod,
sondern den Tag im Herzen.

Jewish Cemetery

Forest of stones, no fancy graves, nothing to kneel before,
and nothing to hold flowers. The stones are so close, one choking
out another, each one inseparable from the others,
and for the living a passage is granted no wider than a crack;
empty of sadness. Whoever reaches the exit has not death
but rather life in her heart.

Poliklinik Prag

Da ist alles umsonst. Kostet nichts mehr.
Nur die krank sind, Kein Reichenhaus, kein Armenhaus,
nur ein Krankenhaus für die Kranken, kostet nichts,
alles umsonst, kein Vortritt und keine Privilegien,
da sind alle krank und klopfen an wie ans Paradies
und taumeln wie vorm Paradies und atmen kaum

Prague Polyclinic

There everything is gratis. It costs nothing more.
Only the sick are there, no rich house, no poor house,
only a sick house for the sick, costing nothing,
everything gratis, no priority and no privileges,
everyone there is sick and knocks at the door of paradise
and reels as if standing before paradise and hardly breathes.

Terra Nova

Ausruhen in einem dunklen Gesicht
in einer schwarzen Hand
ruhen in einem Wort ich komm um vier
warum bist du nicht
gekommen, ruhen
Rache üben an allem, was weiß ist
weiß war, weiß sein wird,
Rache und Trauer üben
in einer langsamen Hand
in der Kohlengrube
im dichten Gefunkel
von einfach gut tun,
es besser tun, verschränken
was zu verschränken ist,
umbilden, was zu bilden ist
in dem ausgegangenen Ofen, in dem
einer auf mein Herz
bläst, damit es wieder anfängt
ein wenig zu glühen,
und Ruß rinnt dabei
von seinem über mein Gesicht,
die Rassen verschränken
damit weiß hell wird
und schwarz dunkel wird
und Lachen hell dunkel,
Lachen

Terra Nova

Resting in a darkened face,
in a black hand,
resting in a word, I arrive at four,
but why have you not
come, resting,
practicing vengeance against everything,
what is white was white, will be white,
practicing vengeance and grief
with a slow hand
in the coal mine
amid the dense glitter
to simply do something good,
to do it better, mixing
what can be mixed,
reshaping what can be shaped
in the extinguished oven in which
someone blows upon my heart
so that it once again
begins to glow a little,
and soot begins to run
from his face onto mine,
the races mixing
such that white becomes bright
and black becomes dark
and laughter a bright darkness,
laughter …

Verzicht

Meine Haut trägt noch einen Atem,
meine Hand hält noch sein Geschlecht
mein Mund wölbt sich noch über Mitternacht
mein Begehr bist noch du
Was ist mein Begehr, wenn nicht du!

Ach wie gut, daß niemand weiß,
willst du mich elend machen,
so fang wieder an,

Renunciation

My skin still carries a breath,
my hand still holds his sex,
my mouth still arches over midnight,
you are still my desire,
what is my desire if not you!

And how nice that no one knows
that you want to make me miserable,
so go ahead and start again.

Immer wieder Schwarz und Weiss

Wieder wölbt sich mein Mund über Mitternacht.
Eine dunkle Zunge rührt in mir einen Ton wach
mit dem ich schluchzend hing, an die, nächtelang
tagelang laß ich Licht ein, und werde nicht rein.
Meine Haut ist farbig von deiner geworden.
Ach wie gut, daß niemand weiß, wie du heißt,
daß meine junge Schwärze herrüht von deiner alten.
von deiner uralten, eingeborenen
Du rufst mich wie die Königin vom Sambesi

Always Black and White

Again my mouth arches over midnight.
A dark tongue stirs a tone inside me
with which, sobbing, I hang upon you all night,
all day I let in light and will not come clean.
My skin has become colored from yours.
How nice that no one knows your name,
that my new blackness rubs off from yours,
from yours both ancient and native.
You call to me like the queen of Sambesi.

Auflösung

Eines Tags, es war gestern, oder, ist auch
gleichgültig, da setzt dieses Gesicht sich wieder
zusammen, da holen die Füße aus, ganz zerbrochen
immer noch innen, eines Tags holt man sich jemand
von der Straße, von wo ist auch gleichgültig,
man betastet und wird betastet, verläßt
sich wieder darauf daß dieses Fleisch hungrig
ist,
aber am nächsten Tag erst, nicht während
es sich vereinigt, sich betreibt, sich äußert,
macht es die Poesie, auf die es schon keinen Wert
mehr legt, es erinnert sich, allein, gesäubert,
es erinnert sich mit und ohne Hilfe des Kopfs
es möchte wieder, es möchte so wieder und
besser lieben, es möchte hat ja das Gefühl,
das ins Fleisch schneidet. zubereitet.
Männer und Frauen, Mann und Frau, das ist gut, das
soll oft sein, und Mann und Mann und Frau Frau,
gut ist nur, was gut tut, es hat immer
gut getan

An einer Kreuzung stehen, nach einer Kreuzigung,
und vor Dankbarkeit nicht wissen, wohin gehen.
Der Weg ist kurz.
In jedem Fall.
Wähl welchen du willst,
es ist gleichgültig.

Ich rufe Dich von der Straße,
komm, hab schwarzes Haar, sei jung,
sei hart, tu weh, hier wo alle blond sind,
terra nova, Africa, ultima speranza.

Dissolution

One day, it was yesterday, or it doesn't matter
when, once again this face put itself back
together, I was back on my feet, though still completely
broken within. One day someone was hauled in
from the street, from where also doesn't matter,
one probes and is probed, still relying
on the fact that this flesh is
hungry,
but then the next day, not while
it draws close, makes love, expunges itself,
it creates the poetry which already no longer has
any value, remembering, alone, cleansed,
remembering with and without help from the head,
wishing to make love once again, wishing to make love once
    again and
make love better, wishing to once again feel
the feeling that cuts through flesh, gets it hot.
Men and women, man and woman, that's good, that
should often happen, and man and man and woman and woman,
good is what does some good, it has always
done good.

To stand at a crossroads after a crucifixion
and because of gratitude not know where to go.
The way is short.
In any case,
the choice is yours,
it doesn't matter.

I call out to you from the street,
come, have black hair, be young,
be hard, hurt me, here where everyone is blond,
terra nova, Africa, *ultima speranza*.

[Ich habe euch, meine Spießer]

Ich habe euch, meine Spießer, hätt ich euer hundert
nie in mich verschränkt, euch ja, meine Männer
den geschwollenen Mund von seiner tückischen Reinheit
befreit, und meinen Schock gelind und wüst, gekostet
genossen. Ich atmete: mehr. Mehr von euch, mehr von mir,
mehr von allem zusammen.

Ich habe ein Ende gemacht mit dieser stummen Meuterei
im Besitz, habe euch verhöhnt, euren Besitz, den Krüppel
den ihr besessen habt, mich nicht, nur diesen toten Rumpf,
diese gelähmte Hand, mehr nicht — Ich atmete immer: mehr.
Die Schmach ist aus mir gegangen in dieser Orgie,
die bürgerliche Infamie mit ihren Demütigungen
der Langweile und des raschschlüssigen Urteils
über ein Fleisch, das so lebendig ist wie sein Geist.

Die Wüste hat meine Augen begegnet mit Sand, von meinem
        verwüsteten
Herzen konnt ich nur vorher sprechen, jetzt ist es verwüstet
wunderbar, die Sandschleier ziehen auf, die Dünen habens
        genommen,
meine Blicke besänftigt mit ihrer unendlichen Zeichnung
mein Gang ans Rote Meer. Mehr sag, ich mehr, mehr noch
        vom Sand.

Diese Infamie, deren Kreuz ich ein halbes Leben lang
getragen habe, bis mir das Kreuz brach, die gewissenlose
Ausbeutung eines leidenschaftlichen Beginnen von Du.

Du, das ist, wo wenig ist, wo die Rasse niedrig Deiner
niedrigen weißen Rasse so ins Gesicht schlägt,
daß Du Deine Abende mit den weißen Großvätern vergißt,
das behält kein Hemd an, was hier ist, das ist so jung wie alt,
das ist wirklich und ohne Rücksicht.

[I did it with pleasure, you prudes]

I did it with pleasure, you prudes, though I should not have
    lowered myself
with the hundred of you, yes you, my men,
my swollen mouth freed of its insidious
purity, and my own sense of shock let go of and laid waste,
    having tasted
with pleasure. I breathed: more. More from you, more from me,
more from all of us together.

I am finished with you after having thrown myself into
this mute mutiny, mocking you, your possessions, the cripple
that you have dominated, not I, only this dead body,
this crippled hand, nothing more — I breathed always: more.
I lost my shame in this orgy,
the middle class infamy with your humiliation,
boredom, and narrow-minded judgment
against the flesh which is as alive as the spirit.

The desert presented my eyes with sand, only from my deserted
heart could I speak before, now that it is a wasteland
it is wonderful, the veil removed, taking in the dunes,
my gaze made calm by their infinite grains,
my path to the Red Sea. More, I say more, yet more sand.

This infamy, whose cross I have born for half
a life, until my back broke, the unscrupulous
exploitation of a passionate beginning from you.

You, that is, where little is, where your race is lower,
where your lowly white race is so obvious that
you forget your evenings with the white grandfathers,
while the one here wears no shirt, and is as young as he is old,
something real and full of abandon.

597

Soziologie

Wie kalt lassen mich diese sozialen Konflikte
Erfahrungswissenschaftlich, um sechs Uhr Abend,
Norm, Herrschaft, und kritische Distanz,

Eine internationale Diskussion,
und das Telefon, es ist sechsuhrdreißig
der Tee kalt geworden, es läßt ihn kalt,
werden und die Zeitungen, die auf
dem Boden liegen, jede Nachricht
ein Schmutzfleck eine Granate, eine züchtige
Obszönität, möchte verbrannt werden,

Es brennt mich, wie soll ich sagen,
daß ich warte auf Anrufen,

Sociology

How these social conflicts leave me cold,
empirical science at six o'clock in the evening,
norms, controls, and critical distance.

An international discussion
and the telephone, it's six thirty,
the tea has gone cold, it's allowed to
go cold and the newspapers that lie
on the floor, each headline
a speck of dirt, a grenade, a chaste
obscenity, asks to be burned.

I have to say that it burns me up
that I wait for a call each night.

Strangers in The Night

Im November, und noch im Dezember
so Lachen muß ich, das war,
ein ganzes Leben für mich,
das Telefon ist blaß
geworden, geläutet hat es auf andre Art,
die Zigaretten haben mich
an den Fingern verbrannt,
und nachher die Vögel die Himmel mit
ihren Südwärtsschreien.
Auswärtig haben wir gesprochen,
und mir ist immerzu Jerusalem
eingefallen, das meine,

Was für eine Grausamkeit,
mich an der Haut zu ritzen,
ins Herz zu treffen
bin ich nicht mehr.
Ich spreche und lache und spreche.
Zu treffen nicht mehr.

Aber die Vögel mit ihren
schrecklichen Schreien.
Ich habe ein Gefühl
hinterlegt, und ich
hatte ein letztes.

Wie müd bin ich und wie lache ich
und ich zeige mich dort, wo die Vögel
geschrieben haben, und ich sage nichts,
ist nichts mehr zu sagen, ist nichts mehr.

Strangers in The Night

In November, and again in December
I have to laugh, that was
quite a life for me.
The telephone has gone
quite pale, it rings in another way,
cigarettes have burned
my fingers,
and after that the cry
of the birds flying south.
We have spoken long distance,
and Jerusalem is always what
I thought of, which was mine.

How horrible
to scratch at my skin,
it is no longer possible
to hurt me deeply.
I talk and laugh and talk.
I can no longer be hurt deeply.

But the birds with their
terrible cries.
I let go of
a feeling, and that
was the last.

How tired I am and how I laugh,
and I drag myself to where the birds
have cried out, and I say nothing,
there is nothing more to say, nothing more.

Nur im November, und sogar im Dezember
ich habe deinen Namen in den Schnee
geschrieben und gejubelt.
Es war die schönste Zeit.
Nicht ich habe zu danken,
der frühe Winter hat ein
Glück gehabt mit mir, mit
uns beiden, vielleicht.
Wo bist du? Das ist keine Frage.
Ich weiß ja. Ich bin alt
und weise auch, das Grab ist geschaufelt,
da täuscht nichts.
Jugend, das ewigliche Licht,
ich habe es nie gesehen
aber ich plädiere für Dich.
Mir ist ein paar Wochen geschenkt worden,
was Jugend ist, und ich habe gewußt, ich
habe keinen Teil daran,
Ich möchte jung sein, [w]eil ich es nie war,
ich bin nur angenommen, nach Katastrophen,
und ich bin geduldet.

Only in November, and also in December,
I have written your name
in the snow and rejoiced.
It was the loveliest time.
It wasn't just thanks to me,
the early winter was also
lucky for me, for
us both, perhaps.
Where are you? That's not a question.
I already know. I am old
and wise, the grave is shoveled,
nothing will be spared.
Youth, that eternal light,
I never saw it,
but I plead for you.
A couple of weeks of youth have been
granted me, and I have known I
had no part in it.
I want to be young, because I never was.
I only arrived after catastrophes,
and I am patient.

Dein Tod, und Wieder

dein Tod, wüßt ich, wie er und warum,
gekommen ist, wär ich schon soviel
stiller, und ich rätsele und
rate, nenne es Verlust,
und mehr und weniger als das,

Wie bist du gestorben,
hinuntergestürzt direkt
direkt aus meinen Armen,
und aufgegeben direkt in
meinen Armen, wo ich
auch hingehe, mich
verfolgen diese fünf Schüsse,
oder waren es doch bloß zwei,
ich nenne es immer fünf,
die du mir zugefügt hast, und
mich nicht ermordet,
sondern doch dich,

Wer ist der Tote,
wenn er stirbt,
wenn sein Geist abfällig wird,
sein Körper unfaßbar,
was wird da bei mir noch bleiben,

nach soviel Jahren immer noch
und immer wieder.

Ich ruhe mich aus,
ein schwarzes Laken, von
[W]orten, und vollgesprochen
Kissen, hinuntergewürgt die
Gläser beinah mit dem Glas.

Your Death, and Beyond

Your death has occurred, I should know
its how and why if only
I were much more
at ease, though I puzzle
and guess, call it a loss
and nothing more or less than that.

How you died
is that you fell straight down,
straight out of my arms,
and were given up straight into
my arms, wherever I
go, these
five shots still haunt me,
or was it only two?
I always say it was five
which struck me, and
did not murder me,
but rather you.

Who is the dead one,
for if he has died,
if his spirit is disparaged,
his body unrecognizable,
what will still remain of me

after so many years
and ever after?

I am at rest,
a black sheet
of words and pillows
that tell all, the drink almost swallowed
glass and all.

An jemand ganz anderen

Daß die Pirellireifen, daß ich nicht,
daß ich, ich laß dich, auch dich,
auf dem nassen Asphalt, der darf
und ich nicht, ich starren auf den Knoten
deiner Krawatte und die Vögel, die
auf der Ausreise sind, die schreien
und jubeln und tödlich, und werden
morgen vergessen. Und ich darf nicht.

Was alles wag ich nicht. Ein Blick
ist zuviel, und die Zitronenscheibe
in deinem Glas, wenn du getrunken hast,
stürzt mich in die Verlegenheit.
Ich darf nachschenken, mehr nicht.

Ich bin aus einem anderen Land,
darf man dann nicht. Ein Blick auf
dein Gesicht bedeutet mein Auslöschen.
ich bin am äußren hängengeblieben,
inwendig hab ich nichts mehr. Ich
rühme nicht die sanften Bewegungen
deiner Gedanken und die Zuspitzung.
Ich schaue, und ich liege ohnmächtig
in einem Satz, den du sagst und
höre deine Stimme das passé defini,
und der konjunktiv, ich weiß nicht,
ob man mehr lieben kann, du sagst auch
: dunque, und ich sterbe und bete an,
während ich vor Träumereien die Rechnung
unseres Abends erhöhe, ich trinke noch
ein Glas und höre, ich höre ich verstehe.
vor lauter Zuhören
daß ich es nicht bin.

To Someone Entirely Different

That the Pirelli tires may hit
the wet asphalt and not I,
that I, I let you leave, also you,
who can while I cannot, I stare
at the knot in your tie and the birds
that are migrating as they cry
and rejoice and are mortal, and tomorrow
will forget. And I cannot.

There's so much I cannot handle. A glance
is too much, and the lemon slice
in your glass after you have drunk
plunges me into embarrassment.
I can only pour another, nothing more.

I am from a different country,
and therefore am not allowed. A glance at
your face means my extinction.
I merely remain on the margins,
inside I have nothing more. I
don't praise the calm movements
of your thoughts and sharp replies.
I look, and I melt
inside a sentence which you say and
I hear your voice, its *passé defini,*
and the conjunctive, and I don't know
if one could love someone more. You also say
dunque and I die and pray
as in my dreams I raise
the cost of our nights, drinking yet
another glass and listening, listening and understanding
through all the noise
that I am not the one.

Ich habe mich aufgelöst und meine
Vergangenheit in dir, und ich sitze am
Telefon und werde pronto sagen, und
ohne Hoffnung, daß es klingt, und
der Hörer wird schwarz werden vor
Angst und der verwickelte Draht
wird etwas wissen von der Verwicklung,
und das Klingeln wird in mein Herz
einen Schmerz von meinem Alter drehen,
und von Orten, an die ich reisen möchte und
einen kampf und ein Auslöschen, ich will
mich auslöschen wenn ich spreche.
Deine Erleichterung, daß ich Sätze bilde und Fehler
mache, ist meine Erleichterung.
Das Gepäck, ein Schutthaufen, wird nicht mehr
bewegt.

I have extinguished myself and my
past within you, and I am on the
telephone and say *pronto*, and
without hope that it's heard, as the
receiver becomes black
with fear and the tangled cord
will know something of entanglement,
and the ringing will register inside my heart
a pain appropriate to my age
and of those places I want to travel to,
and of a battle and an erasure, me wanting to
erase myself when I speak.
Your relief that I form sentences and make
mistakes is also my relief.
The suitcase, a heap of rubble, will no longer
budge.

V GEDICHTE 1964 – 1967

V   POEMS 1964 – 1967

Die radikale Mitte

Dürr, aber nur fürs Auge
Lebensknecht
federleichte Trümmer.

The Radical Means

Wasteland, but only to the eye
that serves life,
feather-light rubble.

Wahrlich

für Anna Achmatova

Wem es ein Wort nie verschlagen hat,
und ich sage es euch,
wer bloß sich zu helfen weiß
und mit den Worten —

dem ist nicht zu helfen.
Über den kurzen Weg nicht
und nicht über den langen.

Einen einzigen Satz haltbar zu machen,
auszuhalten in dem Bimbam von Worten.

Es schreibt diesen Satz keiner,
der nicht unterschreibt.

Truly

for Anna Akhmatova

To one who's never been stunned by a word,
and I say it to you all,
who only knows how to help himself
and only with words —

he cannot be helped.
Not over the short term
and not over the long.

To create a single lasting sentence,
to persevere in the ding-dong of words.

No one writes this sentence
who does not sign her name.

Böhmen liegt am Meer

Sind hierorts Häuser grün, tret ich noch in ein Haus.
Sind hier die Brücken heil, geh ich auf gutem Grund.
Ist Liebesmüh in alle Zeit verloren, verlier ich sie hier gern.

Bin ich's nicht, ist es einer, der ist so gut wie ich.

Grenzt hier ein Wort an mich, so laß ich's grenzen.
Liegt Böhmen noch am Meer, glaub ich den Meeren wieder.
Und glaub ich noch ans Meer, so hoffe ich auf Land.

Bin ich's, so ist's ein jeder, der ist soviel wie ich.
Ich will nichts mehr für mich. Ich will zugrunde gehn.

Zugrund — das heißt zum Meer, dort find ich Böhmen wieder.
Zugrund gerichtet, wach ich ruhig auf.
Von Grund auf weiß ich jetzt, und ich bin unverloren.

Kommt her, ihr Böhmen alle, Seefahrer, Hafenhuren und Schiffe
unverankert. Wollt ihr nicht böhmisch sein, Illyrer, Veroneser,
und Venezianer alle. Spielt die Komödien, die lachen machen

Und die zum Weinen sind. Und irrt euch hundertmal,
wie ich mich irrte und Proben nie bestand,
doch hab ich sie bestanden, ein um das andre Mal.

Wie Böhmen sie bestand und eines schönen Tags
ans Meer begnadigt wurde und jetzt am Wasser liegt.

Ich grenz noch an ein Wort und an ein andres Land,
ich grenz, wie wenig auch, an alles immer mehr,

ein Böhme, ein Vagant, der nichts hat, den nichts hält,
begabt nur noch, vom Meer, das strittig ist, Land meiner
    Wahl zu sehen.

Bohemia Lies By The Sea

If houses here are green, I'll step inside a house.
If bridges here are sound, I'll walk on solid ground.
If love's labour's lost in every age, I'd gladly lose it here.

If it's not me, it's one who is as good as me.

If a word here borders on me, I'll let it border.
If Bohemia still lies by the sea, I'll believe in the sea again.
And believing in the sea, thus I can hope for land.

If it's me, then it's anyone, for he's as worthy as me.
I want nothing more for myself. I want to go under.

Under — that means the sea, there I'll find Bohemia again.
From my grave, I wake in peace.
From deep down I know now, and I'm not lost.

Come here, all you Bohemians, seafarers, dock whores, and ships
unanchored. Don't you want to be Bohemians, all you Illyrians,
Veronese and Venetians. Play the comedies that make us laugh

until we cry. And err a hundred times,
as I erred and never withstood the trials,
though I did withstand them time after time.

As Bohemia withstood them and one fine day
was released to the sea and now lies by water.

I still border on a word and on another land,
I border, like little else, on everything more and more,

a Bohemian, a wandering minstrel, who has nothing, who
is held by nothing, gifted only at seeing, by a doubtful sea,
    the land of my choice.

Prag Jänner 64

Seit jener Nacht
gehe und spreche ich wieder,
böhmisch klingt es,
als wär ich wieder zuhause,

wo zwischen der Moldau, der Donau
und meinem Kindheitsfluß
alles einen Begriff von mir hat.

Gehen, schrittweis ist es wiedergekommen,
Sehen, angeblickt, habe ich wieder erlernt.

Gebückt noch, blinzelnd,
hing ich am Fenster,
sah die Schattenjahre,
in denen kein Stern
mir in den Mund hing,
sich über den Hügel entfernen.

Über den Hradschin
haben um sechs Uhr morgens
die Schneeschaufler aus der Tatra
mit ihren rissigen Pranken
die Scherben dieser Eisdecke gekehrt.

Unter den berstenden Blöcken
meines, auch meines Flusses
kam das befreite Wasser hervor.

Zu hören bis zum Ural.

Prague, January '64

Since that night
I walk and speak anew,
sounding Bohemian,
as if I were home again,

where between the Moldau, the Danube
and my childhood river,
everything owns a part of me.

Walking, it's all come back step by step;
seeing, observed, I've learned again.

Bent over, blinking,
I hung by the window,
saw the shadowy years
withdraw over the hill
in which no star
hung in my mouth.

Across the Hradčany,
at six in the morning,
Tatra snow shovelers
with their chapped paws
cleared away shards of this icy blanket.

Beneath the shattered slabs
of my, yes, my river too,
the liberated water appeared.

Audible as far away as the Urals.

Eine Art Verlust

Gemeinsam benutzt: Jahreszeiten, Bücher und eine Musik.
Die Schlüssel, die Teeschalen, den Brotkorb, Leintücher
    und ein Bett.
Eine Aussteuer von Worten, von Gesten, mitgebracht,
    verwendet, verbraucht.
Eine Hausordnung beachtet. Gesagt. Getan. Und immer
    die Hand gereicht.

In Winter, in ein Wiener Septett und in Sommer habe ich
    mich verliebt.
In Landkarten, in ein Bergnest, in einen Strand und in
    ein Bett.
Einen Kult getrieben mit Daten, Versprechen für
    unkündbar erklärt,
angehimmelt ein Etwas und fromm gewesen vor einem
    Nichts,

(— der gefalteten Zeitung, der kalten Asche, dem Zettel
    mit einer Notiz)
furchtlos in der Religion, denn die Kirche war dieses Bett.

Aus dem Seeblick hervor ging meine unerschöpfliche Malerei.
Von dem Balkon herab waren die Völker, meine Nachbarn,
    zu grüßen.
Am Kaminfeuer, in der Sicherheit, hatte mein Haar seine
    äußerste Farbe.
Das Klingeln an der Tür war der Alarm für meine Freude.

Nicht dich habe ich verloren,
sondern die Welt.

A Type of Loss

Jointly used: seasons, books and music.
The keys, the tea cups, the breadbasket, sheets
    and a bed.
A dowry of words, of gestures, brought along,
    used, spent.
Social manners observed. Said. Done. And always
    the hand extended.

With winter, a Vienna septet and with summer I've
    been in love.
With maps, a mountain hut, with a beach and
    a bed.
A cult filled with dates, promises made
    as if irrevocable,
enthused about Something and pious before Nothing,

(— the folded newspapers, cold ashes, the slip of paper
    with a jotted note)
fearless in religion, as the church was this bed.

From the seascape came my inexhaustible painting.
From the balcony, the people, my neighbors,
    were there to be greeted.
By the fireplace, in safety, my hair had its most exceptional
    color.
The doorbell ringing was the alarm for my joy.

It was not you I lost,
but the world.

Enigma

für Hans Werner Henze aus der Zeit der Ariosi

Nichts mehr wird kommen.

Frühling wird nicht mehr werden.
Tausendjährige Kalender sagen es jedem voraus.

Aber auch Sommer und weiterhin, was so gute Namen
wie »sommerlich« hat —
es wird nichts mehr kommen.

Du sollst ja nicht weinen,
sagt eine Musik.

Sonst
sagt
niemand
etwas.

Enigma

for Hans Werner Henze at the time of A

Nothing more will come.

Spring will no longer flourish.
Millenial calenders forecast it already.

But also summer and more, sweet words
such as "summery" —
nothing more will come.

You mustn't cry,
says the music.

Otherwise
no one
says
anything.

Keine Delikatessen

Nichts mehr gefällt mir.

Soll ich
eine Metapher ausstaffieren
mit einer Mandelblüte?
die Syntax kreuzigen
auf einen Lichteffekt?
Wer wird sich den Schädel zerbrechen
über so überflüssige Dinge —

Ich habe ein Einsehn gelernt
mit den Worten,
die da sind
(für die unterste Klasse)

Hunger
          Schande
                    Tränen
und
                    Finsternis.

Mit dem ungereinigten Schluchzen,
mit der Verzweiflung
(und ich verzweifle noch vor Verzweiflung)
über das viele Elend,
den Krankenstand, die Lebenskosten,
werde ich auskommen.

No Delicacies

Nothing pleases me anymore.

Should I
fit out a metaphor
with an almond blossom?
crucify the syntax
upon an effect of light?
Who will rack their brains
over such superfluous things —

I have learned an insight
with words
that exist
(for the lowest class)

Hunger
        Shame
                Tears
and
                        Darkness.

With unpurged tears,
with despair
(and I despair in the face of despair)
about so much misery,
the sick pay, the cost of living,
I will get by.

Ich vernachlässige nicht die Schrift,
sondern mich.
Die andern wissen sich
weißgott
mit den Worten zu helfen.
Ich bin nicht mein Assistent.

Soll ich
einen Gedanken gefangennehmen,
abführen in eine erleuchtete Satzzelle?
Aug und Ohr verköstigen
mit Worthappen erster Güte?
erforschen die Libido eines Vokals,
ermitteln die Liebhaberwerte unserer Konsonanten?

Muß ich
mit dem verhagelten Kopf,
mit dem Schreibkrampf in dieser Hand,
unter dreihundertnächtigem Druck
einreißen das Papier,
wegfegen die angezettelten Wortopern,
vernichtend so: ich du und er sie es

wir ihr?

(Soll doch. Sollen die andern.)

Mein Teil, es soll verloren gehen.

I don't neglect writing,
but rather myself.
The others are able
God knows
to get by with words.
I am not my assistant.

Should I
arrest an idea, lead it off
to a bright sentence cell?
feed sight and hearing
with first-class word morsels?
analyze the libido of a vowel,
estimate the collector's value of our consonants?

Must I
battered by hail,
with the writing cramp in this hand,
under the pressure of the three hundredth night
rip up the paper,
sweep away the scribbled word operas,
annihilating as well: I you and he she it

we you all?

(Should? The others should.)

My part, it shall be lost.

NOTES TO THE TRANSLATION

BORROWED TIME

Fall Down Heart: "Hymettus" is the name of a mountain that overlooks Athens from the east, and which is famous for its honey and marble.

Reigen: This is also the title of a play by Arthur Schnitzler, written in 1900 and first published in 1921. Causing an uproar in Vienna because of its blatant sexuality, it was subsequently banned. Schnitzler then insisted that the play should not be performed until fifty years after his death, a wish culminated by the first performance given in Vienna by the Akademietheater in 1983.

Autumn Maneuver: In the postwar era, NATO troops stationed in Germany routinely conducted "autumn maneuvers" each year.

Borrowed Time: In German, "der Sand" is a masculine noun, thus creating a distinct gender relation between the sand and the loved one that does not carry over into English. Hans Höller points out a strong echo in this poem with Brecht's "Aus einem Lesebuch für Städtebewohner" (See Höller, *Das Werk*, 22).

In Twilight: The first line in German makes use of the idiom, "die Hand ins Feuer legen," meaning to swear or guarantee that something is true.

Early Noon: Numerous critics have pointed out that stanzas 4 and 5 contain strong echoes of Goethe's lyric "Der König in Thule" from *Faust I*. "Am Brunnen vor dem Tore" is also the first line of Wilhelm Mühler's "Der Lindenbaum," which Schubert set to music in *Die Winterreise*.

Great Landscape Near Vienna: stanza 6 — "Limes" is the name of the system of Roman fortifications along the banks of the Danube which represented the northern defense line of the Roman Empire in present day Austria. Hans Holthusen was the first to observe the similarity between Bachmann's depiction of Vienna in stanza 7 and the portrait of the city in Carol Reed's film, *The Third Man* (See Holthusen 32), a film which also provides the title and inspiration for the central chapter of Bachmann's novel *Malina*. Meanwhile, George Schoolfield astutely observes that the character Orson Welles famously portrays in the film is named Harry Lime, thus rendering a more sinister feel to Bachmann's construction of "Limesgefühl."

Stanza 11 — "Maria am Gestade" is the name of a church located on the banks of the Danube canal in Vienna that is also prominently featured in *The Third Man*.

A Monologue of Prince Myshkin to the Ballet Pantomime "The Idiot": The speaker and all of the characters portrayed are from Dostoevsky's novel *The Idiot*. The basic plot line that Bachmann draws upon is the competition between Prince Myshkin and Parfyon Rogozhin over Nastasya Filippovna, who is eventually murdered by Rogozhin. For a time, Aglaia is also romantically linked to Myshkin, though he ends up rejecting her, while Ganya Ivolgin, Totski, and General Epanchin are figures from the Petersburg society that prey upon the well meaning, yet naive Myshkin. It's interesting to note that the one major character not referred to or portrayed by Bachmann is the consumptive idealist, Ippolit.

The composer for the pantomime, Hans Werner Henze, also collaborated with Bachmann on two operas, as well as setting several of her poems to music.

INVOCATION OF THE GREAT BEAR

Of a Land, a River and Lakes: The first line of the poem derives from the title of a Grimm fairy tale, "Märchen von einer, der auszog, das Fürchten zu lernen." Bachmann, however, does not follow the plot of the tale in constructing her own tale or myth over the length of the poem.

Section VII, stanza 6—"Wacholder" is a brand of schnapps.

Invocation of the Great Bear: The bear referred to is that of the Big Dipper constellation, otherwise known as Ursa Major. Here the bear is not only spoken to, but also speaks at the start of the second stanza.

My Bird: Hans Holthusen was the first to point out that the owl is associated with Athena in Greek mythology, the goddess of wisdom, war, and the arts (See Holthusen 47).

Curriculum Vitae: "Rose Red" in stanza 2 is a figure from another Grimm fairy tale whose sister's name is Snow White.

The Blue Hour: stanza 3—"Sternthaler" is a little girl in a Grimm fairy tale by the same name. Having given away her bread, shoes, and dress to others more needy, she becomes rich when she collects the stars falling out of the sky in her slip. "Sternthaler" is also the name of a 19th-century German coin.

Songs from an Island: This poem was set to music by Hans Werner Henze, carrying with it the same title.

In Apulia: The title refers to a region in southeastern Italy.

At Agrigento: Agrigento is a town located in southwestern Italy that is also the site of Greek temples.

Songs in Flight—The epigraph is from Petrarch's "Triumph of Love." Ernest Hatch Wilkins translates the passage as "Hard is the law of Love! But though unjust/ One must obey it, for that law prevails/ Throughout the universe, and lasts for aye" (*The Triumphs of Petrarch*, Chicago: University of Chicago Press, 1962, p. 26).

Section III, stanza 1—The Sporades are a group of Greek islands located in the Aegean Sea.

Section IV, stanzas 2 and 3—Posilipo and Vomero are hillside regions on the outskirts of Naples. Camaldoli is a mountain just north of Florence.

Section XIV, stanza 1—The Toledo is the central river of Naples.

Section XV—Holthusen observes the strong links between this section and Rilke's *Sonette an Orpheus,* "I,19" (See Holthusen 51). Kurt Bartsch also observes a link between "Sinken um uns von Gestirnen" and Robert Musil's play *Die Schwärmer,* which Bachmann helped adapt for the radio.

EARLY AND LATE POEMS

I Poems 1945 – 1956

Included in this section are poems, both published and unpublished, written up through the time of Bachmann's second book of poems. Roughly half the poems that appear here were published in journals or in the four-volume collected *Werke* which appeared in 1978. The rest appear in German and English for the very first time and can be found in the Bachmann Archive located in the Österreichische Nationalbibliothek (ONB) in Vienna. In the following notes I list the "Blatt" or page number in the archive for those poems appearing for the first time. The page numbers represent no fixed chronology of production or arrangement, for the archive was composed quite haphazardly after Bachmann's death. However, I have tried to group poems together in accordance with shared thematic concerns and similarities in typeface that distinguish different parts of Bachmann's career. A more precise arrangement and dating of the poems must await an authoritative critical edition in German.

Anxieties: ONB, Blatt 6188. In the twelfth line of the poem there appears the words "enden los," which is a typo for "endlos" in German.

[The Night Unfolds the Sad Part of the Face]: ONB, Blatt 397-397A.

In War: ONB, Blatt 144.

Liberation: ONB, Blatt 400a.

[On the Brow of the Year]: ONB, Blatt, 402.

Libraries: ONB, Blatt 399.

Waiting Before the Doors: ONB, Blatt 401.

Unappeasable: ONB, Blatt 392.

Between Yesterday and Tomorrow: ONB, Blatt 387.

Tomorrow I Will Leave: ONB, Blatt 396.

Purgatory: ONB, Blatt 394.

Rejoicing: ONB, Blatt 407.

Without Hope: ONB, Blatt 186.

City: ONB, Blatt, 321A.

Where To?: ONB, Blatt 189.

II Poems 1957 – 1961

Included here are poems written after the publication of *Invocation of the Great Bear*, but prior to Bachmann's split with Max Frisch in 1962 and subsequent breakdown. Except for the first poem and the two poems before and after "You Words," which appear here in German for the first time, the poems of this section were previously published in the 1978 collected *Werke*. Below I list the page number in the archive for each of the poems that appear from it.

William Turner: ONB, Blatt 479.

Hôtel de la Paix: This is the name of a hotel in Paris where Bachmann lived in the fall of 1956 during an extended illness.

Aria I: Both this and "Safe Conduct (Aria II)" were set to music by Hans Werner Henze in an orchestral piece titled "Nachtstücke und Arien nach Gedichte von Ingeborg Bachmann."

Dialects: ONB, Blatt 208. The last line in the German is followed by the word "wo" which I have left out.

The Tightened Lip: ONB, Blatt 208 – 209.

You Words: Nelly Sachs (1891-1970) was born in Berlin and lived for many years in Sweden. She was awarded the Nobel Prize for Literature in 1966.

New Under the Sky: ONB, Blatt 370. In line 7 of the fourth stanza I interpret the words "Herlust" and "Herrscht" in the original to really be "Verlust" and "Herrschaft."

Lay Down Your Weapons: ONB, Blatt 254.

III Poems 1962 – 1963

The poems of this section are those written predominantly in response to Bachmann's breakup with Max Frisch in the fall of 1962 and her subsequent breakdown. Hospitalized in Zurich and Berlin, as well as seeking the advice of doctors and cures throughout Europe, Bachmann turned to poetry as a means to express and grapple with her physical and psychological anguish. The result is that many of the poems were written in haste and later abandoned, though Bachmann held on to the manuscripts and produced several drafts of some of the poems at different times.

The publication of such intense and personal material after an author's death often raises troubling questions. However, Bachmann's heirs decided that there were too many important ties to Bachmann's development as a writer to keep the poems locked up in the archive. Thus in 2000, Isolde Moser, Heinz Bachmann, and Christian Moser (Bachmann's sister, brother, and nephew, respectively) published *Ich weiß keine bessere Welt* (Piper), which collects the poems written during Bachmann's breakdown and gradual recovery from 1962 to 1964.

Rather than simply reproduce this massive grouping of 103 poems in translation, I have separated them into two sections, based on what I perceive as an important shift in their focus which Hans Höller first called attention to in his book, *Ingeborg Bachmann: Letzte, unveröffentliche Gedichte, Entwürfe und Fassungen*. Though he sights "Sound Barrier" ("Schallmauer") as marking the shift in Bachmann's concerns from her inward struggle with loss, anxiety, and addiction to a more outward engagement with the world by seeing her own illness as a metaphorical representation of society's historical ills, I have chosen the poem that precedes it, "The German Miracle" ("Das deutsche Wunder") to open a new and separate section of the poems from *Ich weiß keine bessere Welt* that follows this one.

While many of these poems show Bachmann at her weakest as both a suffering individual and a writer struggling to hold onto her voice, there are also important developments going on in her thinking that foreshadow and link to some of the basic assumptions underlying the *Todesarten* cycle. Indeed, one can date Bachmann's "recovery" to *Ein Ort für Zufälle*, her acceptance speech for the Georg Büchner Prize, written in the summer of 1964 and delivered that fall. In a draft to the speech, Bachmann declares that illness must be seen as an "expression of defeat in the face of reality" (cited in Hans Höller's *Ingeborg Bachmann*, (Reinbek: Rowohlt, 1999) 125, (my translation), yet the malaise is also one experienced in relation to the society at large. It is this crucial linkage between the sufferings of the individual and the deeper social ills that have helped to produce them which Bachmann's poems of 1962 to 1964 gradually work towards.

To augment the personal nature of Bachmann's struggle, I begin Section III with four previously unpublished poems from the archive that seem to me to speak directly to the relationship with Frisch and anticipate its end. As before, I indicate their page numbers in the archive in the notes below. The rest of Section III and all of Section IV consist exclusively of poems from *Ich weiß keine bessere Welt*. In neither section do I alter the order in which the poems are presented in that volume.

Finally, given that these translations are from unfinished drafts, at times I have had to make choices between alternative readings and have supplied punctuation and capitalization in English where it seems to me likely or implied in the original, while also maintaining the original punctuation and spelling in the German. In addition, Bachmann's heirs have called attention to words that are somewhat illegible or unreadable in the original by underlining them in the German, which I list in the following notes. Where they have left blanks for words that cannot be read, I have indicated the same in both the German and English. The notes to *Ich weiß keine bessere Welt* offer even more information about handwritten corrections and stray lines that appear on the manuscript pages, but I will leave it to readers to consult those on their own. Further information about precise dating and the ordering of the poems will again have to await a critical edition in German.

Your Voice: ONB, Blatt 490. The end of the third line contains the alternative phrase "der Gast, der kommt." Similarly, the second stanza that appears here is preceded by a draft stanza that reads, "Was du auch sagst: ich werd es nie begreifen,/ und zwischen dem Vokal und Konsonant/ fühl ich den Hauch, der Liebe Niederkunft.// eh deine Stimme herrlich niederkommt." In addition, after the last version of the second stanza I use here, there appears the phrase, "Ich rate." It is possible that this indicates the beginning of a new version of the same poem, or a different poem. As a compromise, I have chosen to split the poem into two numbered sections, utilizing what I take to be the latest versions of alternative readings.

Prayer for Transformation: ONB, Blatt 470.

My Love After Many Years: ONB, Blatt 466. The title contains the alternate phrase "vielen Jahren" for "langer Zeit." My utilization of the first in translation is from a preference in tone in the translation.

Waiting Room: ONB, Blatt 277.

I've Misplaced My Poems: "los planetas" in the third stanza is misspelled as "las planetas" in the original.

Everything Is Lost: In manuscript this poem is preceded by two stanzas that read, "Ich habe die Gedichte verloren/ sie allein nicht, aber zuerst" and "Gedichte sind verloren gegangen/ nicht sie allein, aber zuerst das Gedicht/ dann der Schlaf, dann die …." In addition, Bachmann's heirs indicate that the words "verbriefte," "hinten," "Weiten," "er," and "Erstummter" in the second stanza, as well as "Erstummten" and "einpuppt" in the third are somewhat illegible in the original.

Island of the Dead: The words "gescheiterten" in line 13 and "das" in line 17 are somewhat illegible in the original.

The Night of the Lost/ The End of Love: Liking the way that these two alternative titles worked together, I've chosen to maintain both in the translation. The word "feingewirkte" is difficult to read in the original.

Until We Meet Again: Who Plaga is or the poem referred to remains unknown. The name is also difficult to read in the original.

Blackness: This is titled "Ein Tag" by the heirs and begins with the line "Ein Tag, von dem du nichts erzählen wirst," followed by "Schwarzsicht," which seems to be the beginning of a separate poem. I have chosen the second as a title for the poem, as it is centered above the poem, and thus could indeed be a title, and because it speaks to the poem itself. In addition, "den" in line 4 and "Gestank" in line 6 are difficult to read in the original.

Question: The heirs title this poem "In Memoriam K.A. Hartmann" and use "Frage" as the first line. However, as "Frage" is centered over the poem, and the poem begins with a question, it makes sense to me that it could also be read as the title. Meanwhile, line 15, "der uns einübt schon ins Gewahrsam" is somewhat illegible, as is the last word, "verbracht." K.A. Hartmann (1905 – 1963) was a German composer who defied the Nazi regime and yet managed to live out the war in Germany.

Diavolezza: This is the name of a cable car in the Ticino region of Switzerland. It also means "devil" or "devilish" in Italian. In line 18, "treibt" is questionable in the original.

Gloriastrasse: This is the street in Zurich where the Bircher-Benner Clinic is located where Bachmann was hospitalized for a time in 1962. In line 33 of the second version, "Flaschen" is somewhat illegible. In line 17 of the third version, the phrase "wahsinniger Anblick" is hard to read.

Day Nurse, Night Nurse: In line 7, the phrase "am Bett" is somewhat illegible. There are also two lines after the end of the poem that I do not include here. They read, "Nadeln bis ans Heft/ ins Fleisch bohren."

For Ingmar Bergman, Who Knows About the Wall: The word "düngt" in line 40 is uncertain.

[I Should Disappear]: The word "dahin" in line 2 is somewhat illegible, as is "mich" in line 16.

My Cell: "hatte" in line 2 is difficult to read, as is "da" in line 5 and "o" at the beginning of the last stanza.

[I Have the Quill]: "*Ma tu*" and "*A ci*" are Italian and mean "But you" and "To here," though the last is grammatically incorrect and could mean "To us." Also, "nichts" in line 18 is somewhat illegible.

The Life Line: In line 15, "an" is difficult to read.

Gently and Softly: "Gently and Softly" are the opening words to Isolde's final monologue before she expires over the body of Tristan in Wagner's opera. In the last two lines of the second version of this poem, the words "Am," "noch," and "gehaßten" are somewhat illegible. In the third version, "Tot ist alles. Alles tot." is also a quote from *Tristan and Isolde*. Also in the third version, the word "eingenährt" is a likely misspelling of "eingenäht" in German.

Watch Out: The word "nur" in line 23 is somewhat illegible, as is the phrase "Auge weckt mich wieder" in line 40 and the word "abzustürzen" in line 42.

[It Occurs to Me What the Last Days Mean]: The word "zum" in line 3 is difficult to read, as are the words "ihnen" and "Blutenbuch" in line 12 and "dem" in line 15. Though in line 4 the heirs seem to have trouble making out "an" and "Taube," these seem to me clear and I have chosen to render them as such here.

Alla piu umile, alle piu umana, alla piu sofferente: The title phrase means roughly, "To the humblest one (feminine), to the most human one, to the one who suffers most." The epigraph means "to live ardently and not feel pain" and is by the Italian poet Gaspara Stampa (c.1523 – 1554), who is best known for a sonnet cycle written to her lover, Count Collaltino de Collato. The "Bridge of Angels" mentioned in the eighth stanza is located in Rome, while "*O Scarpia, davanti a Dio*" is spoken by Tosca in Puccini's opera as she leaps to her death after realizing that Scarpia has betrayed her and ordered the death of her lover, Mario Cavaradossi, who is also the "Mario" of stanza nine.

The Penal Code of Gaspara Stampa: The phrase "nur Menschen gestattet" in line 5 is somewhat illegible, as are the words "ausgespuckt" in line 12, "zufassen" in line 32, and "geht" in line 43.

Un altra notte ancora senza vederlo: This means "yet another night without seeing him."

[Always to Live Among Words]: In line 14, the word "in" is unclear in the original.

Suspicion: The word "dir" is difficult to read in line 9 of the original.

Pious and Wicked: The word "gradsein" in line 12 is somewhat illegible.

At the Berlin Telephone Exchange: At the time Bachmann wrote this, it was common to go to a post office in Germany to make long distance telephone calls.

[That It Was Worse Yesterday Than It is Today]: The word "diese" in line 25 is somewhat illegible.

IV Poems 1963 – 1964

As mentioned in the note to the previous section, the poems contained here continue the order and arrangement set down by the heirs in *Ich weiß keine bessere Welt*. I have chosen to split the poems into two sections to call attention to a subtle but important shift from the inward to the outward in Bachmann's focus. Through the dates that head these two sections, I also wish to imply a progression in Bachmann's health and outlook in the winter of 1963/64 that would allow her to complete the vital work on *Ein Ort für Zufälle* the following summer. However, it is important to emphasize that such dating remains a critical conjecture that awaits more precise dating and organization from a German critical edition. What is clear is that by January of 1964, Bachmann was well enough to make a journey to Prague, followed by a return visit there in February. Both of these trips proved revelatory in convincing Bachmann that she had found a way to leave her pain behind and begin anew. Her journey to Egypt and the Sudan later that spring underscored her sense of her own recovery, however precarious, and would provide the setting and experience for the early drafts of *Das Buch Franza* and what would become the *Todesarten* cycle. That transition, however, first begins here in these poems.

The German Miracle: The word "Geschichte" is unclear in line 23. Also, because there is a distinct separation in spacing and subject matter between the sixth and seventh stanzas of the poem, I have chosen to split the poem into two sections. It is even quite possible that these represent two different poems, with the second possibly carrying "Secret Agents" as a title rather than as a first line.

Sound Barrier: In line 25, "ausgerissenen" is somewhat illegible.

Silent Night, Holy Night: In line 13, "geklebt" is somewhat illegible.

[Someone Shall Be Saved]: This poem appears on the same page as ["Who Picks Me Up?"]. Rather than see it as an extension of that poem, I have set it off in its own right, mainly because of its distinct content and the fact that "Es soll gerettet werden" is centered above the lines that follow it, thus making it appear more of a title than a line unto itself. Meanwhile, "eh" in line 3 is hard to make out, and quite possibly can be read as "als."

Night of Love: Above the title appear the lines, "Wiedergefunden hab ich/ in einer Nacht der Liebe/ wiedergefundem," which I have not included here.

Return Home via Prague: "Heimstätte" in line 4 is not entirely legible.

Dissolution: The word "zubereitet" in line 16 is unclear.

[I Did It with Pleasure, You Prudes]: The word "raschschlüssigen" in line 13 is unclear. Also, Bachmann's use of the phrase "wo die Rasse niedrig Deiner" in the last stanza is an allusion to a line from Arthur Rimbaud's "Une saison en enfer": "Je suis de race inférieure de toute éternité," which Bachmann also alludes to in *The Book of Franza*.

Strangers in the Night: In the penultimate line, "angenommen" is somewhat illegible and is probably a typo for "angekommen" in the German. Also, in the fourth stanza, "geschrieben" is probably a typo for "geschriehen" in the German.

To Someone Entirely Different: The word "kampf" in line 41 is hard to make out.

V Poems 1964 – 1967

These last seven poems represent Bachmann's poetic output during the early years of her concentrated work on the *Todesarten* cycle. They are also some of the most important and beautiful poems that she wrote, and they represent her clear return to full poetic mastery. The only previously unpublished poem that is clearly part of this group is "The Radical Means," which is the only poem to share the same typeface as "Truly" and appears here for the first time.

The Radical Means: ONB, Blatt 2484.

Truly: Bachmann met Akhmatova in Rome in late 1964 and published this poem in 1965. In 1967, Bachmann left her publisher, R. Piper Verlag, in protest against their publication of Akhmatova's selected poems in a translation done by Hans Baumann, a poet embraced by the Nazis. After publishing *Malina* with Suhrkamp Verlag, she later returned to Piper.

Bohemia Lies by the Sea: Bachmann refers to Shakespeare's *Love's Labour's Lost* in the third line, as well as *The Winter's Tale* and the fact that Shakespeare was criticized by Johnson for saying in the play that Bohemia lies by the sea when, in fact, it does not (See Bartsch 132-133).

Prague, January '64: The Hradčany is the name of the central square in Prague.

Enigma: Hans Werner Henze's "Ariosi" is a musical setting of poems by Torquato Tasso (1544 – 1595). Kurt Bartsch points out that "Nichts mehr wird kommen" is a line from the "Peter Altenberglieder" of Alban Berg, while "Du sollst ja nicht weinen" comes from Mahler's Symphony No. 2. (See Bartsch 130).

INGEBORG BACHMANN: A CHRONOLOGY

1926
Birth on June 25 in Klagenfurt, Austria.

1945–50
Study of law, then philosophy at the universities of Innsbruck, Graz, and Vienna. Degree awarded by the University of Vienna in 1950 for a dissertation titled "The Critical Reception of Martin Heidegger's Existential Philosophy."

1948–49
First poems published in *Lynkeus*, edited by Hermann Hakel.

1951–53
Scriptwriter at Radio Rot-Weiß-Rot in Vienna.

1952
First reading at the Gruppe 47 gathering. Libretto for the ballet pantomime *The Idiot*, with music by Hans Werner Henze.

1953
Receives the Gruppe 47 Prize. *Die gestundete Zeit*, poetry, published by Frankfurt Verlaganstalt. In summer lives on the island of Ischia with Hans Werner Henze.

1953–57
Principal residence in Rome.

1955
Die Zikaden, radio play, produced in Hamburg. Invitation to take part in international seminar at the Harvard Summer School of Arts and Sciences, led by Henry Kissinger.

1956
Spends February to August with Hans Werner Henze in Naples. *Anrufung des großen Bären*, poetry, published by R. Piper Verlag, Munich.

1957
Awarded the Bremen Literature Prize.

1957–58
Works as a dramaturge for Bavarian Television and Radio in Munich.

1958
Der gute Gott von Manhattan, radio play, broadcast in Munich and Hamburg. Meets the Swiss writer Max Frisch and moves to Zürich.

1959
Awarded the Radio Play Prize of the War Blind. Delivers acceptance speech titled "Die Wahrheit ist dem Menschen zumutbar."

1959–60
Delivers the first lectures for the poetry chair at Frankfurt University concerning "Fragen zeitgenössischer Dichtung."

1960
Libretto for Hans Werner Henze's opera *Der Prinz von Homburg*. Moves back to Rome with Max Frisch.

1961
Das dreißigste Jahr, stories, published by R. Piper Verlag, Munich. Awarded the Berlin Critics Prize. Translations of Giuseppe Ungaretti published by Suhrkamp, Frankfurt.

1962
Breakup with Max Frisch. Hospitalization in Zürich.

1963
Residence in Berlin through 1965 with support of Ford Foundation.

1964
Travels to Prague in January and February. Travels to Egypt and the Sudan in late spring. Awarded Georg Büchner Prize. Her acceptance speech, "Deutsche Zufälle" is later published as *Ein Ort für Zufälle* by Klaus Wagenbuch, Berlin, with thirteen drawings by Günter Grass.

1965
Libretto for Hans Werner Henze's opera *Der junge Lord*. Meeting with Anna Akhmatova in Rome. Return to Rome as principal residence until the end of her life.

1966
Reading tour of Germany in which she reads from the *Todesarten* cycle for the first time.

1967
Leaves her publisher, R. Piper Verlag, in protest of the publication of translations of Akhmatova's poems by Hans Baumann, a former Nazi poet.

1968
Awarded the Austrian State Prize for Literature.

1971
Malina, novel, published by Suhrkamp, Frankfurt.

1972
Simultan, stories, published by R. Piper Verlag, Munich. Awarded Anton Wildgans Prize of Society of Austrian Industrialists.

1973
Death in Rome on October 17. Burial in Klagenfurt.

SELECTED BIBLIOGRAPHY

I. Works by Bachmann

Die gestundete Zeit. Frankfurt am Main: Frankfurter Verlaganstalt, 1953. Munich: Piper, 1957.

Anrufung des grössen Bären. Munich: Piper, 1956.

Der gute Gott von Manhattan. Munich: Piper, 1958.

Das dreißigste Jahr. Munich: Piper, 1961.

Gedichte, Erzählungen, Hörspiel, Essays. Munich: Piper, 1964.

Ein Ort für Zufälle. Illustrated by Günter Grass. Berlin: Wagenbach, 1965.

Malina. Frankfurt am Main: Suhrkamp, 1971.

Simultan. Munich: Piper, 1972.

Werke. 4 vols. Ed. Christine Koschel, Inge von Weidenbaum, and Clemens Münster. Munich: Piper, 1978.

Frankfurter Vorlesungen: Probleme zeitgenössischer Dichtung. Munich: Piper, 1980.

Die Wahrheit ist dem Menschen zumutbar: Essays, Reden, Kleinere Schriften. Munich: Piper, 1981.

Wir müssen wahre Sätze finden: Gespräche und Interviews. Ed. Christine Koschel und Inge von Weidenbaum. Munich: Piper, 1983.

"Todesarten"—Projekt. 4 vols. Ed. Monika Albrecht and Dirk Göttsche. Munich: Piper, 1995.

Ich weiß keine bessere Welt. Ed. Isolde Moser, Heinz Bachmann, and Christian Moser. Munich: Piper, 2000.

II. Works by Bachmann in English

In the Storm of Roses: Selected Poems of Ingeborg Bachmann. Trans., ed., and intro. Mark Anderson. Princeton: Princeton UP, 1986.

The Thirtieth Year. Trans. Michael Bullock. London: Andre Deutsch, 1964. New York: Holmes & Meier, 1987.

Three Paths to the Lake. Trans. Mary Fran Gilbert. New York: Holmes & Meier, 1989.

Malina. Trans. Philip Boehm. New York: Holmes & Meier, 1990.

The Book of Franza and *Requiem for Fanny Goldmann.* Trans. Peter Filkins. Evanston: Northwestern UP, 1999.

Letters to Felician. Trans. Damion Searls. Green Integer, 2004.

III. Works on Bachmann

Achberger, Karen R. *Understanding Ingeborg Bachmann.* Understanding Modern European and Latin American Literature, ed. James N. Hardin. Columbia: U. South Carolina P., 1994.

Albrecht, Monika and Dirk Göttsche. *"Über die Zeit schreiben": Literatur- und kulturwissenschaftliche Essays zu Ingeborg Bachmanns "Todesarten" Projekt.* Würzburg: Königshausen/Neumann, 1998.

------, eds. *"Über die Zeit schreiben" II.* Würzburg: Königshausen/Neumann, 2000.

------. *Bachmann Handbuch.* Stuttgart: Metzler, 2002.

Bareiss, Otto, and Frauke Ohloff. *Ingeborg Bachmann: Eine Bibliographie.* Munich: Piper, 1978.

------. "Ingeborg Bachmann: Bibliographie 1977/78 – 1981/82." *Jahrbuch der Grillparzer-Gesellschaft,* III/15 (1983): 173–217.

------. "Ingeborg Bachmann: Bibliographie 1981/82 – 1985". *Jahrbuch der Grillparzer-Gesellschaft,* III/16 (1986): 201–275.

------. "Ingeborg Bachmann: Bibliographie 1985 – 1988." *Jahrbuch der Grill-parzer-Gesellschaft,* III/17 (1991): 251–327.

------. "Ingeborg Bachmann: Bibliographie 1989 – 1993" in Pichl, Robert and Alexander Still Mark, eds., *Kritische Wege der Landnahme. Ingeborg Bachmann im Blickfield der neunziger Jahre.* Vienna, 1994.

Bartsch, Kurt. *Ingeborg Bachmann.* Stuttgart: Metzler, 1988.

Beicken, Peter. *Ingeborg Bachmann.* Munich: Beck, 1988.

Bender, Wolfgang. "Ingeborg Bachmann," in *Deutsche Literatur der Gegenwart,* ed. Dietrich Weber. Stuttgart: Kröner, 1976. 584–604.

Böschenstein, Bernhard and Sigrid Weigel, eds. *Ingeborg Bachmann und Paul Celan: Poetische Korrespondenzen.* Frankfurt: Suhrkamp, 1997.

Brokoph-Mauch, Gurdrun. *Thunder Rumbling at My Heels: Tracing Ingeborg Bachmann.* Riverside: Ariadne, 1998.

Brinker-Gabler, Gisela, and Markus Zisselsberger, eds. *If We Had the Word: Ingeborg Bachmann, Views and Reviews.* Riverside: Ariadne, 2004.

Bürger, Christa. "Ingeborg Bachmann's Emergence from Aesthetic Modernism." *New German Critique* 47 (1989): 3–28.

Gölz, Sabine I. "Reading in Twilight: Canonization, Gender, the Limits of Language — and a Poem by Ingeborg Bachmann." *New German Critique* 47 (1989): 29–52.

Hapkemeyer, Andreas. *Ingeborg Bachmann: Entwicklungslinen in Werk und Leben.* Vienna: Verlag der Österreichischen Akademie der Wissenschaften, 1990.

Hoell, Joachim. *Ingeborg Bachmann.* Munich: Deutsche Taschenbuch, 2001.

Höller, Hans, ed. *Der dunkle Schatten, dem ich schon seit Anfang folge — Vorschläge zu einer neuen Lektüre des Werkes.* Vienna: Löcker, 1982.

------. *Ingeborg Bachmann: Das Werk. Von den frühesten Gedichten bis zum "Todesarten"-Zyklus.* Second Editon. Frankfurt: Hain, 1993.

------. *Ingeborg Bachmann.* Reinbek bei Hamburg: Rowohlt, 1999.

Ingeborg Bachmann. Eine Einführung. Munich: Piper, 1963.

Johnson, Uwe. *Eine Reise nach Klagenfurt.* Frankfurt: Suhrkamp, 1974. English trans., Damion Searls. Evanston: Northwestern UP, 2004.

Koschel, Christine, Inge von Weidenbaum, eds. *Kein objektives Urteil — nur ein lebendiges: Texte zum Werk von Ingeborg Bachmann.* Munich: Piper, 1989.

Lyons, James K. "The Poetry of Ingeborg Bachmann: A Primeval Impulse in the Modern Wasteland." *German Life & Letters* 17 (1963-1964): 206–215.

Marsch, Edgar. "Ingeborg Bachmann," in *Deutsche Dichter der Gegenwart*, ed. Benno von Wiese. Berlin: Schmidt, 1973: 515–530.

Mayer, Matthias, ed. *Interpretationen: Werke von Ingeborg Bachmann.* Stuttgart: Reclam, 2002.

Modern Austrian Literature. Special Ingeborg Bachmann Issue, 18, Nos. 3-4 (1985).

Pichl, Robert. "Voraussetzungen und Problemhorizont der gegenwärtigen Ingeborg-Bachmann-Forschung." *Jahrbuch der Grillparzer-Gesellschaft,* III/14 (1980): 77–93.

------, ed. "Ingeborg Bachmann. Registratur des literarischen Nachlasses." Vienna: Institut für Germanistik, 1981.

Remmler, Karen. *Waking the Dead: Correspondences Between Walter Benjamin's Concept of Remembrance and Ingeborg Bachmann's Ways of Dying.* Riverside: Ariadne, 1996.

Schlotthaus, Werner L. "Ingeborg Bachmann's Poem 'Mein Vogel': An Analysis of Modern Poetic Metaphor." *Modern Language Quarterly* 22/2 (1961): 181–191.

Schoolfield, George C. "Ingeborg Bachmann," in *Essays on Contemporary German Literature*, 4 vols., ed. Brian Keith-Smith. London: O. Wolff, 1966. 4: 187–212.

Stoll, Andrea, ed. *Ingeborg Bachmanns "Malina."* Frankfurt: Suhrkamp, 1991.

Text + Kritik 6. Ed. Heinz Ludwig Arnold. Munich: Edition Text + Kritik, 1980.

Text + Kritik, Sonderband. Ed. Sigrid Weigel Munich: Edition Text + Kritik, 1984.

Text + Kritik 6. 5th edition. Ed. Heinz Ludwig Arnold. Munich: Edition Text + Kritik, 1995.

Weigel, Sigrid. *Ingeborg Bachmann: Hinterlassenschaft unter Wahrung des Briefgeheimnisses.* Vienna: Zsolnay, 1999.

Witte, Bernd. "Ingeborg Bachmann" in *Deutsche Dichter,* 8 vols., eds. Gunter E. Grimm and Frank Rainer Max: Stuttgart: Reclam, 1990, 8: 339–349.